The Parliament of Poets

Also by Frederick Glaysher

Into the Ruins: Poems

The Bower of Nil: A Narrative Poem

The Myth of the Enlightenment: Essays

The Grove of the Eumenides: Essays on Literature, Criticism, and Culture

Letters from the American Desert: Signposts of a Journey, A Vision

Crow Hunting: Songs of Innocence

Edited

Robert Hayden, *Collected Prose*; *Collected Poems*

The Parliament of Poets

An Epic Poem

Frederick Glaysher

Earthrise Press

I wish to thank the Fulbright Commission for a Fulbright-
Hays grant in 1994 that enabled me to study in Hong Kong,
Taiwan, and China, including at Beijing University and the
Buddhist Mogao caves of Dunhuang, and I thank the National
Endowment for the Humanities for a 1995 Summer Seminar on
Hindu and Muslim culture and literature at the University of
North Carolina-Chapel Hill. I could not have written this epic
poem without the knowledge and experience they made
possible.
www.fglaysher.com

Library of Congress Cataloging in Publication Data
Glaysher, Frederick, 1954-
    The parliament of poets : an epic poem / Frederick Glaysher.
    294 pages ; 24 cm
ISBN   9780982677889 (hbk. : alk. paper)
ISBN   9780982677865 (ebk.)
1. One poem.   2. Epic poetry.
PS3557.L37 P37 2012   811/.54   2012942399

BISAC Subject Headings: POE014000 Poetry/Epic, POE005010
Poetry/American - General, POE000000 Poetry/General

Earthrise Press®
P. O. Box 81842, Rochester, MI 48308-1842 USA
www.EarthrisePress.Net

In memory of Robert Hayden

CONTENTS

Preface

The Detroit News headline for Monday, July 21, 1969, reads, "Footprints on the Moon!" I can still vividly recall watching it happen on black and white TV, as a teenager, along with my family and the many millions around the world. It fired my young fifteen-year-old imagination like nothing else I had ever known. I had always been thrilled by the entire space program, my father having worked on making the Apollo 11 heat shield for the reentry capsule. And then the incredible event itself, in prime time TV, "one giant leap for mankind." I was there with the astronauts, walking on the moon.

For that day, my family saved the complete front-page section of *The Detroit News*. Eventually, it became my copy of the great event that dad and all the nation had worked for, the greatest technological achievement of human history. As the years went by, I found myself still thinking about our human visit to the moon, going back and re-reading that section of *The Detroit News*, as it has increasingly yellowed and brittled and frayed. The writer of the front page article made one revealing comment which he seemed to think everyone would understand and agree with: "it was not necessary to send poets to the moon." What? The falsehood and injustice of that comment increasingly struck me, as my study of poetry and culture deepened with the years. Who did these Johnny-Come-Latelies think they were? The hubris and arrogance of Scientism seethed in that one sentence, the "two cultures" implicit in it. Poets have been on the moon for millennia.

It was the *in medias res,* "in the midst of things," the great structural device from the ancient epic poets, that took me decades to figure out, repeatedly pouring over Homer, Virgil, Dante, and Milton, and every other epic poet and form, struggling again and again for the right structure. It proved to be the hardest part of the epic form, a seemingly insurmountable challenge over which I stumbled, trying one idea after another, rejecting sketch after sketch, setting my notes aside knowing *that* way and *that* idea wasn't it, wouldn't work.

And then it came to me, while I was attending to some mundane task of life, and I rushed to my study to write it down, lest I lose it after all those years. I knew I had it with the certainty of *that's it! get it down on paper, before the phone rings or whatever, before it's gone forever*—surprise, relief, elation.

From Aristotle, I knew that the plot of *The Parliament of Poets* was the backbone of the book itself, the very crux, first and foremost, for it to work, to draw the reader into it, and to play on the great tradition, evoke it, honor it, raise everything to a higher level of seriousness and import.

And so, after over thirty years of study and thought, endless notes, more than four and a half years of writing, it is now time for readers to decide and judge. The fate of the book in their hands. Have I found and made and sung an epic vision worthy of them? Of humanity? Of you, O Gentle Reader?

Introduction

I derive the title *The Parliament of Poets* from both Chaucer and Attar, which suggests my focus is both Western and non-Western human experience. I seek to sift, ponder, and sum up not only American historical experience but the human experience of the major regions of the globe under the impact of modernism.

In a world of Quantum science, Apollo, the Greek god of poetry, calls all the poets of the nations, ancient and modern, East and West, to assemble on the moon to consult on the meaning of modernity. The Parliament of Poets sends the Persona on a Journey to the seven continents to learn from all of the spiritual and wisdom traditions of humankind. On Earth and on the moon, the poets teach him a new global, universal vision of life.

One of the major themes is the power of women and the female spirit across cultures. Another is the nature of science and religion, including Quantum Physics, as well as the "two cultures," science and the humanities.

All the great shades appear at the Apollo 11 landing site in the Sea of Tranquility: Homer and Virgil from Greek and Roman civilization; Dante, Spenser, and Milton hail from the Judeo-Christian West; Rumi, Attar, and Hafez step forward from Islam; Du Fu and Li Po, Basho and Zeami, step forth from China and Japan; the poets of the Bhagavad Gita and the *Ramayana* meet on that plain; griots from Africa; shamans from Indonesia and Australia; Murasaki Shikibu, Emily Dickinson, and Jane Austen, poets and seers of all Ages, bards, rhapsodes, troubadours, and minstrels, major and minor, hail across the halls of time and space.

As the Guides show the Persona crucial sites around the globe, such as Chartres Cathedral and the temples of Asia, Angkor Wat and elsewhere, the nature of social order and civilization in the regions of the past is explored. Modern twentieth century historical experience in all its glory and all its brutal suffering is fully confronted. The modern movement toward a global civilization is recognized and celebrated for the unprecedented future it opens to human beings. That transcendent Rose symbol of our age, the Earth itself, viewed from the heavens, one world with no visible boundaries, metaphor of the oneness of the human race, reflects its blue-green light into the blackness of the starry universe.

Undergirding my writing is the gradual, continuing development of international federal institutions. The defeat of communism and the numerous crises since then demonstrate that the slowly, painfully evolving authority of a cooperative United Nations, or a seriously developed successor institution, remains the only hope for a comparatively peaceful world.

During one period of my life I read well over two hundred books on the League of Nations and the United Nations. For the most part they were dry technical manuals or histories of primary use to diplomats and scholars. Conversely, through the actions of concrete characters, epic poems interpret history. Global social and political conditions have more than sufficiently changed to warrant a fundamental reevaluation of what has become prevailing literary and cultural thinking.

The Verse

As Milton emphasized, the masters of ancient epic poetry, Homer and Virgil, did not rhyme their poems. While their measures were different from ours, they agreed by their practice that rhyme was not essential to epic poetry. Rhyme would be a nuisance adding nothing of significance, even detracting from the music of epic song, found in its rhythmical language, blending rich vowels and consonants in harmonious agreement with flowing thought and action, like Niagra Falls in its descent, or Milton's verse paragraphs.

While my line tends to the iambic pentameter, depending on thought and need, allowing for variety, lest a slavish adherence become tedious, I relish the feminine ending, an extra half foot of measure to the ten syllables of blank verse, after the iamb, the most beautiful form in the English language.

A Prefatory Ode

To the Right Honourable Patron,
or Corporate Sponsor,
Who Never Materialized

My Lordship,

I had always hoped that you'd show up,
but you never did, much to my woe.
Ted Turner must have deleted my emails,
or some underling swiftly hit the button.
And now, it's way too late. I feel like
Samuel Johnson with his *Dictionary of
the English Language.* "Thank you, Sire,
yet I've come this far alone, and now I'm not
about to stoop to panhandling for coin."
Like everyone today, I've got the Internet,
and don't need you, and your condescension.
My shoes are old and worn, but my own.
I stand in them proudly under God's blue sky.
Like Johnson, I throw yours out the window.
Meeting also with an indifferent
literary period, I resolved
to create a new and better one, thinking
long and hard on how it was done in the past,
Cervantes, foremost, pointing the way,
with his lance, seated on Rocinante.
It would be like Lord Chesterfield who only
showed up with the dough when it was no longer
needed, wanting to take all the credit.
Would that I had only labored on
my epic a mere seven years, like Johnson,
instead of the thirty it required—since
the people deserve nothing but the best,

no matter what the personal cost to me,
and you, Sir, have done nothing to help—
not even informing me of the location
of your house that I might have appeared before
its door, with hat (had I one) in hand,
the other held out! No, you have delayed
much too long, and, again, I say,
I spurn you, as you spurned me, when most in need.
You have done me one favor, though, for
no longer do I harbor thoughts that the
Example of noble Patronage might return,
having done it all on my own, through
solitary devotion and long labor
for the glory of God and epic song,
that she might not perish forever from
the Earth, nay, revive, rally, and lead the eyes
of men, in the dark night, to the rising beauty
of our shining orb, seen, for the first time,
in its fragile delicacy, from the moon.

Your Lordship's,
or Most Honourable Chairman,
Executive of the Board,
doubtless a mega-billionaire,
I say,
Your Most Humble, Impoverished,
Servant of the Muse,

The Poet of the Moon

Gazing from the moon, we see one Earth, without borders, Mother Earth, her embrace encircling one people, humankind.

The Parliament of Poets

BOOK I

THE ARGUMENT

The first book proposes, in brief, the whole subject. In the midst of things, the Persona stands on the moon with the assembled poets of all nations, ancient and modern, called by the Greek god Apollo and the Nine Muses to consult on the meaning of modernity and modern Nihilism, the belief in Nothing, the dark vision of the time. Cervantes, seated on Rocinante, welcomes the Poet to the moon. A throng of poets and writers, East and West, accompany Cervantes, Du Fu and Li Po, Vyasa and Tagore, Basho and Saigyo, Rumi and Attar, Shakespeare and Samuel Johnson, Keats and Wordsworth, Jane Austen, African griots and shamans, Balla Fasseke, Merlin, Job, and many others. All consult on the threatened state of humanity, how to find and affirm a worthy vision of life, meaning, and purpose. They consult and agree they shall strive together to help the Persona by guiding him on his Journey.

O Muse, O Maid of Heaven, O Circling Moon,
O lunar glory of the midnight sky,
I call on thee to bless thy servant's tongue,
descend upon thy pillar of light,
moonbeam blessings, that from my mouth
may pour out at least a fraction of the love
I hold for thee, sweet blessings, for service
to God's creation, and His Creative Word,
the Bible's thundering verses, Brahma
of the Upanishads, Allah, the Compassionate,
Buddha's meditative mystery,
Confucius and the Dao. O Great Spirit
of the many peoples and the tribes,
if I have ever sacrificed for thee, long years,
drinking water from a wooden bowl,
hear my appeal and inspire me to sing

the tale supernal, upon the moon,
The Parliament of Poets, assemblage
of thy devoted ones, God intoxicated,
survey the cosmos and the centuries.
O guide us, Divine Light, in consultation,
that I might draw back the curtain of time,
explore the many mansions of thy kingdom,
East and West, meet in thy shining grace,
acknowledge all factions and antinomies,
ephemera of passing light, into night,
the lunar globe raise our gaze from Earth,
grant us perspective to view anew our plight,
our fate upon this blue-green globe,
this spinning ball of pain and joy, delight,
so that we may find the path to peace,
O Great Being of the eternal universe,
near and far, immanent and transcendent,
Nature's finest glory and Beyond,
wrap us in the endless cosmos of your Love.
     In the mid part of the moon, I stood,
in the midst of the Sea of Tranquility,
looking around me from rim to curving rim,
the brilliant moonscape against the blackest
black of space, stark blackness, polarities
of light and night, where a human footstep
marked a giant leap forward, in lunar dust,
For All Mankind, footsteps still all about,
undisturbed, untouched by decades of time,
destined to remain for all time, eternity,
or as near to it as we can imagine,
unlike what Robinson Crusoe found,
an ephemeral footprint on a beach,
here with instruments and a flag unfurled
in the solar wind, half a Lunar Module,

the descent platform left far behind,
the glory of the moon and all creation.
  And then I saw him sitting upon his nag,
Rocinante, Don Quixote, a lance resting
across his saddle, as he leaned forward,
from next to a crater, gazing my way.
At first, shock overwhelmed me, finding myself
where I was, disoriented, disbelieving,
how could it be? I stood there without
an encumbering spacesuit, lightly clad,
in my old corduroy jacket, worn beyond
its prime, breathing in the atmosphere of the moon.
The Man of La Mancha plodded slowly on his nag,
even as I began to realize we were
not alone. A crowd of people were coming
toward me too. How could they have gotten
here as well, I wondered, my own presence
and Cervantes, still a mystery, unexplained,
beyond belief, amazement, deeply stirring,
shaking my very being, as I recalled
my flight to the moon. A creaking leather
saddle woke me further to his nearness,
as he leaned closer to me, looking annoyed,
eyeing me from his mount, "So you've finally
made it up here. What's taken you so long?
Don't give me any of your excuses.
We've all been waiting for you. Here they come.
Snap out of it and collect your wits."
  At the head of a throng of people
massing across the Sea of Tranquility,
I began to discern other old friends,
long known but never met face to face,
only in ink, the printer's art, or used to be.
In the front of the crowd, drawing near, I saw
Du Fu wrapped in Confucian reserve and robe,

exiled, forced to wander and beg, seeking food,
crumbs at the door of the great,
hoping for an appointment from the emperor,
dreaming of a great man who would bring down
the River of Heaven to wash away
the blood of weapons, never to be used again.
Flowing behind him his robes stirred up
the moon dust, like a mist about his feet,
standing still a distance away, saying,
with elevated dignity, "You who
have been to Chang-an, welcome to the moon."
Next to him stood Li Po, friend and fellow poet.
Bai Juyi followed both, a voice for the people,
daring to speak of injustice to the emperor,
his fame reaching all the way to distant lands,
far to the East, Korea and Japan,
a Lay Buddhist of the Fragrant Mountain.
The scent of the same fragrance came from
the Japanese poets next to him, Basho,
like a monk but dust of the world upon him;
Saigyo, a monk who left his military clan;
Zeami, playwright of the court, whose plays
lay bare his time, cutting through to
another realm, like a samurai sword;
Milarepa, the Tibetan poet,
clad in cotton, wrapped in selfless practice,
detached but from Buddha's teaching of dharma.
Another fragrance, too, rose petals and poppies,
Attar and Rumi, the journey of
the hoopoe to the Simorgh, the Beloved,
delirious, whirling in a vortex of longing,
and Naguib Mahfouz, wearing a cravat.
They and many other poets flowed into
the landing site, Samuel Johnson and Thomas Gray,
Henry Vaughan and George Herbert, Dryden,

Shakespeare and Marlowe, Ben beside them,
jostling and pushing forward, Shelley
and John Keats, William Wordsworth, Longfellow,
Robert Burns looking ready still to raise a pint
for "auld lang syne," his mountain daisy and rose,
while Welsh bards stood on a rock with Taliesin,
spreading out around space junk left behind,
between and among the old instruments,
the hardware of Tranquility Base.
I could see now poets of the Book,
Job of tested patience, long suffering;
Dante, the man who had been to Hell,
Milton, who justified the ways of God,
song of the conquering evolution
of the soul, the battle of good and evil,
choosing through free will, God's holy gift;
Rumi's Indian brother, reincarnated,
Kabir, weaver of a Muslim-Hindu cloth,
warp and woof of the One, free of duality;
Vyasa, Kalidasa, and Tagore,
all had come from their ashrams to the moon;
and standing nearby, Sin-liqe-unninni,
"O Moon God, accept my prayer," who entered
into the spirit of *He Who Saw the Deep*,
out of the libraries of Babylon, Sumer,
raised the song of Gilgamesh and Enkidu,
their journey through Mesopotamia.
From every land and clime, all around, they stood,
poets of every continent, jostling
for a sight of the poet from Earth,
ahead of his time, new arrival, not yet
translated to the Spirit of the universe.
African poets and shamans, griots
of ancient songs, singers of rituals,
nobly held their instruments, flutes

and calabashes, drums, ready to play
as though Balla Fasseke were about
to step forward to sing the tale of
Sogolon's son, Sundiata, unifier of
Mali and much of the Africa of his day;
Aimé Cesaire saluting Africa,
Léopold Sedar Senghor, the widening world.
In "Moonglow" Christopher Okigbo,
naked before Mother Idoto.
And from the Americas, too, were tellers
of tales, Hopi and Navaho, Lakota,
Odawa and Iriquois, Mohican,
American tribes beyond telling, Incan
and Aztec, Aborigines of Australia,
drums and didgeridoos, island peoples.
All stood quietly on the moon, watching,
pressing to see this most curious of sights,
a supposed "white" man from the suburbs,
not long from morning prayers, plunked down on the moon.
   Together, Merlin and Queen Mab stood
before the crowd, he holding out his staff,
she clothed in Nature's bountiful plenty,
catching the eye of many a poet and seer.
Speaking the thought of many present,
addressing Cervantes, Merlin asked,
"What is this embodied spirit doing
here amongst us, disturbing the serenity
of our lunar home? How can this be?
Is this one of your quixotic jokes?
Did you bring him here, and what's the point?"
Cervantes, leaned slightly back in the saddle,
Rocinante snortling, giving her head
a little shake, her mangy mane taking
awhile to resettle in low gravity.
All eyes moved from Merlin to Cervantes,

who replied, once peace and quiet had resumed,
though how and why the heavenly realm,
that poets have occupied from time
immemorial, could be compromised,
still seemed to hang upon the lips of many,
glared from their eyes, full of curiosity.
Cervantes, cocking back his head with authority,
swept his eyes over the assembly
of poets, the pressing multitude, began,
"We have all experienced the loss of the
Living Presence, in modern times, even
those who would go backward show loss.
Our people all lose their way, bewildered,
science usurping the glory of the moon,
our domain, where most of us dwell even now.
Just look around at all the trash
the astronauts and scientists left behind,
scattered about the beauty of this plain.
All man's science and technology
cannot understand the moon, mighty symbol
of eons, visible sign uplifting men's eyes
to the heavens. You all know I speak the truth.
Many of our people, and even some of us,
cling to nostalgia, but it is not the same
as that deep experience of the Divine."
Lifting his lance into the air, waving
it about, Rocinante leaping apace,
raising her forelegs, Cervantes exclaimed,
"Obeying Lord Apollo, I challenge you!
I call here a Parliament of Poets!
In high consultation, we shall find the way
back home, to the depths of man's soul,
what we have all known and sung about for our
peoples, that they might find wisdom through delight.
To put it simply, not a one of us

can bear what's put down on paper these days,
or rather computer screens and digital bytes,
so I invited all would-be poets,
tossed the gauntlet down before them,
find a way to reach the imagination
of humanity, raise a new song.
He alone chose it," waving his lance at me.
"The age produces poetasters by droves,
little songsters, lost in self, despicably
trite, cynical and despairing ditties.
This man has sacrificed for the Muse,
begged and sought her beauty, and she is here
to tell you so, if you think otherwise."
He ended, glancing toward Calliope,
all eyes following, her beauty, ever
youthful, in her wisdom, inspiring
vision in her small band of devoted ones.
Discreetly she acknowledged Cervantes' words,
bowing her head gently, in her diaphanous
gown, all the Muses behind her on the moon.
And then Cervantes said, "That is why
I called you all here and sent a guide
to lead this embodied poet to the moon.
Exceptional times require exceptional means.
We must all pitch in and help this poet
or our cause may be lost forever.
And every one of you knows you fear it,
watching what they're doing down there,
the way the world goes, from bad to worse.
Put aside the old rules about embodied spirits
not allowed amongst us. The astronauts
didn't worry about that, did they?
It's too late now. The urgency of the hour
must bring us together, For All Mankind.
We have all arrived. Let us begin."

Above the lunar landscape, in answer
to the Man of La Mancha, astride
Rocinante, a deafening roar went up,
cheering assent, in the universal
language of the world, a crescendo
nearly blasting him out of the saddle,
terrifying his nag, causing her to tremble.
Cervantes looked on, knowing something had been
achieved, some new possibility was
lingering in the rarified lunar air.
   Then stirred Celtic Merlin, stepping towards
Cervantes, his staff in his right hand,
saying, "We've accepted Cervantes' challenge,
and his terms, and now I counsel we must
select someone to preside over our
deliberations. The high import of
our purpose requires our united choice.
Despite the caviling of his friends,
Job spoke the truth even to the face of God.
We can rely on him to tell us if
we stray. I urge all to consider him,"
stepping lightly aside as he ended.
Cervantes replied, "Job's vision is beyond
reproach, and no one debates he clung to
his integrity, held his ground against
the onslaught of every conventional mind,
even as we must do now on the moon,
this extraterrestrial globe, jewel in the sky.
We poets have owned it for millennia,
and must not cede it to wayward scientists
and plunderers of the Earth, who would
extend their selfish exploitations
throughout the universe, debasing everything
they touch, like Minos for a golden coin,
corporate greed gone intergalactic.

Meaning is the deeper fact, the deepest
fact and basis of the harmony of life,
amongst ourselves and all the starry cosmos."
  Having heard enough of praise, Job stepped forward,
saying, "I thank Merlin and Cervantes,
for thinking of me, and their good words.
I must decline the offer, however meant.
I believe we must look to someone of
wider sensibility, more universal.
My time was long ago, now the remote past,
tied to an early stage of civilization.
We now must aim at the entire globe."
Murmuring surprise and agreement rose
on all sides, recognizing Job's wisdom,
as poets discussed with those nearby who might
lead the deliberations forward,
but every proposal met with difficulties.
No one seemed universal enough.
Every poet had his limitations,
for history limits everyone's experience.
And then Rumi of the Sufi path, Pir
to many on the mystic way, spoke out,
"He's here to learn. Put him in charge of
consultation. He can ask what he needs to know.
Let each instruct him as best they can,
to and fro, we the ancients, he the poet
groping for the door, the path of his own soul,
as it must always be, for each and every one."
  All around, the poets seemed pleased, nodding
assent, talking among themselves, neighbor
to neighbor, a plan, perhaps, was plotted down.
When I saw that this idea was gaining ground,
I felt more than a little apprehensive.
How could I lead the poets of the past?
How could I stand before them, the truly great,

whom I revered, my masters and sustainers,
great souls who had achieved where I could only dream?
Who am I but one long tested, found wanting,
a would-be poet, if not poetaster,
wishing Robert Frost's arduous ordeal
had been mine, a mere twenty years of the dark pit,
now thrust upon the moon to my surprise.
And yet I still yearned to learn from them,
the more I considered it, liked the thought,
for what had I been doing all those years
but talking with the dead, while I poured over
their books and poems, thinking always about
their craft, noting their charms and style,
choice of words and turns of phrase, relishing
the beauty of their thought and high import,
their souls splayed upon the printed page.
A bit like Cervantes, or I should say,
Cid Hamet Benengeli, if not Pierre Menard,
in my study, falling asleep, over my books,
waking up Don Quixote! Shades of Borges!
Extend the conversation, so it seemed,
right and fit, the method of the ancients.
      Standing next to me, elbowing me in the ribs,
Melville said, with a mocking seaman's drawl,
and a sparkling eye, "What 'da ya say, matey?"
waking me for the moment from reverie.
I sighed, replying, "All right. I'll try to ask
questions that do not waste your time and are
worthy of all of you, my masters,
whom I acknowledge, one and all. Help this
would-be servant of the Muse, lost of late,
aye, needing your tutelage, delighting wisdom,
lunar apprenticeship rekindling my hope
to intone a high and elevating song
before the Nine Sisters of our art."

"Now we've got a plan! We know how to proceed,"
bellowed Chaucer, conducting, as it were,
some ministration for the king, royal
negotiation with the French, a parley
among pilgrims on their way to Canterbury.
Far back from where I stood, a poet shouted,
loud and direct above the lunar din,
"Now what's your first question? Let's hear it!"
Another broke in, with an emendation,
"Wait! Half of us will never hear him from
over here, with Rocinante shuffling about.
We can barely see him over all the heads.
Get him on top of that piece of space junk.
Good for something after all. Can't they go
anywhere in the solar system without littering?"
he muttered, trailing off. And then I realized
he was Villon, back there with a bunch of
rough-looking French poets, passing around
a bottle of wine, Raminagrobis,
Moliere, Baudelaire, and Rimbaud, a crowd
of cut throats, Cyrano de Bergerac
with his bottles of hot air and mouth to match.
I wasn't about to argue with them,
especially once Rabelais starting rolling
on his back, his bare arse sticking upward
while he showed his countrymen how he couldn't
even light his own farts, on fire, on the moon,
for lack of oxygen, howling with each blast!
Cursing him with vigorous oaths and protests,
angry poets gave the fumes a wide berth till
the solar wind dispersed, carried them away.
Turning from the rollicking French, I heard
an irascible Samuel Johnson say,
"Solar system? Try universe! More than
one piece of radioactive space junk

is out there now, but what else can be
expected of scientists who lack a
vision worthy of humanity?"
William Blake, with a scathing look, shot back,
"Well, he's here to give it to 'em, if they'll
listen. Fat chance that, getting over their
seventeenth century retreat into the
Royal Society, cleaving the soul in half.
None of them would ever listen to me,
and look where they've got us now! Near collapse!"
"Pity the poor scientists. They had to use
rockets and machines to get up here."
"Well, it took imagination, too, though
some might not want to admit it, making
us perhaps one in the end after all."
"Oh, they'll deny it, some at least. Just for spite.
We don't need to worry about them, nay-sayers."
Next to Judeth Shakespeare, whose books have been lost,
Jane Austen upbraided her countrymen,
"Do you men always have to fight and quarrel!
Have we come all this way for more of that?"
She then looked toward Cervantes, gallant knight,
a damsel in distress, seeking help, waking
him up to perform his duties, by default.
"All right! All right! Gentlemen, and gentlewomen,"
Cervantes pleaded from Rocinante's back,
motioning me towards the Lunar Module,
or what was left of it, the descent platform,
still shining gold and orange in the brilliant light.
As I climbed the rungs up the LM,
I thought, correcting the illiterate grammar,
"One small step for a man, one giant leap
for mankind." Ignorant astronauts, mere
technicians, mangled the opportunity
for deathless words of immortal stature.

There it was, between the rungs, as I climbed,
the plaque attesting before the cosmos
that America's journey to the moon,
President Kennedy's resonant voice,
ringing in my ears, *was* For All Mankind.
Standing on the platform, I turned, surveyed
the lunar landing site, filled with thousands
of poets from every land and clime,
every religion and path of wisdom,
every race and tribe, seers and shamans,
singers of the ages, all looked back at me,
who must have seemed a curious spectacle,
a poet without a poem, seeking instruction,
wanting to ask the masters for advice,
petitioning before them on the moon,
of all places who would ever have thought.
Took a hare-brained poet to come up with that!
I shuddered, despite myself. Many saw it,
so I thought, as I began to choke, deeply
stirred, realizing more so where I found myself.
Then Cervantes said, urging me along,
from my moon-dreaming, "All right! You're here!
What do you want to know? Let's hear it!
I proclaim the Parliament of Poets
now in session. Speak up! We're listening."
  "I, I, I," I stammered, swallowing hard,
searching for something that might merit their
attention, weighing my mind, searching inside.
"Go on!" a heckling poet jabbed into
the non-existent air. "Though we have eternity,
you don't!" sending off a roar of laughter,
putting me more at ease, despite the
thousands of eyes intent upon me.
Then came back to my mind what I've often
struggled with, trying to peer into the future,

that perennially human impulse,
thinking always of Virgil's *Aeneid*
and his prescience. Who better to ask than he
for the resolution of so many woes
of our age? "Okay, I'm launching out forward.
A question for Virgil, if I may be so bold,"
seriousness entering my voice, welling up
in me, seizing the moment, lest it be lost.
"Virgil, we can't tolerate an Augustus
in our age. What shall we do? And how?
For thirty years I've studied and thought,
strived to understand. What do you advise?
Tyrannies and oppressors, Marxists and fascists,
we've already had. Only madmen would
want to go back to anything like that,
and yet order erodes, deteriorates,
moral decline and decadence deepen,
a Slough of Despond draws in everything,
empire grows, looms, corporate plutocracy,
oligarchies of the billionaires, with
no commitment to any nation or people,
global, exploiting the masses everywhere,
reduced to wage slaves, with wages going down,
stripping entire nations of their wealth.
Plato's luxurious city global now,
spanning the Earth, trampling the poor and humble,
and what used to be the middle class, much
under duress, sinking below the waves,
enervated civilizations losing the
will to live, young men and women even
the will to procreate, make a life together."
   Tall and severe, laconic, Virgil stood
among the Greek and Roman poets,
Orpheus, still grieving for Eurydice,
Homer, Demodokos, and Anacreon; Horace,

Theocritus, Momus, and Symmachus;
Apollonius, poet of the Argonauts,
Callimachus, Alexandria's librarian,
Lucretius, who said of Iphigenia,
sacrificed before the Greeks sailed for Troy,
religion could cause so much evil and woe;
Ovid, lush tales of metamorphosis;
Catullus, still longing for Lesbia;
Seneca, Plautus, and Petronius;
Statius, the late echo of epic song;
Propertius, Juvenal on the Forum;
even Cicero was there, whose "Dream of
Scipio" was a poet's dream, earning him
the right forever to stand upon the moon.
I could not keep my eyes from drifting to his hands.
All the Roman great stood with Virgil,
who moved with *gravitas* toward me,
weight of vision, master of masters, whose
Aeneid I had labored over, its choice Latin
a living, immortal tongue, the beauty
of which no dust can ever sully, as long
as our fragile planet circles the sun,
before me, in toga, sizing me up.
Oh dreadful sense of unworthiness!
Our gaze met, as my question lingered,
unanswered, in the lunar vacuum,
and then he looked around briefly at the
Parliament of Poets, returned his gaze to me,
looking me in the eye the entire time,
"'Know Thyself'—You know you've found your theme.
No Augustus for your age, but men speaking
to other men from all around the world,
seeking to resolve the upheavals of the day.
Consultation not unlike what we conduct
here on the moon, seeking wisdom's way.

The Mediterranean Lake has become the globe.
Have greater confidence and hold yourself aright.
Remember the plenitude of humanity.
For you this is the way back to Earth.
The deeper questions lie beyond this one.
You know that too," he said, with finality,
turning, and walking back beside Homer.
As he reached his place, blind Demodokos
was led toward me, by a young squire,
holding out in one hand a wooden bowl,
saying, "From Delphi's Pierean spring,
I proffer water so pure it can inspire
song to make even Odysseus weep.
Like Iphigenia, accept your sacrifice."
Shaken by his words, I yet reached for the bowl,
quaffed from the high spring of mountain water,
my eyes from his blind eyes again to Virgil's.
Determined not to swoon like Dante, or
further betray myself, I still felt Virgil's
reprimand, high counsel, truth of his words,
so brief yet to the point, to an apprentice,
Demodokos now standing with Phemios.
Granting the empire its proper place,
but moving on, whence true order flows,
I swung away from the assemblage,
looking behind the Lunar Module,
the Earth high above the curving horizon,
a small blue-white ball, our home, against
the blackest black of space, vast space,
wondering whether I could prove worthy
of the theme, shoulder such a load,
like Milton move beyond heroic song,
the tales of knights and kingly courts,
caparisons and jousts, mighty battles,
Beowulf's halls of kings and drinking mead,

sing a vision beyond the Augustus of an age,
or the rule of the greedy wealthy, seeking
only their own welfare, not the common good,
find the path into the regions of the soul.

BOOK II

THE ARGUMENT

A young Lakota Indian brave dances a hoop dance upon the moon, for the assembled poets, seers, and medicine men. Black Elk and Chief Seattle set forth the sacred vision of Mother Earth. Black Elk guides the Persona back to Earth and the ancient cave of Lascaux. The ancient philosophers and the Golden Bough. The cathedral cavern. An Australian aborigine, Japara, "moon man," carries the Poet to Everywhen and Kulama, ceremony of renewal. Catalogue of the ships.

A great war cry went up, drums tom-tommed
a deep bass sound of tightly stretched hide,
chanting of many braves, pounding of hearts.
Clearing a space, poets made room for a
young Lakota Indian brave, strong and virile,
raising a hoop before him, dancing the
hoop dance of his people, the hoop dance of
all the peoples of Mother Earth, far above,
while all stood round, the poets and seers,
shamans and singers, griots and troubadours,
bards and rhapsodes, watching him, pounding moon dust,
mesmerized, for he danced in another world,
the world, as it were, of the moon,
behind him all could see the hoop of the Earth,
beyond the hoop of the hoop of the moon,
within the hoop of the moon's own hoop,
the hoop of our rotating solar system,
the hoop of the spiraling Milky Way,
the hoops of the innumerable galaxies,
the hoop of the endless universe.
His long braids spun with the planets,
spinning on their axes, as he weaved
in and out and through nine hoops,

and the pounding of the drums pulsed
through the arteries of the universe.
First one way, and then the other,
his moccasins dancing through moon dust,
feathers proudly worn, hide loin cloth,
pipe-bone breast plate, and head dress, transfixing
everyone by the energy of his dance.
Seen by all, an even more astounding
sight took place, as he slowly changed into an
ancient medicine man, standing proud and noble,
holding a sacred coup stick, a medicine
wheel, with seven feathers, suspended from it.
The youth was gone. Black Elk stood before us.
"Behold the Earth!" he commanded, gesturing
with his coup stick, directing our gaze,
rising like a hoop of many peoples.
"It is holy, being endless, broken
like a ring of smoke. The broken hoop
begins to heal, to encircle the Indian
nation, all nations, once again, heal."
All the universe seemed to listen.
In a sacred manner, wide as starlight,
though broken and scattered, Black Elk
moved toward me, lifting his coup stick to Earth.
"The Holy Tree will heal and flourish.
Poets and shamans, bring the people back
into the sacred hoop that they might walk
again the red road in a sacred manner
pleasing to Wanka Tanka, the Great Mystery,
Gitchie Manitou, the Great Spirit,
the Great Father beyond all the names of
my people, the Spirit of the Universe."
    Looking out over the Sea of Tranquility,
at the sea of faces following his every word,
Black Elk said, "Though nations are in despair,

teach this poet your strong medicine that he
might help humankind walk the good road again."
Coming down from the module, I stood
before Black Elk, struggling with emotion,
speechless, overcome by the vision of his words.
Black Elk began chanting, raising the hoop,
raising the vision of man, not white,
nor red, but human, before the universe,
the good Earth spinning in the background.
And then he said, "It is hard to follow
the great vision in the world of darkness.
Many men get lost among the shadows."
Turning round to all the assembled poets,
on all sides, Black Elk said, "We must be the
pathfinders for this poet, guide him
through the forests of memory on the right path.
Even I despaired for my people,
thought the people's beautiful dream had died,
I to whom was given so great a vision.
Sometimes dreams are wiser than waking.
We know the center is not dead, cannot die.
The Great Mystery watches all his children.
Help this poet tend the Sacred Tree,
bloom again at the center of the hoop.
If your medicine is strong, pour it forth."
    And then from the Indian hunting party,
another chief stepped forward, Chief Seattle,
in full regalia, a head dress of eagle
feathers and brocade, flowing down behind him.
Standing next to Black Elk, Chief Seattle
said, gazing at our planet, "Every part
of Earth is sacred to our people,
pine needles and sandy shores, dark woods
and meadows, the humming insect
and the howling wolf. All are holy.

The Earth is our Mother. What befalls her,
befalls the sons of Earth. Earth does not belong
to man, man belongs to the Earth.
The Great Mystery has woven this web.
Man is but a strand within it.
Our God is the God of all people.
The Earth is precious to Him. To harm the
Earth is to heap contempt upon Him.
We must preserve the land for all children.
There is only One God, and we are brothers
after all. Black Elk, you must teach this poet
your strong medicine. Take him to the caves below,
before our people, time before time,
before we crossed the land and ice,
into the deep caves of the past.
As into a sweat lodge he must go,
teach him the ways of Earth people,
so that his tongue may chant the song
that will help the World Tree grow again,
at last a great circle of peace hoop the globe."
With those words the great chief passed back into
the hunting party, his words in the moon air,
leaving all pondering deeply what he had said.
    Black Elk broke the silence. "The Great Chief
has spoken. The path is laid before us.
I and he who must tell the tale shall leave.
The rest of you remain upon the moon.
Consider what, in your turn, you must teach.
Choose your lessons wisely, guide him aright.
Help him become a living Dream Catcher,
through which all that is bad will pass,
while hooping the will of the Great Spirit,
as far as a brave can serve Him for
the good of the tribes and many peoples."
Ending, Black Elk turned to me, gesturing

to grasp his wrist, saying, "Come," holding
aloft his coup stick, with firm shakes on high.
Near the medicine wheel, I closed my hand
around his wrist, feathers brushing across,
and as I did, I felt a strength I had
never known, a tingling sensation,
feeling more alive than I had ever been.
Swiftly we rose from the surface of the moon,
leaving behind the Parliament of Poets,
as Indian war cries sent us on our way.

   Long flight traversed in timeless time,
not knowing where Black Elk had been directed
to take me, I wondered on the way,
in silence, as we traveled toward Earth,
moving through the blackest black of space,
Earth growing ever larger, her earthshine
in the bright white light of eternity,
beckoning us on, lighting our way,
passing the Hubble telescope, wondering
if below they could see us, though it was
pointed at galaxies far away in Fornax.
Many destinations ran through my mind,
a holy mountain in the Dakotas,
Sioux Nations, Oglala, Lakota, others;
a forest and oceanside in the Northwest,
where Sacagawea, after traveling
a long way, too, guiding Lewis and Clark,
saw the Great Waters and the beached whale;
totems of many families, Manataka,
Sitka, Haida, Kwakiutl, peoples
and tribes, the Three Fires, Odawa,
Ojibwa, and Bodewadmi, "The Keepers
of the Sacred Fire," makers of the
ash tree baskets that my grandmother loved;
and my neighbors in Arizona, Hopi

and Navajo, Chemuevi and Mojave.
What would America be without the
Naragansett, Penobscot, Mohawk;
the great League of Iroquois, Oneida,
Onondaga, Cayuga, Seneca,
Tuscorora; Huron and Cherokee,
Klamath and Crow, Arapahoe, Miami,
Chickasaw, Nes Perce, Kickapoo;
Apache and Mandan and Shoshone;
on plains and in deserts, valleys and woods,
the Indians embraced the Earth,
Inuit, Hualapai, Ahwahneechee,
Anasazi, Pima, Arikara, Tukudika.
So many gone, hundreds long ago,
from the six-hundred tribes, many nations,
proud, upright people, under the sun.
Many days below the moon to recite
their names, and tell their stories, tales of woe.
Like Black Elk, listen like a chickadee,
lost nations barely surviving, spread like
a forest across North America,
like a trail of tears from coast to shining coast.
  Suddenly we plunged into Earth's atmosphere,
Black Elk shielding me as we flew,
his medicine wheel before us, yet to
my surprise we weren't heading for America,
but Europe, native home of the white man.
Although I wanted to question Black Elk,
glancing at him, concentration etched
his face, as we entered the rainbow
colored fireball of reentry, streaming
around us, a fiery furnace of trial,
burning away at the dross of my soul,
rocking and shaking us violently,
I clung to my guide as never before,

trusting he knew how to get us through
the sheltering sheath of Mother Earth,
back home, back to her consoling embrace,
and through, through we broke into the atmosphere,
slicing into the encapsulating bubble,
fragile and airy, blue sky of Earth,
bumping and rolling, rocking into a glide,
as we descended downward toward Europe,
and then toward a corner, toward France.
Looking now more relaxed and calm, Black Elk
said, aside to me, smiling slightly,
"The land of the people who were good to me."
We soon landed in a forest, along
the side of a mountain in a valley,
in a small clearing. As I let go of
his wrist, Black Elk, without looking at me,
began to walk towards the end of the clearing,
where an overgrown path led up the mountain.
At the edge of the forest I saw a dove,
pecking on the ground. Black Elk now spoke.
"I will wait here for you. You must choose
to follow the dove to a Golden Bough.
If it is your fate, break it from the tree.
It will light your way in the world below."
As I swung round back to the white dove,
it flew into the shady oak forest, at
the base of the mountainside, ahead of me.
Leaving Black Elk, I hurried to catch up.
"O my guide," I thought, "do not let me lose you,"
as through the undergrowth I zigged and zagged,
after it, finding myself in a thick wood,
sunlight barely filtering in, as though
I had entered a cave below the earth.
At the far end of a shadowed tunnel
of wood, along the path, in a slight clearing,

robed figures stood, severe, somber.
Celtic priests and priestesses, druids.
One spoke. "We come to witness if you be
the one who can slay the ruling king,
feeble and sullied, lead aright, renew,
invigorate the declining dominion.
Since only poets and singers belong
on the moon, dancers and musicians,
we receive you here for your love of wisdom,
with masters of our later tradition.
Only through this sacrifice and struggle
can you receive and prove the gift of song."
And I saw then next to the druids,
the philosophers, Thales, Heraclitus,
Parmenides, Plato and Aristotle,
Empedocles, Anaxagoras and Pythagoras,
Roman Epictetus, Marcus Aurelius,
Plotinus, a Greek and Roman pantheon,
stretching far as I could see into the woods.
Blind Tiresias, servant of Apollo,
staff in hand, stood quietly nearest to me.
Recognizing others, close to my heart,
I yet had to beg leave, following the dove,
up the hill to the right away from them,
till the dove alighted upon a branch of
a young tree surrounded by mighty oaks.
Just below the dove's perch shined a Golden Bough,
made more so by a ray of golden light,
penetrating the green canopy of
the ancient wood, older even than the Celts.
Placing my hand upon a nearby tree,
leaning into it, feeling its spirit-bark,
I realized that this was Virgil's fabled bough.
Stepping to the tree, I reached above my head
and snapped it from where it grew, below

a mistletoe entwining a higher branch.
Bough and leaf shone with a brilliant glow,
lighting my way down through the forest,
past the ancient druids and philosophers,
hailing me as I ran by in triumph,
holding high the Golden Bough in front of me,
to where Black Elk awaited my return,
at the edge of the glade. He watched me
as I approached, proudly bearing the bough.
Sizing me up, he said, "Now you are a brave,"
fixing his eyes on me as his words sank in.
I felt them as the highest praise, and vowed
inside, that I would suffer any ordeal
rather than let him and others down.
   He turned into the woods, up the mountainside.
We went some distance, a steep ascent,
turning the lower foot sideways to wedge
our progress up the steep and rocky grade,
lest we slip and lose ground, falling back to
the valley floor, now ever farther below,
until within a narrow crevice in the rock,
we made our way in, opening further
into the mountainside, the light from the
entrance fading, while the Golden Bough
began to glow brighter, lighting our way,
deeper underground, down into the
under-regions of the Earth. At last,
from the narrow passageway, we reached
a small space of about ten feet across,
with boulders scattered about, piled together.
Black Elk stood still and said, "Sit down
and put the branch inside your jacket."
As I followed his instructions, we were
plunged into the darkest dark I'd ever known.
And then he began to chant a native tongue.

A low, melodious prayer resonated
in the small chamber, filling it with
soaring intonations, intermixing in
antiphonies echoing throughout the cave.
I followed him, or tried, I could not tell,
but stumbled along in the deep recesses
of my heart, following his prayer, feeling
his absorption in another realm,
traveling there with him, tagging behind.
Black Elk began to speak. "For over
ten thousand years after the people crossed
the ice and snow, on their winding journey,
they prayed always to the Great Spirit,
and He encircled them in his great hoop,
through forest and mountain and desert.
Part of my vision in this Land of the People
Who Were Good to Me, that I have always
held sacred, never spoke of until now,
is of my people, our people, before
Wanka Tanka took them on that journey.
Our peoples reach back to what now I must
teach you. Red man and white man,
all the tribes of Mother Earth passed through
the entrance of the caves. Here you must learn
what has been forgotten, in the heart,
not only in the head." His words, in the dark,
while I sensed he was not far from me,
his words seemed to come from another world,
one before time, primordial, almost
before the beginning of the human race.
"That you might teach others, the Great Spirit
gave me a vision of bringing you here.
Long out of memory, I remembered it
when I saw you on the moon, you who taught
the Hopi and Navajo, Chemuevi and Mojave,

trying to learn from them, we teach you now,
what you failed to understand from them,
the intaglios of the desert you sought out,
etched into the Sonoran Desert rock."
His medicine wheel then began to glow
until it was as bright as the Golden Bough
had been. He made a movement to proceed,
so, standing, I withdrew it and held high
the bough, as he led me to another passage,
leading deeper underground, wider now.
To my surprise, markings and paintings
on the walls, hand prints silhouetted in
ochre, vulvae, engravings and symbols.
Unknown to me before. I wondered what
they were and what they meant. Time
immemorial seemed writ there as we passed.
Next we flowed into a vast cavern,
with both our lights burning brilliantly,
illuminating all the walls and ceiling
of a gigantic amphitheater of the soul.
  Black Elk spoke, "Many times longer than my
people journeyed, our ancestors journeyed here;
here our ancestors understood all life is sacred,
the work of Mother Earth." Holding up his
coup stick, with the medicine wheel,
he rotated around where he stood, throwing
the light upon the walls and ceiling, where
I saw with a catch of breath, an astounding
array of creatures, bison and ibexes,
rhinoceroses and bulls, grazing horses,
cows, male and female reindeer,
mammoths and felines, parts of whales,
sweeping in a vast migration across
the field of time, across the temple of
the cave, the cathedral of the ages.

In silence and awe, reverence, we stood
and gazed and gazed and gazed, and gazed some more.
And when Black Elk spoke again in the cave
of Lascaux, it was with a new tone in
his voice, as one speaking of holy things,
mysteries too great for man, beyond us,
yet we seek to understand what we can,
grasp and convey what insight one might have.
"Here young braves became warriors, became men,
left behind their foolish ways for the ways
of their people, their tribe. Here they learned
to respect the creatures of Mother Earth,
before the hunt, to consecrate their acts
to the round of life. Through death, to live,
to live to die, like men, worthy of their tribe.
Here the landscape of the human soul,
carrying from here the Mother Goddess,
image of their service, sacrificing self,
the great beasts sacrificed, too, for man,
man himself sacrificed for woman,
their children, the sacred mystery of life.
Here cave men first learned to paint their dreams.
This is the womb of the human race.
Time and eternal power meet to serve
the Eternal One and creatures of time.
After millennia, here in the womb
of Earth, human creatures were reborn,
the human animal became man.
We people began to understand,
but now have lost the vision of this place.
We and nature are one, together, whole.
Separated, severed, alone, we die.
The dance of life and death upon these walls,
man and animal, nature in antiphony,
unity, the Great Spirit master of all.

You know it's in your DNA, genome.
You trace back here, your haplogroup, some cave
painter, shaman, a glassmaker even then."
Lowering his glowing medicine wheel,
he stopped and looked back toward the entrance,
waiting for me to absorb his meaning.
I knew then that modern man's arrogance
had forgotten the unity of life,
life and death in cosmic oneness,
man divided against himself and woman,
desecrating Nature, piling the bison
skulls to the sky, raped and exploited the
land without regard for balance, harmony,
as though we were the center of the universe,
not part of the Great Mystery's creation.
I shook to my bones, shaking and shivering,
not from the cold of the cave, deep and dark,
but the frigidity of the modern soul.
   Black Elk motioned it was time to leave.
I left the Golden Bough on a boulder,
he plucking a leaf and handing it to me,
leading the way, back up the narrow passage,
the medicine wheel lighting our way.
When we came out into the light, our eyes
squinting to adjust, Black Elk said,
"Here I leave you. Another medicine man
shall take you where you need to go,
decreed by the poets on the moon.
My people call. Your way from here is long.
May the Great Spirit guide you, Poet of the Moon."
And before I could protest, he was gone.
And I, I was alone, wondering where I was,
how I'd ever get back home, scarce able
to believe all that had happened, what I had
witnessed and been left trying to comprehend.

And then I saw to my shock what appeared
to be the bones of men in front of the cave,
littering the slope, thrown out to the vultures,
returning to and feeding the great beasts,
cast out for neglecting the Mother Goddess
and her children, what the Antler-man evoked,
in cave paintings and forgotten rituals,
but still I shuddered at the inhumanity,
wanting now to flee that place in haste,
and thought of some American Indians,
torturing and mutilating their captives,
like my ancestor on the Pennsylvania
frontier, scalped, a tomahawk in her head.
    While I struggled to come to terms with my thoughts,
I saw a figure, in the woods, frightening
to look at, given my new discovery,
so different was he from all that I have
known and been, a naked man out of an
ancient time, primordial, older than
the caves, of black and muddy complexion,
holding a spear, covered with white stripes and dots,
painted all over his body, bristly,
woolly hair, staring at me, as I tried
to recover from my shock of horror,
desperate to judge his intent. Head hunter?
An ancient shaman from an ancient land?
I mulled over Black Elk's words. Drawing near,
he spoke, as out of a dream, "The poets
on the moon have sent me to lead you on.
Out of The Dreaming, I am Japara,
'moon man,' my face scarred like the moon at night,
and I have come to tell you the story
of our bands, on the land, from Everywhen.
Do not fear. I have come to take you there.
Gently he walked toward me, like a hunter

toward a skittish deer, saying, "Hold my
arm firmly and we shall go from here."
   Stunned by the appearance of the man,
I scarce knew what to do, but could not stay
there, thinking of the bones, such horror,
while this guide seemed mild, though primordial.
I awoke from my fear, his demeanor
winning me over, despite my daze and thoughts,
as I slowly moved towards him, grasped his wrist.
Before I knew it, we were ascending,
ascending to find a new home for the soul,
that ancient forest and cave far below.
I barely could look at him as we flew,
for fear that fear would cause me to let go,
his dark and ancient visage so unknown.
In a vortex, time swirled, carrying us
along, I and my new companion,
and then I noticed from that great height
the oceans seemed to be lower, continents
nearly covered in ice as we passed from
the hemisphere, his outstretched spear steering.
Much land and sea swept by, while at times,
camp fires below, and ants, here and there.
After a long while over water,
I saw ahead an enormous island,
brown and reddish, even from that great height.
I wanted to ask him where on such a vast
continent we were going when suddenly
it became clear he was heading for its
center, dry and red, a desert, so it seemed,
other deserts came to mind that I had known.
"We go to where The Dreaming can be told,"
he said, leaving me still wondering
where that might be and what it was.
Over land we flew, a few rivers,

some dry beds, that snaked their way across
both lush and withered terrain. Lowering
towards the ground, small groups of people,
here and there, a mere handful clinging
to life, scattered across the vast expanse.
Even further towards the center,
in the distance, a looming mountain,
an enormous red rock abruptly rising
from the land, unlike anything around it.
More at ease, I looked at Japara,
asked him with my eyes, an annoying tourist.
He explained, "Uluru, but we go beyond,
into The Dreaming," and soon it lay behind,
out of sight, as we sped forward somewhere.
We were nearly touching the treetops and
brush, brush mostly, if not scrub.
Ahead, a band of people, women cooking
over a fire, children ran about,
some sat in a circle, next to a lean-to,
tending to some handicraft or task.
Suddenly we were seen and a stir went up,
with Japara waving his spear, shouting
in a tongue I could not understand.
Lightly, we set down not far from them,
the desert dust rising slightly around us,
as we found our footing on Earth again.
Gesturing toward me as he spoke,
Japara seemed to be introducing me
to the clan, many of whom eyed me
apprehensively, as a stranger dropped from
above. I now could understand Japara
as he greeted them in their native tongue.
"This is the shaman I told you about,
from the moon, from Everywhen, where the
people have forgotten The Dreaming,

the sacredness we experience and live in.
He must learn and tell the tale once again."
A thrill went through me at his words,
hope rising that he might know better than
I myself, so weak and given to despair.
Addressing all the clan, he said, "Tonight
the golden ring forms around the moon,
and Kulama, ceremony of renewal.
Prepare." Japara led me away to
a lean-to by a gum tree, where I fell
into a deep sleep, dreams of oblivion,
all that I had been through flowing through my mind.
When I awoke it seemed I had slept long
and late into the day, for the sun was
already nearing noon, and women
and children were busying about,
tending to one duty or another,
preparing yams for the evening feast.
The men were gone. In a time before time,
I arose from the lean-to, which was shielding
me from the sun, looked about, and saw
Japara and a hunting group of men,
giving the game to the women, as they passed.
Japara greeted me from a distance.
"We have had a good hunt while you dreamed.
The women will prepare the food. Come with
me and the men where we can properly tell
you the stories," several of them behind him,
still amazed at the sight of me, as I at them.
We seemed beings from different galaxies.
   Japara led me away from the camp
and into the desert behind the lean-to,
and away from most of the women, with
only a few following behind us.
At a clear place of desert sand, free of brush,

where a circle and fire pit had been dug,
not far from caves and a lake, Japara
made a sign and we all sat in the circle.
A short silence fell upon us. No one moved.
   One of the women, Mimbardda, began
to speak, sweeping the sand smooth and level
with a stick, drawing two men in the sand.
I felt that something of great importance
was about to be told. All stayed silent.
"In the beginning, Jindoo, the Creator,
sent two wise spirit men to shape the Earth,
from the far end of the Milky Way,"
which she drew in the sand above the men.
"They shaped the sea, the earth and the sky.
And then Jindoo sent Seven Sisters,
stars of the Milky Way, the Pleiades,
to beautify the Earth with flowers and trees,
birds and animals, every creeping thing,"
drawing the Seven Sisters near the men.
Younger men and women now joined the outside
of our circle. Mimbardda continued,
without any sense of interruption.
"While they worked, one of the younger sisters
fell in love with the two wise men,
following them into the bush one day.
Darama, the Great Spirit, had warned them
that if such a thing happened they could not
return to the Milky Way, so while the one
woman had to stay, the others rose to the stars,
and the two spirit men remained behind
and became human, like us, losing their
special powers, feeling longing for their home.
They became parents of the Earth who made
laws and ceremonies, the parents of
people, the desert people, and all our bands,

Toogee and Warlpiri, Nanda and Ola,
Kokowara, Tiwi, Yolngu, Arunta,
Barkandji, Butchulla, Targari,
Dangu and Ewamin, Gaari, Inqura,
Rembarunga, Nakara and Maduwongga,
Maya, Kalali, Pongaponga,
Alawa, Jandruwanta, and Arabana,
bands of many names, man and woman.
People spread throughout the bush, all directions,
many tongues and kinship from our parents."
The sun moved deeper into the afternoon.
"O desert people, O stranger from afar,
four-hundred bands and more spread over the land.
This is why we have knowledge and respect
for the universe." Drawing a mountain,
"The Great Spirit, Jindoo, Ngurunderi,
Guthi-Guthi, Darama, the Spirit
of many names, Yuin-Monaro.
He came down from the sky and saw
that there was no water that could be seen,
so from Mount Minara he called Weowie,
the Rainbow Serpent in the mountain.
Guthi-Guthi called, 'Weowie, Weowie!'
And the water serpent came out,
traveled over the land, making water holes,
streams, billabongs, and lakes throughout the land."
As Mimbardda continued to recite
The Dreaming into the night, more villagers
joined us, widening the circle, and later,
the circle revolved like the stars, above,
dancing, singing and chanting, drums
and didgeridoos, sonorously lifting
the hearts of all, swirling circles, dots on
the faces around me, circles in the sand,

twirling time, Dreamtime, Everywhen, now.
A young couple had disappeared together.
   The women began to remove the yams
from the fire, unearthing them, people
eating, here and there a circle of people,
sharing sustenance of life. The glow of
the fire lit the surrounding darkness, night sky.
As people watched, Japara, with his spear,
quietly motioned me aside, and then
into the desert bush, where he said,
"It is time that we return to our home,
the moon, where you have more to learn and know."
He held out his arm to me, and, with all
fear long gone, I understood, taking hold
of my brother's wrist. Through The Dreaming,
we soared, rising in the night, the glowing
circle down below, fading smaller, while
the brilliant moon loomed larger as we flew,
heavenward, moonman and moonman, homeward bound.
   And while we sailed thoughts came to mind.
And so I shall name the masters of the ships,
they, who, like Japara and I, launched out,
from land to ocean, from Earth to space, following
the longing of their hearts, past voyagers,
the ancient mariners and captains of ships,
Egyptians up the coast to the cypress forests
of Lebanon, the Argonauts seeking
the Golden Fleece, Odysseus his homecoming,
the Phoenicians their port, Norsemen plowing
the sea, Chinese charting a route to India,
traders on the Red Sea, Oceanic islanders,
Columbus sailing in the Niña, the Pinta,
and the Santa Maria, finding instead
of the Land of Spice, a new world of hope,
built on the stolen foundations of death.

Vasco da Gama sailed around the Horn
of Africa, losing ships; Magellan
sailed around the world, with five,
but only one returned to Spain, without him,
while Hudson sought the Northwest passage,
discovering ice pack and a mutinous crew.
Such were the old explorers, against all odds,
while modern ones ride the high sea of space.
Though the astronauts were aided by ground control,
making at times the difference, they were
still up there all alone, a long way from home.
The first man in space was the Russian Gagarin,
flying in the Vostok, a mighty ship,
putting him and five comrades later into space,
Titov, Nikolayev, Popovich, Bykovsky,
and the first woman, Tereshkova.
Vying with them, the Seven Mercury ships
celebrated the Freedom of Man from Earth,
rang the Liberty Bell, for Friendship,
Faith, an Aurora never seen before.
Shepard, the first American, suborbital;
Grissom did it again in space,
"Godspeed, John Glenn," the first man in orbit,
Carpenter, a second spin around the orb,
Cooper, the longest flight to date; Shirra
doubled Glenn's revolutions, while Borman
and Lovell stayed up there for fourteen days.
Gemini blasted off ten manned missions,
with some of the same astronauts,
while rookies joined the ranks, Young and McDivitt,
Conrad and Gordon, Aldrin, pushed outward,
space walks and rendezvouses and dockings,
longer and longer, ever further into
the unknown, away from the blue planet,
sailing always forward, not content to sit still,

though seemingly secure, risking everything,
life itself, in the quest to know, explore.
Apollo, that Greek god, wanting man on
the moon, was next, beginning in the Attic way,
three heroes, Grissom, White, and Chaffee,
lost on the launch pad, leaving the Earth
without their ship. America forged on,
no greater spur than failure and tragedy.
Eiselle and Cunningham, Anders and Schwikart,
replaced the fallen, for eleven days
circling the planet, Apollo 8
looped around the moon, Apollo 9 tested
the Lunar Module. With Apollo 10,
Charlie Brown and Snoopy swooped low over
the barren rocks and runway of the moon.
Apollo 11 achieved Kennedy's mission,
putting two men on the moon, with time to spare.
Japara and I were hot on their trail.
What is the human being that can do such things?
How has he acquired such capacity?
Where is it taking him on his journey?
Who sits at the controls of the ship of life?

BOOK III

THE ARGUMENT

Japara and the Persona return to the moon. The Parliament of
Poets continues. The nay-saying druid questions the fitness of
the Poet, many rallying to his defense. The dark pit. The
journey from Earth to the Moon. The flight with the Birds of
Paradise and the poet Robert Hayden. Twin Towers of
ascending light. The Nine Muses and Lord Apollo. What is
woman?

O Divine Essence and attending Muse,
  give my tongue thy blessings that I may find
  the words to describe the glories of thy Being,
help all mankind, threatened by ourselves,
turn again to peaceful contemplation,
prayer uplifting human vision to
the Great Mystery of the universe.
  O Reader, how can I tell you about
the voyage to the moon? How convey
the glories that I saw there, above the
earthly realm? There the sun always shines,
its glowing rays intensely light the way,
so brilliantly that all the stars are overwhelmed,
all lesser lights give way, as in obeisance,
and one sees but the blackest black of space,
not threatening and fearful, serene as God
in high bliss contemplating his own nature,
the marbled Earth floating through creation.
  And so Japara and I approached the moon,
scarfaced man to the scarfaced Man in the Moon,
the Sea of Tranquility, from still far
above the surface, growing closer, like
a Lunar Module seeking its landing site,
the pocked surface of the moon ever nearer,

craters with white rays spewing out for miles.
Beyond ground control, on manual now,
we zeroed in, and I could see from above
a great throng assembled, even larger
than when I had left with Black Elk for the
regions below, below the earth itself.
Now back to the supernal realm I came,
Japara my guide and protector from
the scars of life and precarious woe.
   Masters far beyond numbering were there,
poets and seers, bards and balladeers,
Italian sonneteers, Greek pastoralists,
the singers of Middle Eastern ghazals,
the storytellers of all Ages, generations,
answered the call to parley on the moon,
For All Mankind. So deep was I struck by
the sight, I felt a surge of emotion
that would have taken away my breath
had there been any air to lose, hit me
full in the chest, nearly the afflatus,
coming on, almost relinquishing
my hold on Japara's sustaining arm.
"Hang on," he shouted, "you're not safe yet,"
glaring at me; tears coming to my eyes,
I to him, "I don't know if I can do this."
"You've come this far! Out of The Dreaming,
the spirits call you on," filling me with hope,
flying farther, alighting among the throng.
   It seemed every poet from every land
and every time was there, numbers beyond
reckoning flooded the plain, ranged across it,
standing or sitting in groups, coteries,
together with their old friends and supporters,
the ways of the literary world, East
and West, as the story goes, truth be told.

Exactly why I could never fit in,
small, derivative, politics, not art,
the university become a coterie,
no longer trying to reach the people.
Most chatting amongst themselves, self-obsessed,
while Black Elk and Chief Seattle were watching
our descent, gently down before Cervantes,
leaning in the saddle, on Rocinante,
one hand on the pommel, the other hoisting
his lance, next to him, Du Fu and Bai Juyi,
Job and Dante, Virgil and Milton,
Homer and Vyasa, Tagore and Kalidasa;
Rumi and Hafez stood there with Attar,
all then watching as I gathered my wits,
wondering what now my journey would bring,
so grand the scope, so wide the breadth,
expanding before my all-too-human eyes.
   At that moment, Cervantes shifted in
the saddle, the Spanish leather creaking,
with a clatter of his armor, space suit now,
as it were, while he roared out to the poets,
"Tally ho, compadres, he returns,
the Lunar Knight of Mournful Countenance!
Traveler, time immemorial, you have seen,
and time remains, flowing through the regions
of this timeless space. Grasp it if you can,
can tell what it is, accept the imaginary
for what it is. The only thing that is real,
what we have before our eyes. Life but a dream.
To imagine that things in life are always
to remain as they are is to indulge
in fantasy. Nothing that is human is eternal.
You have the best guides. Others stand ready,
rally to the defense of all that we are,
all we have been. Grow your will to the charge,

for a true knight picks up the gauntlet."
And with those words a deafening roar went up,
acclamation shaking me to the core.
What great moment and import I felt,
laid upon me, so unworthy, and yet
all events demanded more of me, led on,
consternation, struggling within my soul.
How could I dare to stand with Homer,
Virgil, Dante and Milton, bards, East and West?
Off to the side, one seemed to detect my
inner turmoil, finding diversion, perhaps,
therein, toying, as it were, with a boy.
"Why him, and how did he get up here to begin with?"
Shocked, many eyes looked over at him,
a Celtic bard and druid, robe flowing
in the solar wind, embroidered with
a pattern of another time, gray locks
below his shoulders, challenging me
before Cervantes and all assembled there.
"Step forward," Cervantes commanded me,
a wider clearing now opening for us,
Japara leaving my side. "Tell us all,
for those who may not know, the story
of how you came here to the moon,
your long path through the ordeal of sacrifice,
hoping to win the favor of the Muse."
I thought of Odysseus, rehearsing the
tale of his long voyage, through stormy seas,
to the king and queen, lords and ladies.
I choked, tried to hold myself together,
before that illustrious assembly, a wave of
emotion surging over me, like the raging
waves on a shore of Lake Superior blown
by the northwest winds across two-hundred miles,
pushing a wall of water, thundering down

upon the narrow eastern channel of
Whitefish Point, sweeping all before it,
sinking many a ship to the deep,
as once the Edmund Fitzgerald and her men.
I struggled all inside for words. How answer
such a question? What words but truth
could possibly suffice for such a crew?
And so admitted, "I am all unworthiness,
yet still cannot but seek to serve the Muse,
a hope begun, I know not where, perhaps
a story around a campfire, a mother's tale,
a grandmother's love of books, a mother's trip
to the library, many times; a poem
in early boyhood read, a rousing rhyme
of Tennyson's or Kipling's, a song of
glory and sacrifice, men giving their lives
for other men, to protect the tribe
and little ones, a school room story hour,
or a lonely beach with Robinson Crusoe.
I don't really know, but ask you now to help
raise the song that men now need, help me find it,
teach it to me, if any of you have
ever bowed the knee to lofty song,
to the Muse of your far-flung land,
that I may take it back to Earth and write it down.
We see from where we stand the plight of
Mother Earth, our peoples all imperiled
and adrift, endangered. Ask the Muse!
I know not why she laid this thing upon me,
but I cannot rest until I get it out
and set it down, for others, is my hope,
and if found worthy, a laurel from her hand.
What poet can say anything else but this?
Bléssed gift, the greatest of any land!"
And there I choked, tears streaming down

my cheeks, but held my head aloft among
those who knew the weight of what I spoke,
over their heads I could see the Earth rising,
as though it were the sun on a newborn day.
A meditative silence looked back at me.
All eyes fixed deep upon my soul,
my words hanging upon the non-existent air,
mulled over in the heart of every bard.

   Sweeping his long lance to the side, Cervantes
pointed to the left, to a large burly one
that I knew, met again upon the moon,
saying, "We've heard as much from him,
Robert Hayden, with whom you apprenticed
for a while. What can you tell us about
all that?" Before I could think or find words,
Bob moved forward and said, "He need not speak
to all that. We came together to the moon,"
changing the direction of discourse,
for the druid burst out, "That's what I really
wanted to know. He's still embodied!
How'd he ever get up here," scowling slightly,
while he shook his locks of gray. Cervantes
turned back to me, "Well, all right, go ahead,
but the scientists aren't going to like it,
the too literal-minded at least.
They think they have a monopoly on space travel."
A chorus of guffawing laughter could
be heard scattered around Tranquility Base.

   I fidgeted. I didn't really want
to relate all that but could feel there was
no way to avoid it, standing on the carpet,
so to speak, of the moon. I had to comply,
launched into it. Ah, not a pretty story,
but the truth, to say, somewhere in the
mid-point of my life I was thrown into

a dark pit, sank into a Sea of Despond,
blacker than the blackest night, a swamp
barren of solid soil, whereon one might
plant one's foot, move firmly out and up,
as one might climb a steep, precipitous
mountain. I often floundered in despair,
blindness, confusion, lost as the lost of
every world, forlorn, alone, clinging by
but a shred to a weak and desperate
hope that somehow I might find my way
above the murky foam, be led or guided
from that muck, rise above like a lotus
on a stagnant pool, find beauty to lead
me back to land, yet once again, take me
from that dark pit, free me from the bonds
where I hung, as by clanking steel chains,
upon a dank and anciently hewn stone wall,
a torture chamber from where no music
came but the screams of men and women
upon the rack of life, the victims of
some potentate, despot, strangling tyranny,
fascist dictator, crushing and brutalizing
the humanity out of them, out of ourselves.
Thus, I found myself sunk, entrapped,
in such a feculent quagmire, conundrum,
that I could not find or figure my way out.
Forever lost, it seemed, not knowing
how to find the good, the beautiful, the true.
And then slowly I began to apprehend
that there, in chains, I hung with others.
Not alone, but many prisoners were
there with me. Our state seemed universal,
a writhing throng, now appeared on all sides,
bound, in every posture of agony,
suffering, extreme maltreatment, undeserved,

and I was but one of the multitude,
the realization of it touching me
to the quick, compassion suffusing me
when I saw others were worse off, writhing
on a bed of coals, cruel instruments,
and other diabolical engines of hate.
At the center of that seeming dungeon
hung one Prisoner, serene, who seemed
beyond it all, above, wrapped within
a mystery, a glory upon his face.
"Thus far, and no farther," I then heard.
And found I stood upon the floor, strewn with
filth and crawling things, a stench unbearable,
the background of it all, gallows calling.
A voice then said, "You may go, since you chose.
Your test is set before you. It begins."
The chamber door opened a crack, letting in
enough light that I could see the way out,
won somehow beyond my ken, deserving,
but so it seemed, my destiny, my fate,
from which I could not shirk, so forward
I walked to the open door, not knowing where
or to what it led, but felt strangely calmer,
at peace even as I strode toward it,
feeling in my heart the justice of it all.
I looked no further upon the denizens
of that pit, nor the figure at its center,
but walked toward the door and through it,
into a land I had no memory of,
but found green and wide, with trees and creatures,
stretching out before me on every side,
a garden like paradise, as it should be.
Memory of that place began to fade away.
  I found myself sitting in my study, dozing
over a book, Cervantes' *Don Quixote*,

surrounded by volumes of world classics,
the Japanese *Manyoshu* and the Indian
Bhagavad-Gita, Saigyo and Basho,
Wu Cheng'en's *Journey to the West*,
Rumi's love for Shamsi-Din, Attar's
for the Simorgh, epics of Africa,
the poems of China, ancient and modern,
the magic of Borges' *Ficciones*.
In my mind's eye, I ran my fingers over
their spines, hunting for a book, a title,
lost somewhere, in knee-high piles on the floor,
or my haphazard placing on a shelf,
next to Michigan's poets, Robert Hayden
and Theodore Roethke, or Robert Lowell
and Elizabeth Bishop, Philip Larkin,
all that confessional, small postmodernism,
the Nihilism of Deconstruction,
nauseating high priests of Nothingness,
rabid atheism, riding the tide,
self-righteously beating its fanatical chest.
    And then "Injun Joe," so-called, by white settlers
of my little town of Rochester, appeared before me,
the last Indian left, agéd and feeble,
long ago seen for the last time heading out
of town, up North Hill, to where the Indians camped,
near water, under oak trees. It always
seemed to me it could have been my backyard,
a sloping hill down to the creek and pond.
Even he, Injun Joe, stood in my library,
shaking my arm, awakening me, walking
out the back of the house. Rubbing my eyes
and head, I shook off my daze, setting aside
my book, followed through the family room door
out onto the deck, along the flagstone path,
to the circle patio under my apple

and oak trees, in the midst of peonies
and wild flowers, fragrant in the late spring air,
above the ground cover, blooms and blossoms.
Sitting down on the stone bench I looked up
the hill for Injun Joe but he was gone.
No sight of him under my old oak tree,
until I, too, follow Joe over the hill,
elsewhere than Earth, to happy hunting grounds.
  In my backyard, sitting on a stone bench,
I saw and heard birds and beasts of every kind,
amazing creatures for Michigan, tigers
and antelope, bison and mastodons,
ibexes roamed the hill to the pond, browsing,
along with moose and bear and deer,
on the lush, green grass around its banks,
as out of an ancient cave painting, Lascaux.
They all belonged with me, I with them.
Beauty everywhere, bees spreading pollen.
I thought upon that path of the Navajos,
"Beauty before me, beauty behind me,
beauty all around me, I'm on the pollen path,"
and rolled it over and over in my mind,
scarce knowing what to think or whom to thank,
blessing beyond blessing, surrounded me.
And then birds began to alight around me,
a few at first, become a flock, Robins
and thrushes, chickadees and golden finches,
downy-headed and red-bellied woodpeckers,
doves and hawks, parrots, toucans, orioles,
bluebirds and pelicans, seagulls and eagles,
cranes of every type, flamingoes strutted
about my backyard, nightingales sang,
peacocks fanned their tails, juncos hid under
the bushes from falcons and osprey,
still not willing to take any chances;

the Aztec quetzal bird with feathers of green,
the blue-throated nilkantha, a feather falling,
moon-birds, cakora, cakravaka, thirsty
devotees of Krishna chasing Radha.
More birds than I can name, had ever seen,
or known to exist, rare and exotic,
blended together in sumptuous symphony.
And then I saw a glorious hoopoe alight
upon a branch of the nearest apple tree,
among the white blossoms. All the birds
drew silent, watching her, as did I,
wondering why and what would happen next.
And so she spoke, "We seek the Simorgh,
and shall take you to her, a marvelous bird,
beyond the ken of man, beyond this world,
this tinseled dome." A hush profound fell upon
us all, at the idea, there in my backyard,
all trying to imagine her beauty.
The hoopoe breaking the silence, saying,
"We shall aid in carrying you aloft.
We birds of flight, instruct you, prepare for a
journey most rare, a journey to the moon,
what no man or poet has ever achieved.
Fairy folk of every land shall come for you,
your guide, shall be here too, master, friend, father,
mentor, pir, brother, ordeal beyond this world,
up to the starry sky. Often a journey
begins before one realizes it.
Just so now, we sing our song for you,
a new song, if you will, for every land
and clime, that you might raise, if you prove true,
accepting what's been laid upon you,
casting all else aside. You chose. Now further
the test abide." With that the hoopoe rose
into the air, all the birds rising with her,

trailing behind, in a great swooshing vortex
of feathered wing, circling round my meadow hill,
ascending higher with each pass, nine times,
up and around, nearly drawing me in,
as when a whirlpool off a rocky coast
will suck in every boat and floating thing,
drawing it deep down to the ocean floor,
as off the coast of Japan's tragic shore,
but this one, made of air, seemed formed to draw
me aloft, from earth to sky, tugged on me;
I thought for sure it would pull me
off the ground, but then subsided, as they
rounded the ninth gyre and blended back
into the air, over the trees, disappeared
as suddenly as they had come.
I found myself alone in the meadow,
like Quixote in the Cave of Montesinos,
the trees and grass and bushes swaying
gently in the freshening breeze,
my heart lifted to a different world,
in my backyard, my glade of trees,
where under I sat stunned, amazed.
    While I was trying to absorb it all,
a figure emerged from far down the hill,
where I could see two trees close together,
like double slits in the rolling landscape,
dressed in a jacket and vest, a decorous
bow tie, near the pond, incongruous,
out of his element, holding a tall black spear,
with a broad, wide blade, tapering to a point.
Walking towards me, I noticed he adjusted
his bow tie with one hand, peering through
bottle-thick glasses. "Egads!" I exclaimed,
"Bob, is that you!" remembering the day,
by chance, walking across the campus Diag

I had seen that figure in front of Angell Hall,
recognizing me too, as he smiled back,
two poets, one now grown older, both lessoned
by time. We laughed, looked at one another,
shaking hands, embraced. Stepping back, I said,
"Bob, that spear is just so not you!" And he,
grabbing and fanning his lapel, as was his wont,
"I'll have you recall I was the young poet
who aspired to fulfill Stephen Benet's prophecy
of an American Black poet with
a spear, chanting a song for his people,
and I still honor that, though complex for some."
Laughing together again, I shot back,
"They still don't get you, that you're human."
"Forget that crowd!" he scowled, adding,
"You, my friend, have done what you told me,
taking my breath away, gasping, as I recall."
"Oh, yes, I remember. It consoled me
for many years, even as your words,
'My God, you're going to have such a difficult time,'
have proven all too true with every passing year.
What a young fool I was to think all I had
to do was serve Robert Frost's twenty years!"
Laughing on the patio, he said, "Many
poets make that mistake. Enough of that too!"
waving his hand, sweeping it all away,
a gesture that only he could make.
"I will name their names and they shall come,
come for us, carry us heavenward to the moon.
I have come to lay my Black Spear down,
by Roland's horn. Do you think they'll be able
to get that? Howlingly funny!" he roared,
the old understanding passing between us,
my friend and mentor, I, still, his apprentice.
I hazarded, "The clichés are even

thicker now than when you were..." catching myself.
He just smiled and said, shaking his spear
in the air, "Boy, step aside, and let a
real poet show you how to get to the moon."
What a sight we were, there in the meadow,
a large, eccentric Black man, and a poet
worn down by life and all its poignant pains,
my body evincing signs of mortality.
The old bond felt so strong, as he began,
"Scientists and engineers don't own the moon.
I once saw their flags and footprints, intricate
rubbish left behind. We're rescuing it from them!
We poets were there first! I call, spirits!"
Both arms now flung forward, shaking in the air.
"I invoke your names, and from every land and time.
Hah! We poets are not the ones to worry about,
but scientists, bereft of any guiding vision!
Technicians without souls! Without a human heart!
We poets reclaim what is rightfully ours,
and so, great spirits," he bellowed into the air,
shaking his spear again, with new found fervor,
such that I reeled back, "I call you to come forth.
You shall carry us homeward to the moon.
All fairy folk come forth, juju man and
woman, watchers of the moon who knew its lore,
fays of every land, peries of Persia,
houri, genii on flying carpets, carry us
like Buraq, from Mount Qaf to the moon.
Lead our camel across the sands of time and space.
Egyptian Thoth and Greek Endymion,
Queen Mab, with all your crew, Puck and Titania,
Oberon, Robin Good Fellow, Tinkle Bell,
Welsh Fees, angels and cherubims, seraphims
of the Holy Temple, Roman Fata,
Valkyries of Valhalla, fleet-footed Mercury,

come down from Mount Olympus,
aid us Greek gods, if ever you assisted
human beings, we need you now,
Phoebus Apollo, bear me witness and hear
me out, your servants stand here in this grove,
raise them to the inspiration of the moon,
where you call all the poets of every land
to assemble. Zeus, wing our earth-bound feet
like Perseus, gird us to battle Medusa;
like Arthur, kept by the fairies, keep us safe,
safe upon our journey. Poesy is in need.
Take us to where we can look on Mother Earth,
reigning in the night of space, imagination's
greatest image, newly acquired, begrudgingly
admitted, obtained fortuitously,
despite themselves, by bumbling scientists
and fighter pilots, cosmic hieroglyph,
they knew not how to decipher thee.
Repair now to the poets' round table,
that bards and minstrels, poets and seers,
rhapsodes and griots, shamans and priestesses,
may consult in high intoxicating tones
of artful song, the meaning of our fate,
the fate of all humanity in this dark,
Nihilistic age." Surging into his appeal,
he bellowed all the more into the heavens,
"Divine beings come forth, convey us to the moon,
hear our petition now upon this meadow green,
this sward, pixies and gnomes, elves and brownies,
kelpies and korrigans, leprechauns,
the African flying tortoise, Mbeku,
flying shamans of the Incans,
carry us from Earth to the moon."
With a thud, Bob planted the end of his spear
down on the earth. I looked at him standing,

gazing into the sky, nearly blind as he was,
and knew he saw deeper and farther
than many men with two good eyes.
And then something began to happen,
those he summoned began to appear!
Together we could see them. The Fairy Queen
trailing her, or, er, his crew, came twinkling in,
apsaras and gandharvas from the East,
sphinxes and griffins, out of a thousand and
one nights of dreaming, the noble vulture
Garuda from standing guard in India,
Mother Goose's proverbial Man in the Moon,
her storybook cow that jumped over the moon,
Fenghuang, the Chinese phoenix bird, along with
the Russian Firebird, and their Greek consort,
all came down to serve the Fairy Queen
who deftly exercised her royal sway,
looking at Bob, intoned in silver notes,
"My lord, you called, and we have come to do
your bidding, poet true and valiant,
pure of heart, thy melodious song, nectar
to our breast, we thirst to hear your words
that guide us aright, poet-seer, though judged
legally blind by bureaucratic ignoramuses,
we know better, that thy penetrating sight
perceives what other men unwisely neglect.
And so we are here, guided, to be your guides,
and up toward the empyreum,
carry thee and thy charge to heaven's light,
great symbol of majesty's highest rule,
light saving us from pitch-black darkness,
raising men's minds above the lowly Earth.
Light in all its glory we shall ride,
moonbeams from the moon on high shall
safe passage grant; our road, supernal physics'
deepest insight into light, the energy

and mystery of the universe. I come
to petition further on your behalf." Spreading her
tender hands out toward the crystal sky,
she demurely began her appeal.
"True Light, if ever you have sought to guide us,
guide now, that these poets may assemble
on the moon, your orb, bejeweled in brightest light,
in time of darkness, enlighten our minds;
this corporeal one, especially,
requires your transcendent energy.
Let us rise, within thy brilliant light enwrapped,
vision visionary, all mystic beings attest,
rise, elevated by thee." She gestured us
closer. "Together, poets, stand," and in the
evening light, we now could see, the day, as we
spoke, having passed, into night, moonbeams upon
the meadow of my backyard, shimmering light,
ascendent energy of the far-off moon.
The hoopoe and all her flock having sailed
back over the trees, swirling around the circle,
joined and accompanied by Queen Mab's crew,
fairies and genii and magical beings;
Robert and I found we were rising in flight,
lifting off like a Saturn V rocket
from Cape Canaveral, not in a violently
shaking roar, but in fluid bird song.
   Queen Mab and Japara were at our lead,
bearing us aloft, light speed, for the moon,
and we within a shining beam, a tower
of light, Twin Towers, soared heavenward,
beyond time and Earth, accompanied by all
the multitude of birds and fairy folk;
together the angle of ascent achieved;
Daedalus and Icarus flew with us,
Icarus falling to Earth as we neared the sun.
Looking away, Bob murmured, "O Daedalus,

fly away home, O fly beyond Africa";
Pegasus heading back to Olympus;
Phaeton returning to his father's house;
Jason and the Argonauts launching out,
Prometheus flying back for fire,
dolphins sailing for Byzantium,
the White Tiger of the West for peace,
Bob and I like crows stroking for the moon.
I thought who needs warp drive when I've got Queen Mab,
my escort and midwife of my dreams;
and so she brought us here, to fairyland,
Japara and all the other wondrous folk,
even where you see us now, before you,
the Sea of Tranquility, all tranquil here,
earthly turmoil left far behind, place of pain
and human strife, so it seems, unending.
    After I finished, a long spell of silence
followed my tale. Cervantes spoke first.
"So he found me and my nag on the moon,
and the rest of you, gentlewomen and men.
Well, druid, are you satisfied? He needs
the help of all of us if he's to succeed.
All our peoples suffer for lack of vision.
We must rally together or we'll fall
before the onslaught of our modern foes,
run amok in the confusion of the age,
its noxious fare, the misbegotten guides."
The druid, struggling inside, eyed me,
up and down, sorting out things in his mind,
not quite yet resolved, quipping defiantly,
"You know the pagans aren't going to like the way
you're treating me." And I, "What makes you think that?
Would I give you such a large role
if I only wanted to beat up on you?"
    A new voice was heard, from a flowing cape,
"Of the same line, I, Merlin, vouch for him.

There's vision in him and a poet's tongue.
Let it be settled now so that all may
strain together in the great battle ahead.
Those who think otherwise, think again."
Resigned, the druid's demeanor changed.
"Master Merlin, you have my yea!"
And a cheer went up from all assembled,
filling my soul with a rush of moon air,
even as I felt my burden resume,
but with new hope that was never there before.
   And then a pulsating globe of light
appeared next to Merlin and Cervantes,
within a majestic lady in a silken gown,
holding a Greek tablet and stylus,
stepping out among the poets, followed by
eight other women, surpassing beauties,
all in diaphanous gowns, goddesses.
The first was even she, Calliope,
daughter of Zeus and Mnemosyne,
memory of her I shall never lose. No man
could look upon such a woman and forget her,
inspiring epic, foremost of the Muses.
The others gathered gracefully behind her.
She, the loveliest of the Muses, said,
"Now that we all have resolved to help
find the way to wholeness once again,
we come to urge you forward, to spare no pain,
shirk no suffering to gain this immortal prize,
but you must choose it every inch of the way,
for Lord Apollo demands every ounce
of devotion from his acolytes, but
beware lest you think it comes solely from yourself."
At the mention of his name, Apollo himself
appeared next to her in radiant aurora,
nearly blinding us with his intensity,
Calliope and all the Muses, to him,

curtsied, with feminine grace and style, catching
his eye and all the men standing by who watched.
He discreetly accepted their deference,
indicating to the Muses to continue;
Clio of history's great narrative art,
Euterpe, dame of tragedy and lyric,
Polyhymnia, Terpsichore, Melpomene,
and striking Erato, startlingly beautiful,
to say nothing of the passion of her verse;
Thalia of comedy's lightly lifting touch,
and lastly, Urania, Muse most apropos.
Like sweetly choice fruits from the gardens
of the world, each seemed not only Greek
but a hybrid of exotic, faraway lands,
not far away or strange anymore,
Africa and India, China, Japan,
Polynesian and Latina females
stood before me in feminine beauty,
under the sustaining sunlight of the moon.
Calliope, turning sideways to her sisters,
motioned to me, saying, "We shall grant him
our favors, abundant, copiously,
if ever granted to a poet and a man.
His task requires all our charms and skill,
if it is to succeed, as we all desire."
I was so dumbfounded I could not speak,
kept my head slightly bowed before them,
Greek goddesses of beauty and intelligence,
yet seemingly from every clime on Earth,
exquisite varieties of womanhood,
vibrant, gentle, tender, loving, chaste,
yet alluring, composed, confidently endowed;
that something different about women,
that only they have, struck me, deprived me
of all resistance or speech before the silken robes
of the panoply of their pageantry.

I heard Bob near me gasp, mouth agape.
Not a poet on all the plain breathed a word.
No one moved, not poet or Muse.
A profound silence hung in the moon air,
an unearthly stillness about the plain.
Together we all experienced it.
We were not alone. There was a Presence,
an Unseen Presence of Divinity,
and even Lord Apollo stood reverently.
We could feel and sense it without need of words.
Hearts were in unison as seldom known,
a resonance, as of far-off music, near,
the lunar music of the spheres,
heard and flowed out and over everyone,
pervading, sustaining all creation.
As that high pitch diminished and passed,
no comment or word on it was possible,
all groping about inside themselves.
Looking around in wonder and awe,
I noticed Aphrodite's acolyte,
Sappho, standing next to the Nine Muses,
she looking every part the Tenth, and by her
side Jane Austen and Emily Dickinson,
Gabriela Mistral, Muse of Chile,
women who knew the value of marriage;
women who threw all their passion into art.
Along with them Cynthia and Artemis,
Dido and Beatrice, Radha and Sita,
and I could see too Murasaki, Nimue,
Guan-yin and Shakuntala, Durga or Kali,
Virgin and Madonna, Saraswati,
Mary Magdalene and Dulcinea,
Pocahontas and Sacagawea,
pathfinders and guides, mothers and helpmates,
equals, superior to man in many ways,
their gifts and charms a balancing complement,

Gaia Mater, Venus, Juno, Kannon,
all the way back to the Neolithic caves,
statues, ochre hand prints, shell necklaces,
embellishing worship of humanity,
symbol of the Human Divine within.
Standing closer to them, Jane Austen said,
"Men all too often think women are nothing
but dancing girls and conquests, appendages
to their vanity and pride, mere metaphors.
Those ways of old are rightly passing away.
Anything is to be preferred or endured
rather than marrying without affection."
Stunned, I yet stammered, looking at all of them,
"Many no longer want to marry, man or
woman, commitment thrown to the winds,
along with children, if not tossed in a ditch,
mother and child abandoned, forgotten,
or many never ever even born.
A fate all too common in many countries.
To all the old ways of abusing woman,
the modern world has added its own,
so many afraid of starting life together,
no longer knowing how to begin. But, yes,
not a metaphor, or merely, though recall
the protective role of female sanctity,
so that woman might not become Circe,
nor men in their own way lose all restraint.
I choose Penelope, an earthly woman,
real, not a mirage, she of the poet's name,
love's own form, a blend of what we are.
Not a goddess on a pedestal, enshrined,
untouchable. I don't want a theory.
I want a woman in my arms, my wife,
pressed against me, and I close to her,
like luscious, ripe pomegranates I can pick,
within reach, touch and gently caress, kiss,

our hearts drawn together in mutual love."
Jane blushed, disconcerted, discretely stepped back,
holding her shoulders as she went, pursing.
I bit my manly lip for speaking loosely,
for never did I intend to hurt her heart,
yet thought, what is woman? Man without her?
To hold the woman whom one loves,
what greater joy in all the universe?
Though she be more, what greater metaphor?
As man, too, is her lasting conundrum.
Nature endowed her with that beauty
to ensure the survival of the species.
Through the harmony of man and woman,
the Universe become aware of itself.
Yet I knew I'd misspoken, squirmed before
Phillis Wheatley, and British women writers,
poets, playwrights, Aphra Behn whose satire
had women justly ranting against the time,
an Indian queen lost like Pocahontas,
Aemilia Lanyer who read "many a learned Booke,"
writing defenses of Eve and Pilate's wife,
Mary Sidney, Elizabeth Cary, Mary Wroth,
Elizabeth Gaskell, Mary Shelley, Edith Sitwell
and Virginia Woolf, Christina Rossetti,
Margaret Cavendish, her scathing tongue
flailing hard the Royal Society.
    A crude voice then interrupted my thoughts,
the druid, again, saying under his breath
to Rabelais, "Gawd, a hectoring wench,
even up here on the moon. Always trying
to wrap a man around their little finger!
Well, he gave it to her, he did. Shut her up!
Don't give me any of that sentiment.
I know what I used to do to teach them
a thing or two! Put 'em on their back!
That calms 'em down! Ha! Ha! Ha!"

Rabelais and the French poets joined in,
passing around a bottle, laughing hard.
"Put that bottle away!" yelled Cervantes,
bringing us back to the matter at hand, saying,
"Muses and gentle ladies, forgive the term,
if it now offends, permit me to speak.
My words so unworthy, yet as one who
actually ascended Mount Parnassus,
as my poem attests, drinking from Delphi's spring,
humbly, with all humility, as you suggest,
there are many windmills, shall we say,
that we must attempt to assail and conquer,
for time grows short on Mother Earth.
Evil knights and monsters stalk the planet.
With your blessings, Nine Muses, goddesses
of surpassing delight and enchantment,
illustrious kinswomen of the shelf,
each and every one, to leave none out,
I call the fairy folk and genii, Merlin
and Queen Mab, out of The Dreaming,
this life of dreams, dreams of life,
moon visions, as it were, with your permission.
I, in utmost sincerity, petition thee
to continue your copious blessings, as we
sally forth, servants of you all, as we are."
With heads held aloft and elegant mien,
the Muses drew together, then disappeared
in sparkles of rainbow light, rising above
the plain, wafting toward Earth, high above,
followed by their train of feminine acolytes.
We gathered there were all astonished.
Cervantes, recovering first, turned around,
sweeping his eyes over the crowd, searching,
until he found who he was looking for, shouting,
"And so now, druid, you know how he came
to the moon the first time! Shut your mouth!"

BOOK IV

THE ARGUMENT

Beyond *in medias res*, Tagore guides the Persona to India, to the
ashram of the sage and epic poet Vyasa in the Himalayan
foothills, to the field of Kurukshetra, and, in sight of Mt
Kailash, to Shiva Nataraja. Kabir. The epic struggles of the
Ramayana. Hanuman carries the Poet of the Moon to Angkor
Wat in Cambodia.

Mother Earth, far off, across timeless space,
enwrapped in her blueish-white beauty,
the diaphanous gown of her own glory,
high above the horizon, guided our thoughts,
as we looked around at one another,
there upon the Sea of Tranquility,
groping in wonder, wondering what journey
might lie before me, gift of her bounty.
   A lilting poet's voice cut through the silence,
a silence deeper than ever known on Earth.
"Oh, you Westerners are really too much,"
Kalidasa said, shaking his head lightly
from left to right and back again.
"All your dualistic struggles, antinomies.
We Indian poets should take him next.
We should teach him the yoga of our ways."
   Cervantes leaned back on Rocinante,
puckered his lips, not quite a smile, then a trace,
saying, "That's the spirit! Forward, charge!
Slay them while we may! Now there's a poet!"
looking all around, at flabbergasted faces.
To whom Kalidasa discreetly replied,
"There's a greater poet than I who should
guide him, a Bengali gurudev,
master of the deep soul of our people.

Rabindranath Tagore is here, will know
better than I the modern ways of dharma.
Too self-effacing to put himself forth,
I ask you all to urge him on this journey."
All looked beside Kalidasa, at Tagore,
standing where he belonged, long white hair and beard,
old, dressed in a humble, simple, flowing robe.
In his eyes and presence, a spirit felt,
a shining aura of his inner soul.
Tagore looked straight at Cervantes, saying
nothing, but deep eyes met deep eyes, thinking.
Cervantes broke off, turning round, announcing,
"Let all acclaim and charge Tagore with this task
of knightly pilgrimage to his homeland."
A shout went up from every poet's soul,
as eyes went to Tagore, who stepping forward,
said, "I accept your will as though it were
the Infinite One, and shall lead him on
the path he must needs tread, if he is to learn
what we in our consultations have agreed.
May Brahman and the gurus guide our steps.
We needn't linger longer, but set out."
Clasping his hands together at the chest,
with a slight bow to the assembled poets,
he moved towards me, holding out his arm.
Long transported to world's beyond belief,
I hesitated not, though I felt amazed,
obeying the master whom I revere,
trying to walk in his ways, raised my hands,
acknowledging his divine being, as he
had ours. With trust unquestioning, I stepped
to where he stood, grasped his wrist, and then within
the instant, we were gone, soaring above the moon,
the Earth circling larger into view,
as we flew toward her, home of all our pain

and love, the diurnal beauty moving through
the deepest black of black, a raja's jewel
worth more than any embellishing a turban.
Again, I felt, how can I say it? Flowing
through me, as we flew, such energy,
fortifying me for all that lay ahead.
As we neared Earth, I could sense her pulse,
the Schuman Resonance, wave upon wave,
of electro-magnetism coming from
the millions of lightning bolts striking the Earth,
surging through me, charging me with each beat,
the Earth itself a revolving Dynamo,
more alive than any man-made machine.
And then far off to the left, I saw the
international space station round the globe,
wondering what crew was in there now,
and what a shock it would be for them to see
Tagore and I together sailing through space.
We could see India from Mt Kailash to
Sri Lanka, greens and browns, her great rivers
not yet visible but down there nonetheless.
Where Tagore was taking me I did not know,
and did not ask, trusting his judgment,
though my curiosity began to grow,
traversing a quarter of a million miles,
at almost the speed of light, the spirit's speed,
entanglement achieved at full throttle.
It became clear we were headed toward
the north, the foothills of the Himalayas,
a river below, winding down the Punjab.
I cast a sideways glance at Tagore to which
he replied, "The River Beas. The ashram
of the great sage, Vyasa, epic poet of
the *Mahabharata*, India's greatest poem.
I at once thought of Vyasa's tale of

India's earliest time, King Bharat,
Shakuntala's son, and his progeny,
their bitter betrayals and wars, dharma
cast aside for worldly tinsel, baubles,
the things we human beings imagine amount
to something worthwhile, unworthy, really,
our swiftly passing lives upon this planet.
    While such thoughts ran through my mind, Tagore
took us lower, over a forest, setting
us down in a glade, between the River Beas
and a small building, some distance away,
nestled in trees, with goats milling about.
Tagore immediately led me towards
the ashram, and then I saw him, sitting
under a great tree, absorbed in meditation.
Vyasa had a full beard, his hair pulled up
into a topknot, three white lines across
his forehead, a red dot in the middle line,
with a string of beads around his neck,
a saffron robe over his shoulder,
the right bare, wrapped at the waist,
a sacred cord across his bare chest.
He opened his eyes as we stopped in front
of him, gently pressing his hands together,
as did we, Tagore bowing and touching
his feet, I following his example.
    Vyasa said, "Rest here travelers from
the strain of your journey. This sacred grove
and this hermitage is almost as sweet
as the heavens from which you've traveled,
four-dimensional travels through time and space.
Such a hermitage nurtured Shakuntala,
with birds, deer, and thick forests everywhere,
a refuge and sustainer of the soul,
a pious grove in which the fairies dance,

as daylight shuts moon-blooming flowers,
and slays the moon outright, they can be seen.
The fragrant lotus of the sacred river
wafts its perfume through the air. Here we hermits
dwell at the foot of the Himalayas,
plunge in a pool of nectar, lead our
self-denying lives. Rest here in the shade
of the asoka tree. My scribe is away,
but I welcome you both." In the shade,
we sat quietly for some time. Nothing stirred.
I felt I had to speak and said to him,
"O Vyasa, help me find a vision worthy
of humanity. The time is so confused.
Passion and violence wrack the entire globe.
The ways of peace and meditation lost."
Unruffled, he replied, "Strive always to teach
humanity dharma and the ends of life.
Time flows like a river but the body
cannot remain steady like a boat.
The soul is a traveler that is forever
in search of its far shore, its goal and aim.
I know that is why Tagore has brought you,
O Poet of the Moon, to my ashram.
To cry over the failings of life is not
the aim. Rid yourself of all attachment.
It is good that man does not know the future.
What is fated will happen, as it should.
Pre-knowledge can be a cause of sorrow.
You are unable to watch what I have seen.
Do not blame your fate for the turn of events.
Man is responsible for what happens.
Fate means only that God knows what will happen,
but He never interferes in human affairs.
Renunciation does not mean running
away, but facing one's problems squarely.

You must choose the path of renunciation.
Only then will the gods help you. The battle
is first in your own soul. Choose sacrifice.
Poet of the Moon, your dharma is heavy,
but Brahman tests every soul with its burden.
Let your action rise to your fate.
Dharma, this is all that I have to teach,
and all you need to learn on your journey
around the world. And so the gods gave me
this hermitage, don't you see?" He ended,
allowing that to sink in, motioned me
towards him. I rose from the woven mat that
I was sitting on and stood in front of him.
From a small bowl of red sandalwood paste,
he anointed my forehead with a red dot,
between my eyebrows. We raised our hands in
namaste, bowing slightly as we did.
Tagore touched his feet, as did I, leading
me away into the forest, where he stopped,
overlooking the river, paused, soon held out
his outstretched arm toward me. In a daze,
I grasped it, lost in thought, meditation,
and from that sacred grove we flew,
high above the forest, eastward, going far.

   We soon were over a plain, a wide field,
where two vast armies were ranked to battle,
legions on either side for war, the carnage
about to begin, so it seemed. Into this,
Tagore led me. Panic surged within me,
as I looked at him, and he peacefully
looked back. Ksatriyas, warriors and princes,
on either hand, girded for the worst,
stood ready to commence. And then I realized
this was the war of the Bharatas,
Kurus seeking to destroy Pandavas

and Arjuna, the rightful heirs of the
kingdom. Not being of the warrior class,
I confess, I felt very out of place,
as we landed on a small hill behind
a red oleander overlooking the site
of the battlefield. Not far away,
I noticed a chariot, alone, between
the armies, Hanuman's flag flying from it,
two figures standing nearby, engaged in talk,
not battle, though some struggle waged in the soul
of one, Arjuna, his charioteer, Krishna,
attired in his glory, indescribable.
Darshan not through a statue but the living god.
Out of sight, or so I hoped, we watched,
strained to listen, the conversation going
back and forth, while I recalled their great words,
treasured deep within my heart, the call to
sacrifice and duty, the warrior's art,
test supreme of every soul, the mettle.
Arjuna put down his bow and arrows,
and I became aware that we were not
alone behind that bush, but now, at my
elbow, to my surprise, I recognized
a most incongruous figure, a prim
New England man, Ralph Waldo Emerson,
dressed in his dark suit, collar and cravat,
smiling serenely upon the scene.
And I recalled and mulled over his lines,
"If the red slayer thinks he slays,
or if the slain think he is slain,
they know not well the subtle ways
I keep, and pass, and turn again.
I am the doubter and the doubt.
And I the hymn the Brahmin sings,"
while nearby Krishna intoned them as well.

"Master," I said, "you were my first teacher,
guide. You opened the way for all of us,
walking away from the cowled churchman.
The time has turned away from the Over-Soul.
Tell me how to go on from here, how to raise
a universal song For All Mankind,
as universal as the morning wind."
Smiling sweetly, gentle tolerance and
forbearance, love and compassion, he said,
"What's a moment of confusion in the face
of eternity? Shrug it off. The Eternal One
is within every man and woman.
You already know better than I that
you must find your own way. Self reliance.
Now watch and listen," turning to the battle.
Resolve strengthened in my startled heart, the call
of duty, as Krishna called to Arjuna,
"Remain poised in the tranquility of Atman,"
and other snatches we were blessed to hear.
Krishna's back now toward us, Arjuna
bowed before him, clasping his hands, seemed
transported to a higher realm, while we
remained below, standing on our feet of clay.
Arjuna bowed down a second time to
Govinda, Lord Krishna, a deep shudder
of emotion ran through my body and soul,
like nothing I had ever felt before,
not physical, spiritual, the only word
that can convey some vague inkling of what
I felt, like wave on wave of surging water,
on a beach, braking over the shore, my soul,
spreading out, much absorbed into the sand,
while most was drawn back into the sea.
   Behind that red oleander, with Tagore
and Emerson, what seemed the longest time

beyond time, till Arjuna rose towards
his chariot, taking up his great bow.
At that moment, Krishna turned towards me,
where I thought I was hidden, hurling
at me on that Kuru field of battle,
"You are a poet; where's the poem?
You bear a vision; where is its rendition?
You have a song; sing it for us.
Let go of the outcome; detach yourself.
You have a duty; where is the action?
Cast away all desire and fear.
You know the asuras, when will you slay them?
Do your duty; leave the rest to God."
  The blackest blackness of time overwhelmed me,
dumbstruck, stumbling backward, recoiling, swooned
almost dead on the spot, judged, found wanting,
more than I could bear, mere mortal,
unworthy of sight of him, Lord Krishna.
Half aware, the sound of charging armies,
the clash of swords and weapons, dimly heard;
the sound of gandharvas, heavenly musicians,
playing on their vinas, lifting me upward,
aided by apsaras, maidens of fresh water,
bathing my forehead, reviving me as we flew,
cries of agony and slaughter below,
receding, far away now, bearing me away,
landing in a pine forest on a mountainside,
a formidable peak in the far distance.
Tagore and I stood there, surrounded by
a ring of gandharvas and apsaras,
healing music rising among the pines.
The quiet of the mountainside imparted
a much needed sense of serenity,
lifting my spirit to a new plateau.

   Tagore then spoke. "You have heard Krishna, now
Lord Vishnu's eighth incarnation, Shiva.
He will come down to us from Mt Kailash,
from talking with squabbling ascetics.
Lord Shiva will speak a different language."
Pointing, he said, "He will come over
that rise. You shall be granted a vision
few souls have ever seen. Learn from it.
Prepare for the Dance of the Universe,"
looking deeply into my eyes, with a
seriousness that made me wonder what
new experience I was about to have,
so far from home, my suburban town,
so typical of modernity, Rochester.
While I looked, I saw a beautiful female
glide down through the pines, along with
and alighting next to Narada, leader
of heavenly musicians. Leaning toward
Tagore, I asked, "Master, who is this being
of surpassing beauty?" "Saraswati,"
he replied, "Consort of Brahma, patroness
of the arts." Standing on a lotus blossom,
floating above the forest clearing,
she began to play the vina, lifting
all into another region of reality.
Suddenly I saw Shiva Nataraja, a vision,
an effulgence of light, in sacred grove,
a whirl of dance, poised within a circle
of fire, on the edge between two worlds,
his swirling locks revolving with his movements,
long coils of hair flying about,
the divine music of the universe,
soaring, as of the heavenly spheres,
whirling, in serenity supreme, beyond
this world, right foot planted firmly on a dwarf

of ignorance, dread symbol of our worldly
nature, sunk so low from the lofty heaven
of our goal. In one hand, he held aloft
a flame of fire, burning away illusions,
our maya; with another, he beat the drum
of creation, marking time, upon a lotus,
his third arm signaling peace, assurance,
dispelling fear, his palm open toward us.
Lord Shiva looked upon us, calm, benevolent,
enjoying his creation, OM the syllable
he intoned through movement, divine energy
flowing, destruction returning chaos
to order. Into and out of samsara,
flowed creation, rhythm of life, joy,
his footsteps relieving the suffering
of his followers, perpetual conflict,
good and evil, knowledge and illusion,
nourishing the universe, Creator
and Destroyer, lover and ascetic,
husband and hermit, his third eye gazed out
on all, so he danced upon the crossing
point of two times, holding us spellbound,
as he whirled upon the flower of wisdom
and enlightenment, enlightening us,
ending one age to begin another,
enumerable kalpas passing as we watched,
his raised leg a sign of liberation,
moksha of the soul, release, from the
burning flames that arched around him,
sat, chit, ananda, truth, consciousness, bliss,
his forth arm crosswise, compassionately
granting his favor to humanity,
releasing all from the round of samsara.
Before his glorious image we all
instinctively bowed down in awe and joy,

submission and surrender, humbling
ourselves before his visionary dance,
Shiva Nataraja, medicine wheel
of Bharat. As he had come to us,
he suddenly began to fade, disappeared,
taking with him the forest circle of
gandharvas and apsaras. Oh, how I wished
I could have followed them, Saraswati, too,
leaving Tagore and I standing together
under the pines, a fresh breeze coming down
the mountainside, as from Mt Kailash.

   Tagore looked at me for a while,
held his head up slightly, saying nothing,
and then walked a few steps away, peering out
towards the valley below, mountains far away.
While he stood there silently, I said nothing,
still too overcome to know what to say,
waiting for him to find the words
that might be right after what we had seen,
experience beyond what words can capture.
With his long hair slightly blown by the wind,
still looking across the valley, through the pines,
his back to me, he said, robe flapping,
"When young, I used to come up here alone.
Slipping away from my father, long ago.
Here, take this bloom of red oleander,
a token of our journey," holding it out.
Nodding, I slipped it into my breast pocket,
still dazed, failing to thank him for his gift,
while he continued, breeze furling his robe.
"I must return to the moon where I belong.
Another guide will come for you before long.
Prepare for him. He will soon be here."
And then Tagore gently faded from my sight,
until I could see the valley and the mountains

across the chasm, part of a path visible,
winding upward through the rocky terrain,
high in the mountains the glaciers melting.
I looked around, and I, I was all alone.
Looking across the valley I thought of
Radha and Krishna, the gopis, what love
means for a man and woman, the Divine,
blue lotus-eyed Radha, her treasured jewel,
her face as radiant as the Moonlight Goddess,
her love the very essence of devotion.
Deep in my heart I reflected on what
had transpired, vowing to find some way
to convey it to the world, if life and time
should be granted to me by the gods.
    The wind picked up, soughing through the pines.
I felt a presence behind me and turned
to see a man emerging from the wood,
thin, but one who held himself with dignity.
As he drew closer, he said, "The poets on
the moon have sent me, and so here I am.
Kabir says, it's too cold on this mountain.
We've got to go elsewhere if we're to talk.
Where doesn't matter. All the world's the same.
Take my arm. We shall go to Kashi,
as good as Magahar or anywhere else."
Slightly smiling, gazing steadily in my eyes,
raising his bare left arm toward me,
the fingers curled but not closed in a fist.
I kept my eyes fixed on him, such a
different man before me, but my heart felt
confident in the way of my guide. I sensed
there was something I deeply shared with him.
Without a word, I reached forward and took
hold of his wrist, still looking in his eyes.
Kabir turned his gaze heavenward, and we

were off, leaving that clearing behind,
flying south out of the forest and mountains.
How long we soared I cannot say but soon
I saw great rivers below me with cities
along their banks, one with great steps down to
the water, with many people on them, and
in the river. Near there we lowered to
a flat plain, where a small village of rustic
dwellings spread out with fields that were dry
and barren. Before a hut, he gently put
us down, gesturing for me to follow him.
Jars and a loom were under a nearby tree.
Stooping, he entered, past bundles and bales.
One room was all there was, seating himself
on a mat by a window. A goat was
in the corner, but baahed, wandering out.
Kabir, not taking any notice, looked
at me a moment, and then said,
"Listen to me, my friend, the Beloved
is within you. He's not in Mecca or Kashi,
He's not in the Quran or the Vedas.
The sacrifices of the Brahmins stink to
high heaven, the Muslims wander in the
mirages of the desert of their imagination.
Hindu and Turk, where did these two come from?
Pandits have all gone astray. Of the mystery
of Ram, what you call God, they all know
nothing. Worthless the Puranas and Hadiths,
false the Quranic law, false the sacred thread,
the Supreme Soul is seen within the soul.
The Moon is within, so is the Sun.
Light, eternal in the Sun, reborn in the Moon.
Neither in temple nor mosque,
neither in rites nor ceremonies.
If thou art a true seeker, thou shalt see

Ram in a moment of time. What are the
ten avatars? No avatar can be the
Infinite Spirit. The yogis, the sannyasins,
the ascetics, dispute one with another.
Brahmas and Shivas, Indras and demigods,
none are the Lord Self-revealed;
the scent of sandal and flowers dwells in
those deeps, the light of sun and moon and stars
shines bright, the melody of love, rhythm.
The universe sings in worship, adoration,
day and night, mingled in the hymn of the heart,
like the mingling of the Ganges and Jumna,
a lotus blooms without water, eternally,
center of the spinning wheel of the universe.
The bee of my heart drinks its blooming nectar.
The moonbeams of that Hidden One shine in you,
in the silence of OM, of the universe.
Music all around, the drum beats, lovers sway,
love songs resound, drink the cup of the Ineffable,
reach the Root of Union, the Sorrowless Land.
He on that path transcends all sorrow.
Merge your life in the ocean of life,
find your life in the supreme land of bliss,
lost in the effulgence of billions of stars.
The Supreme Spirit is near you—awake!
Run to your Beloved, put aside all imaginations.
O brother, my heart yearns for that true Guru,
the vision of Brahma. Drink the sweet honey,
pluck the petals of the lotus of the heart.
All things are created by OM, without form,
without quality, without decay. Seek thou
union with Him, that formless God takes
a thousand forms in the eyes of his creatures.
Pure, indestructible, infinite, fathomless.
He dances in rapture, without beginning or end,
all within His Bliss—Thou and I are One."

"Kabir says all this to you. Carry it back.
Go thou and meditate always on it.
Tell all the world what I have told you.
Follow your thirst for the Infinite!
O brother Sadhu! Mate with the Beloved.
Dance in the delight of a hundred arts.
Your Lord dwells within you. Be the river,
enter the ocean. Let the waters merge.
O friend, awake! And sleep no more.
Leave your bed to commune with the Beloved.
He is dear to me who can call back
the wanderer to his true home, the Union.
Why should we forsake home, wandering?
Home, the abiding place, home, the Attainment.
Stay where you are. All things shall come to you.
Why travel to the moon? There is nothing
but water at the holy bathing places.
The images are lifeless and cannot speak.
What are all the holy books, priests, and scholars?
Kabir utters the words of experience.
All other words are untrue, phantoms.
The moon-bird is devoted to the Moon.
I left off all rites and ceremonies,
bathed no more in holy water,
no longer rang the temple bell, or set
the idol upon its throne, nor worshiped
the image with flowers, incense, or food.
Austerities and yoga please not the Lord.
The man who is kind and righteous, treating all
as his own, attains immortal Being, the
true God is ever with him, dwelling in his heart.
He attains the true Name whose words are pure,
humble, free from pride and conceit.
The yogi reads the Gita, pride swells up.
Hari is in the East, Allah the West.

Look in your heart. There you will find both.
All men and women of the world are His forms.
They are not low born. Kabir is the child
of Allah and Ram. He is my Guru, Pir.
Let us go to that country where dwells the Beloved.
He can never be found in abstractions.
He can never be found in organizations.
He can never be found in institutions.
No matter how grand, pompous, wealthy,
powerful and pretentious, recognize the Lord,
fill your soul with mercy. Renounce the self,
know the Self. This is Paradise, Salvation.
One Love pervades the entire world,
music of the meeting of soul with Soul.
O Poet of the Moon, Kabir says,
get rid of duality, achieve Union.
Go thou and meditate on this. Tell the world."
He sat quietly, as did I, a warm,
serene smile on his lips, looking beyond me,
then raised his hands together toward me,
I to him, heart to heart, we understood.
I rose without a word, walked outside,
past his weaver's loom, back towards Kashi,
all he said revolving through my heart and soul,
like the Milky Way up there beyond daylight.
   Down the road I stopped, surrounded by fields
and bordering trees, pondering in my heart.
A cart then went by, pulled by a poor farmer,
who looked gaunt and impoverished, desperate,
changing utterly the direction of my mind.
I thought of all the wealth I had seen, clashing
on the field of Kurukshetra, no concern
for this man and the poor of India.
The wealthy and their cold hearts, taking all,
reveling in their luxurious decadence.
How many poor have died lying in the road,

where they collapsed in painful exhaustion?
Oh our hardened hearts of indifference!
And while I grieved and bemoaned our human plight,
there was a movement in a tree nearby,
a sound of an animal, awakening me.
I stepped out from where I had been brooding
to discover a remarkable sight,
a large creature strangely half-man, half-monkey,
crowned with a regal headdress, armlets
and anklets, a broad sword on his belt,
necklaces, and a type of open cloak,
chakra blossoms adorning his chest,
a vision out of the *Ramayana*!
He could have crushed me in an instant,
but I felt no fear, despite his size and sword,
Hanuman, Rama's devoted servant
and defender, the Monkey King, his tail
singed from having burned Ravana's capital.
And then he spoke, "Rama sends for you.
We must go quickly. He stands on the shore,
waiting for Nala, the craftsman, to finish
the bridge across the water to Sri Lanka.
We shall talk as we fly." And with those
words, so mildly spoken, he swept me up
in his furry arms, gazing into my eyes.
I grasped his furry wrist, feeling his strength
as it flowed through me, lifting me to a
higher realm, above the fields of Kashi.
A vast panorama of Mother India
flew by me as we sailed through time and space,
through the swirling kingdoms of Kosala,
Kasi, Mathura, and Kunti, past
Chitrakuta, and Sarabhanga, over the
Vindhya mountains to Panchavati and
the Dandak forest, past Kishkinda, where
Jatayu fought for Sita, sacrificing himself,

trying to stop Ravana from abducting her,
home of the monkey army now marshaled
on the far southern shore of India,
past the many places of Rama's valor,
his stringing and breaking the mighty bow
of Shiva, India's Odysseus.
No man could lift it, only Rama,
winning chaste Sita's blesséd hand in marriage.
Hanuman pressed on, Rama's service his goal
and eternal delight, intent on defeat
of the evil Ravana and his asuras,
demons preying on all the innocents.
    I saw below, ahead of us, Rama's bridge,
stretching across the sea to Sri Lanka,
still visible from space, Nala's handiwork,
as on my flight down from the moon with Tagore.
Upon seeing him standing on the shore
of the ocean, with his devoted brother,
Laksman, planning how to rescue Sita,
Hanuman in devotion cried, "Lord Rama!"
Landing before him, Hanuman explained,
"I have brought him here as you commanded,
the Poet of the Moon, fresh from Kabir."
Eternity seemed to pass between Hanuman
and Rama, before the latter kindly said,
"Our enemy Ravana ravages all the land,
destroying sages at their rites, the people,
and all order swept aside by violence, greed,
and passion. Nala's bridge is almost complete.
Valmiki and Tulsidas, all the poets of
the *Ramayana*, await on a hillside,
to watch the battle and the slaying of Ravana,
sing in song our victory For All Mankind,
remind them when they again are threatened.
Take him to Valmiki and return."
Without a word Hanuman obeyed,

scooping me back up, where I stood speechless,
head bowed, not daring to look at Rama.
In a few strides, it seemed, Hanuman had
set me down next to the epic poets on
the far hill, overlooking the ocean, and left.
From where we stood, we could see legions of
monkey warriors, ranked far into the distance,
waiting for Rama and Hanuman's commands.
Soon the troops began to march to battle.
The ten heads and twenty arms of Ravana,
all his army, could not stop Rama.
Ravana's world collapsed. The great vulture
Garuda, too, fought, saving Rama and Laksman.
Ravana's demons fell like leaves before
a strong wind, swept from the branches,
blown away from life, across the ground,
swirling with the dust, and their own cries.
The battle raged back and forth, relentlessly,
Rama's chariot flying the flag of the universe,
with Garuda perched on it, chasing
Ravana's fleeing chariot around Lanka
and the globe, until Rama let fly a
devastating weapon straight into his evil heart,
knocking him off his chariot into the dirt.
All creation changed with that act, revived,
Rama and Hanuman recovering Sita,
welcomed back into Rama's loving arms.
All the battles of history seemed to flow
through my mind as I watched from that high hill,
next to Valmiki and Tulsidas, other poets,
watching and learning, our emotions
soaring with the tides of struggle and victory.
    All soon began the trek north to Ayodhya,
across Rama's bridge, with Hanuman
appearing, saying as he came towards me,
"Now you understand. Every generation

must fight Ravana, the one without, and
the one within. Build a monkey bridge across
the chasm of Nihilism that the
Rakshasas have opened in the modern world.
We must hurry. Rama orders me to
announce his arrival in Ayodhya,
before King Bharat grows impatient.
I am commanded to carry you in
giant strides to a friend. Time runs short."
To which I revealed some apprehension,
Valmiki hastening to say, "Fear not.
You'll be safe. We will meet again on the moon.
Vyasa, Tulsidas, and I shall bring
all the poets of the many versions,
they who are here with us and many others,
all those who inscribed their poems on palm leaves,
Kritivas in Bengali, Nagachandra in Kannada,
Kambar, the Tamil poet, Eknath in Marathi,
Indonesian and Thai, Khmer and Malayalam,
more tongues and cultures than the West even has."
At that, Hanuman scooped me up into his belt,
while growing to his giant size, nearly
reaching, it seemed, half way to the moon.
With a few enormous strides, Hanuman
crossed the Bay of Bengal and Andaman Sea,
setting me down somewhere in Cambodia,
near Angkor Wat, in a clearing of the jungle,
brilliant birds all around, singing in the trees.
Removing me from his pouch, Hanuman
said, "Fear not, my friend Ta Chak will come.
I must head for the ashram of the sage,
on to Bharat, his reign of peace to begin
at last in Ayodhya," raising his
gigantic right hand to me as he vanished.
And I, I was all alone, in a jungle clearing,
exotic birds sang in the flora and fauna.

BOOK V

THE ARGUMENT

An old man welcomes the Persona to Angkor Wat, Cambodia,
guiding him across the bridge, through and around the galleries.
Bayon. The Killing Fields. Bagan, Burma, Valley of a Thousand
Temples. Sun Wukong, the Chinese Monkey King, ferries the
Poet over Tibet, to Dunhuang, in the far northwest of China.

A rustle and a parting of leaves, an old man
stepped out of the jungle, a little frail,
thin and short, walked toward me, saying,
"Ah, so you are the Poet of the Moon.
Hanuman told me I would find you here.
I am Ta Chak, reciter of the *Reamker*,
the *Ramayana* of Cambodia.
Come, I will show you the way," gesturing,
and turning to a path that led through the
foliage, soon coming out onto a dirt road,
which broadened, took us toward the east,
became clearly now a road traveled by
many people, as I followed my new guide.
We came out of the thick jungle, on either
side of the road, and I beheld a sight of
such startling and overwhelming beauty
that I found myself gasping in awe.
Mt Meru, the center of the universe,
majestic towers, rising above the jungle,
set like a jewel in the Buddha's forehead,
four towers surrounding the central one,
an enormous moat on all four sides,
shaped like unopened lotus blossoms
richly imbued with beauty. A long bridge
led to the temple, across a waterway,
the moats keeping out the demons, while Nagas
rose along the way, adorned the bridge,

mythological beings protecting
the pilgrim's path. So overpowering,
I glanced aside at my guide, hoping for
reassurance, as one does, when a young boy,
from one's grandfather in strange and
unfamiliar situations, seeking the
older man's wisdom and experience.
He understood and said, "Angkor Wat,
City Temple, though the city is no more,
long gone, all impermanent in this world,
passing, as we pass, the journey the destination,
and here before us lies what is our own.
From the moon you have come, and from here
to the Buddha you shall rise." He looked ahead
as we continued to make our way across
the bridge, Nagas leaping as we walked.
   At the end we passed through a gate,
entered what used to be the city grounds.
Before us again we saw the five towers,
rising above, upward, into the sky,
more stone than the Egyptian pyramids,
weathered and darkened with time, lichen, moss
everywhere, worn by the feet of millions.
Another long processional walkway
lay before us, as we pressed on, coming
at last to another gate, entering upward
to the three terraces above, and then
into a long gallery before the temple,
extending all around it on every side,
more than a mile long it seemed.
We stopped inside and I glanced from
left to right, trying to perceive where
I was, standing next to Ta Chak, who now
looked quietly at me, saying,
"These galleries are past and present of

the soul, tell the story of the East,
much of the path you've already traveled,
Indra's great vision. Here the record
of the passage through the Khmer ages,
all the Asian kingdoms of by-gone times,
peoples of the morning mist.
They sent you to me to show you these,"
he added, with a tone of nobility,
his head poised, gracefully raised back,
looking me in the eyes, sizing me up.
Despite my feeling so inadequate,
I tried to rise to the occasion,
to see and learn, determined I would go
forward with my guide wherever he led,
strive to understand whatever lesson he deemed
I might be worthy of or need to hear.
I then noticed, behind, on the wall,
figures and carvings, discernible in
the morning sun, though in the shade,
since they were on the western wall,
but open through the colonnade to the
long processional way we had crossed.
    Stepping to the right, and walking slowly,
Ta Chak said, gesturing now at the wall
to his left, "Here, the battle of Kurukshetra,
where you strained to listen to Krishna speak
with Arjuna, saw him set aside his bow,
long ages ago, after which the gods
brought their teachings to our land, their power
not lost on our former and mighty kings,
commemorated here for the Khmer people."
Before me I saw it exquisitely carved
in detail as I gazed and followed Ta Chak,
time hanging still, sense of all else gone.
He reached the end of the western gallery,

turned left around the corner, glancing at me,
the morning sun now illuminating
both of us, and he again gesturing at
the wall, picking up the pace, in the sunlight,
"Here is the army of King Suryavarman II,
founder of Angkor Wat. This temple, too,
his funerary," and he waved toward
the depiction of the great king without
pausing, as we passed along, my keeping step
with him, following his direction, so sure
he seemed to know where he was taking me.
    Ta Chak again turned to the left at the end
of the southern gallery, and there stretched
before us another long passageway,
open to the eastern sky, the sun now
risen above the jungle, illuminating
directly through the colonnade the bas-reliefs
that covered the wall in artistic glory.
Ta Chak directed my attention with his,
waving, saying, "The churning of the milk,
Lord Vishnu and all the gods struggling
with the demons, pulling on the great cord,
for a thousand years, extracting the nectar
of immortality, seizing it, victorious,
Asura demons defeated, Lord Vishnu
ascending above them in triumph."
    Reaching the end of the eastern gallery,
Ta Chak turned left, taking me with him,
as he strolled along the northern wall,
saying, "Lord Vishnu's incarnation, Krishna,
defeats the evil Bana, with all the gods of
Brahman wielding their weapons, upon their mounts,
battle with the demons, as must we all,
Lord Vishnu preserving all from harm,
from destruction." Again turning the corner

to the left, we approached where we had begun,
now back at the western gallery, strolled awhile.
Ta Chak stopped, turned entirely to the wall,
and in an even more reverent voice said,
"Lord Rama, Vishnu's mighty incarnation,
locked in battle with Ravana, the evil
abductor of his wife, purest Sita;
Hanuman, part man, part monkey, leading
the battle, his legions of monkey warriors
defeating Ravana's island kingdom
of Lanka, as you witnessed and know,"
a startled expression appearing on his face,
as he realized the fact for himself,
looking at me afresh, that I had witnessed
such a sight, far beyond my merit
I readily concede, and wanted to say,
but Ta Chak gave forth no pause, adding,
"Oh, great battle in which we all must strive,"
leaning now toward me, with gentleness
of spirit and word that almost tore out
my heart, as I stood next to him, gazing
at the epic tale wrought before us,
in such exquisite detail by artists
so long ago, so far from India,
so far from the realm of heaven, truth be told,
the truest location the mind of man.
Long we stood. Time stood still. In another world.
He allowed me to absorb it all
through every portal of perception,
until I trembled at the overwhelming
power of epic song, wrought in stone,
before me, a vision, ages, long ages ago.
This was the vision that Ta Chak as a boy
had memorized, written on palm leaves,
the epic *Reamker*, singing it for the

Khmer people, from village to village,
for high and low alike, the powerful tale,
words once heard in illustrious halls,
as once revered here in Angkor Wat,
immortalized in images before me,
for all Khmer, for all the world.
From my musings, Ta Chak awoke me, saying,
"Poetry is mightier than the sword,
and can change the course of civilization,"
waving toward the steps, leading me from
the galleries, as I struggled to make sense
of the commanding vision he had shown me.
　　As we stepped out past the colonnade,
the late morning jungle air seemed heavier,
more humid, no longer a visible mist,
the sun high above the horizon.
Ta Chak spoke, still standing on the steps,
"Tell them on the moon I fulfilled my duty.
We must climb higher now," leading me
around and through a maze of passageways
and terraces, until we came out before
a steeply ascending mountain of stone steps,
up to the highest tower of Angkor Wat.
I had to clamber on all fours, my head
in obeisance as we climbed to just outside
the center of the temple, holy of holies,
what once housed a statue of Vishnu,
but long since Buddha, as centuries had
given way to centuries, time flowed
and changed, kingdom to kingdom.
Carefully, at that great height, Ta Chak
faced west, from where we had walked
that morning along the jungle road.
Stretching out before us, past the bridge
and blue moat was a vast expanse of green.

And I saw devatas, temple dancers,
beautiful goddesses, every one of them,
gliding across the reflecting pool,
as though it were the oceans of the world,
elegant head dresses and costumes, jewelry,
shimmering as they danced, and musicians
accompanying them, no man in sight of them
could ever look the other way, and so,
I could not keep my eyes off them,
such beauty on this Earth a blessing,
men and women, the dance of life,
the touch of love exhilarating all hearts,
the balancing act of the universe;
a thousand devatas floated before my eyes,
the beautiful apsaras of the carvings
come alive to dance in song and joy. Aside,
children and fathers watched mothers dance,
fathers holding the hands of the little ones,
with pride and devotion for their women.
Ta Chak spoke, "All the kingdoms followed this path.
Far away, Borobudur in Java,
Bali, Thailand, Malaysia, Laos, Vietnam,
into the archipelagoes, this the path,
to preserve and elevate the people,
from war and suffering, the dread of life,
and so we slew the demons for a time,
always watching and ready to attack,
crawling back up from the depths, from below."
I could hear gamelans above the trees
and thought of shadow puppets on bamboo sticks.
We gazed out together, without speaking,
in all directions, until he gently said,
"Take my arm," as he held it out to me,
and I did not hesitate to obey
my master's command, grasped his wrist firmly,

knowing his intent must be some further
quest. Barely had my hand closed tightly
than we were soaring above Angkor Wat.
All that jungle, soaring north, where soon
he set me down before another temple,
Bayon, covered with enormous Buddha faces,
hundreds of them, surrounded by the same
thick, luxuriant jungle. He intoned,
"Avalokitesvara," gazing in every direction,
in compassion, eyes looking upon
all the suffering, sentient beings.
"Infinite beings. Infinite Buddhas.
Infinite beings. Infinite Buddhas."
Meditative Bodhisattvas in all directions.
Quietly, beyond words now, I gazed,
standing with Ta Chak, in the morning light,
radiance on all the temples of Bayon.
A long time went by, and then Ta Chak,
already close to me, held out his arm,
without speaking a word, carrying me aloft,
over the trees, on to where I knew not.

   Passing many other temples, in various
states of decline and ruin, jungle growing
out of and around the stones, Banyan trees
choking and toppling many, Ta Chak flew on,
to some destination he had in mind,
while I watched the landscape below change
slowly from jungle to farm fields, workers
here and there, tending to crops, mostly rice fields.
He lowered us onto an empty field,
a dry, uncultivated piece of land.
I wasn't sure of the direction,
or why he would have brought me there.
No sight of any landmarks worth our time,

scattered weeds, sparse trees, clumps and mounds, here and
    there.
He stood silently, so I spoke. "Master,
why have you brought me here? What do you mean?
What should I learn from this barren place?"
Tears began streaming down Ta Chak's face, shaking
and sobbing, pitiful to see in an old man,
moving me deeply, wondering why and what
could possibly cause him such grief.
Suddenly it struck me through the heart,
like a fiercely driven machete, by
some heartless man, intent on watching on
his victim's face the flash of horror
as he realizes that he has been done
to death, dropping lifeless to the ground;
even so, I stood in that killing field,
the realization stuck in my guts,
no compassion in the modern world,
Ta Chak's sobs and tears streaming down his face,
overwhelmed by the blow of the realization
of where he had brought me, where millions died,
slaughtered by the madness of modern man,
Pol Pot and those who ran amok with him.
Through the tears now in my own eyes,
I could see through nightmare vision human bones
in the dirt of that field, merely one of many.
Choking sobs, I said, "Oh, master, take me
away from here," his old face awash with tears,
burdened with the sorrow of all Khmer.
He held out his arm, even as he wiped his cheeks
with his other sleeve, as I with mine.
We lifted, heavily, from that place, convulsed,
distressed, perplexed, grieving over
all I had seen and felt, struggling for why,
filled with seething disgust for modern man

and all his violent, contemptible theories,
the decadent ideas of the Sorbonne,
Western decadence in an Asian form,
Asia just as given to decadence.
   Silently, for a very long time, we flew,
neither one saying a word to the other,
horrible memories began to fade, but not forgot,
and I turned to wondering where we were heading,
over jungles and mountains, temples and
cities, passing many boats on rivers.
Finally, Ta Chak, his composure restored,
flew over a mountain into dryer terrain
and a river valley, setting down on a
mountainside overlooking the valley.
We had entered a visionary realm
full of temples, hundreds and hundreds of
temples, spread out as far as I could see,
stupas and pagodas, towers and domes,
as though all the cathedrals of Europe
had been built in a single place.
"The fabled land of Marco Polo, Bagan,"
said Ta Chak. "The land of the Burmese,
the Valley of a Thousand Temples,
four thousand and more filling the valley."
The early morning air, still, interspersed with
dew and mist, encircled the temple spires,
a heavenly realm on Earth lay before us.
I could see over the doors and windows
a purifying flame, burning away
ill will, impurities, and evil forces.
For more than two hundred years the center
of a thriving Burma. Impermanence,
all things passing with time and decay,
even so the time of Bagan long gone.
No matter where man goes, time does not stand still.

Nothing lasting in this world of woe and pain,
change its own refuge and not to be feared,
passing from sorrow and illusion,
in the still moment to Nirvana,
the ultimate truth of Enlightenment,
free of desire, craving, dissatisfaction,
crossing the river is the journey,
enduring movement the destination,
the hope and joy of life lived to the full,
the pilgrim soul traveling to the other shore.
"And there," said Ta Chak, pointing toward
a golden dome reaching to the sky,
"is Ananda Temple," exquisitely
proportioned on an alabaster base,
surrounded by gilded stupas in harmony
with the transcendent currents of the valley.
   Ta Chak said, "Hanuman's cousin
shall be here soon," a lingering gaze into
my eyes. Before I could speak, he rose,
flying back toward where we had come from.
Alone I looked toward the golden spire
and all the ancient valley temples,
most fallen into ruin and decay,
though a few seemed cared for and maintained.
Monks and pilgrims moved about in the distance.
I wondered who could be Hanuman's cousin,
looking apprehensively around the slopes,
where up the mountainside I saw a figure,
smaller than a man, coming toward me,
dressed in brilliant yellow silk, with a
yellow silk cap, a furry little creature.
I recognized him as soon as I saw him.
Sun Wukong, the Chinese Monkey King!
"Greetings, Foreign Devil, I've come down from
the water-curtain cave of Flower-Fruit Mountain,

the Buddha Pure Land realm. Don't worry,
Guan-yin ordered me to take good care of you,"
grinning ear to ear. "So, I'll take you further
on your Yatra, your spiritual journey."
Suspiciously, sizing up all four feet of him,
I said, "Buddy, no monkey tricks, or else.
Got it? I haven't come this far for nothing.
And don't call me 'Foreign Devil.' Haven't you
gotten over that yet? Much of the world has,
or at least is working on it." Glowering,
I added, "Try catching up with it."
Sun Wukong let out a screech of laughter
and turned a little somersault, spinning
in glee. "Ah, Foreign Devil, I understand
you have to get back to the moon. But you
don't have seventeen years, unlike Xuanzang,
the holy scripture-seeking monk of the Tang Court,
taking his time traveling back to Dunhuang
and Chang-an, the Emperor's Capital.
Guan-yin has given me special permission
to fly with you, lucky Foreign Devil."
To which I grimaced, while he continued,
"Oh, sensitive! You're lucky I don't pull out
my needle from behind my ear, changing it
into an iron rod, the thickness of a
rice bowl, and beat you to a pulp. Watch yourself,
or I just might lose my temper, even
after Nirvana. I will lead you to the West,
the West of China, that is, not yours!"
to which he laughed, thinking he was clever.
"Guan-yin called you the Poet of the Moon,
sent to harmonize the nine schools.
Their tripling must be quite a story.
Only three in my day!" he laughed,
turning another somersault, pleased as punch.

To which I replied, "Like your master
Subohti, I would say that to harmonize
the nine schools is a natural thing."
"You're not my master, Foreign Devil.
Don't forget it," itching behind his ear.
I stepped back a little, eyed him warily.
Sun Wukong said, "Look around here at Bagan.
All things are impermanent, as Buddha taught.
Do you doubt it?" Sighing, I replied,
"Alas, no, I've never doubted it, always
felt it," with a fearful shudder of humility.
"Wukong, please guide me. Help me to learn
what you have to teach. Whatever Guan-yin
has sent you to me for." I raised my hands
together, bowing slightly to him, in heartfelt
hope that he might guide me on my way,
though I knew not where it was to lead or how.
He laughed again, a monkey shriek,
followed by a cloud-soaring somersault,
and then he stepped towards me with his
furry little arm held out, impishly.
I took a chance. What else could I do? I stepped
forward cautiously and grasped his furry wrist,
hoping he who guided Xuanzang would guide me.
"I'll spare you my 108,000 mile somersault,
since I doubt you'd be able to hold on,"
rising above the mountainside, carrying me
with him, over the dry valley, temples
and stupas, everywhere overgrown with
brush and scrub and weeds, among fields
and cows and goats, people heading to their crops,
flying around the Ananda Temple,
circling it once, all four directions,
East, West, South, and North,
as we sailed in the air, circumambulating

the golden spire, in the morning sun.
I bowed slightly in my mind, as Sun Wukong
headed north, rising higher in the sky,
toward the pilgrim sun, monkey of the mind.
   Below us a vast expanse of brown and green,
fields and farms, trees and jungle.
And I saw below us a flash of birds,
large white cranes, rising from trees,
heavenward, so it seemed. We flew on.
I knew not where. Whole regions passed far below.
Villages, small cities. Rocky mountains
began to appear, covered with snow and ice.
The Monkey King saw me studying them
and said, "Far to the west lies Mt Everest
and Mt Kailash, the center of the universe,
Shiva's mountain, axis of the world.
In all four directions, the rivers flow,
sustaining all the world." And then I became
aware that we were beyond the frigid cold
of that rarified region, enwrapped in warmth,
in a realm no chill could penetrate.
With smiling eyes, Sun Wukong remarked,
"Dharamsala, where my cousins play in trees."
I caught my breath, as I caught his meaning,
and we passed into even more rugged land,
snow-covered mountains and barren plateaus.
I saw colored flags streaming from a peak,
flying freely in the mountain wind,
five colors, the colors of fire, earth and
water, iron and wood, fluttering cloth,
prayers to high heaven for a safe journey,
mantras reverberating in the breeze,
wafting up to us at that far height,
purifying the air, pacifying the gods,
a land as rarified as the air.

We entered a Shangri-la, Shambhala,
all have dreamed of, peak after peak, the flapping
flags welcomed and called us onward. And then,
the Tibetan poet Milarepa spoke
to me from his deathbed, "Poet of the Moon,
they who are full of worldly desires
cannot do anything for other people,
cannot even be helpful to themselves.
Load your back with hard work, mind with duties.
One cannot foresee the time of one's death.
Seek now the dharma of the human race."
Stirred by him, I cast an eye at Wukong,
wanting to ask him where he was taking me,
for now I realized we were in Tibet,
that poor land beaten down so pitilessly
by ruthless tyrants, conquering violence,
the brutal crushing of a little kingdom,
by those who failed to tame the monkey of the mind,
subjecting its people to destruction.
Then I saw it far below, covering
a mountainside, the Potala Palace,
Tibetan Buddhism's greatest monastery,
home for centuries of Dali Lamas,
homeless now, all homeless, lost and gone.
Before us a city reminding me of
the Beijing I had once visited, long ago,
it, too, impermanent, swept away by time,
already a different Beijing existing.
Flying, cloud soaring, Wukong looked at me,
saying, "A museum now. Like so many
holy places on the Earth, the people's hearts
have turned away from the divine fragrance,
or forced, as the case may be, if not both,
their hold, at least, weakening with time."
We flew on. I shuddered deep inside but not

from the cold around us, rather from the cold
within the hearts of men. I would have wept
but tears would have turned to ice, like men's hearts.
Sun Wukong sensed my inner turmoil and said,
"My great teacher Subohti taught aright,
'Nothing in the mind is difficult, only
the mind makes it so.'" We flew on in silence.
    The mountains and dry, brown plateaus gave way
to a mottled land, with a little green,
very little, the cold high desert plateau
seeming to stretch on and on forever.
Down below there somewhere I thought I saw
a Gulag camp of prisoners, sentenced
to years and decades of manual labor,
scientists and artists, intellectuals,
banished for having a brain and using it.
I could not help but grieve over their plight,
the plight of the people, all of China.
Yet Monkey King pressed north. And then he said,
"Soon you will see it, where you were before."
It struck me like a bolt of lightning,
vajra-like, startling me, Dunhuang oasis,
the Mogao Caves of a thousand Buddhas,
in the desert on the old Silk Road,
where all humanity once had passed,
traveled through, Chinese and Indians, Persians,
Khotans, Greeks and Romans, Muslims, Christians
from Syria, Mongols, blue and green-eyed
peoples, all rode the precarious road
to Mt Mingsha, where monk Lo-Tsun had a
vision of "a thousand Buddhas in a cloud
of glory." From oasis to oasis,
with horses and camels, on foot, carrying
cargo, the riches of the East and West,
foreign devils pouring in from every land,

the heart of man itself the worst devil,
unenlightened by the saving grace of
compassion, of Guan-yin's mercy.
　　The setting sun in the West guided our way
past Crescent Moon Lake, surrounded by sand dunes.
A sight so beautiful I wanted to scoop
up the moon's reflection from the water.
Sailing back to the transcendent oasis,
the light over the Sanwei Mountains sparkled
with the radiance of the thousand Buddhas
housed in the interior of its caves.
Monkey King gently put us down next to
the green trees along the flowing river.
Before us stretched a mile of Buddhist caves,
carved more than a thousand years ago,
by travelers seeking merit with the divine,
protection on their way in all directions,
seeking refuge in the caves as in the
three jewels of Buddhism. Sun Wukong said,
"We'll rest here for the night and enter the
cave in the morning." The moon shone above.
I understood him immediately, outside
the hundreds of caves, when he referred
to only one. Memory filled me with
a shiver, felt deep in my inmost soul.

BOOK VI

THE ARGUMENT

After an arduous journey from Bagan, Burma, up over Lhasa, Tibet, to Dunhuang, China, Sun Wukong, the Persona's able guide, having traveled a different route with Xuanzang, takes him to a Mogao Cave. From there, Sun Wukong flies the Poet to Chang-an, where Du Fu leads him up the many stairs of the Big Wild Goose Pagoda. Bai Juyi lifts him up to Mt Tai and the Azure Clouds, imbibing the beverage of the Three Vinegar Drinkers, savoring its harmonizing nature. Heading east, into the rising sun, past the Kingdom of Silla, ancient name of Korea, to the mountains of Lake Biwa, where Basho and Saigyo rested from their long journeys. Like much of Japan, the view of the lake has changed since Basho was interred at the Temple of Gichu-ji on its southern shore. Basho teaches the Poet of the Moon the oneness of his vision, a Vinegar Drinker in his own way. Saigyo lifts the Persona back to his great metaphor, the moon.

In pre-dawn darkness I awoke, realizing
where I was, slipping away under the grove
to the riverside, leaving Sun Wukong
who seemed asleep in a tree above me.
The dry desert air was still cool, the water
I drank from the river even cooler,
trickling along, over pebbles and sandy bars.
Looking back towards the cliff, I could not
make out separate caves, only a dark bluff
above the trees. Walking back to Sun Wukong,
I thought of the pilgrims of the past, watering
their camels and horses here, encampments
for millennia, merchants and travelers,
emissaries and ambassadors, soldiers
and humble people of all walks of life,

journeying through the desert of this world.
Sitting down quietly a distance from Wukong,
my legs folded under me, I meditated
on all that had happened to bring me here,
once again groping for the sense of it all,
wondered on this journey and its meaning,
sought the center of my being, surrendered
myself to that which has a purpose
greater than what I can understand.
Time trickled by, a stirring in the branches,
sporadic bird song became a flood,
caused me to open my eyes in the dawning light,
Wukong now sitting on a branch grinning
down on me. Unable to suppress a smile,
I looked up at him, relaxing, saying,
"Well, Wukong, the sun is rising, a thousand
Buddhas reign resplendent over the mountains."
He, jumping down, gave a shriek of delight,
"Infinite Being, Infinite Buddhas!"
Laughing and carrying on, he added,
"Maybe there are foreign devils who get it!"
scampering around, somersaulting,
immediately back to his tricks and jibes.
  Now past the early glow of sunrise,
bird song no longer heard in the oasis,
we sat awhile until Sun Wukong said,
standing up, casting his eyes over me,
"It's time. The sun is on the cliff and caves."
Without a word I too stood and looked toward
the bluff, signaled him in silence, followed
him as he led the way, no longer scampering
or flying, but serenely, peacefully out
from under the trees and across lotus blossom
paving stones to the cliff face, where we could
see caves ranked in both directions.

I followed him up and along the stairs
and a walkway, sensing he knew the way,
my Monkey King guide. The heat of the sun
now on us, I could feel the day coming on,
hot and dry as an Arizona desert.
With the sun, we entered the cave, Tang Dynasty,
at its height, sumptuous detail everywhere,
glorious art intimating a world beyond art,
art its servant, glorying in its servitude,
exalting in worship of beauty beyond beauty,
the highest, deepest, true beauty,
the good, the true, the beautiful made one.
Awe, waves of awe overwhelmed me.
I felt it once again. Wukong silently
stepped aside, stayed back out of the way,
allowed me to move forward past the murals,
toward the niche, deeper toward the western wall,
where those before me reigned in splendor, glory,
the Buddha Sakayamuni, his right hand raised
in the mudra of "have no fear," though I was
already far beyond fear, where no fear
can ever reach, taking in all the scene,
his sitting on an octagonal throne,
Mt Meru, as it were, the center of
the universe, cosmic mountain transcending
the worldly plane, far beyond the mountain caves.
Encircled with a nimbus of spiritual fire,
his glowing nature made manifest,
he sat in lotus position, head erect
and calm, peace and nobility emanating,
resonant in his bearing, crowning essence,
long ear lobes intimating the princely world
he left behind, flowing robes. He seemed
to float above the cave floor, above the world,
while his companions stood on either side;

to the left, flanked by Ananda, upon a lotus,
in humility, service his garland and
ceaseless sacrifice, tending to all,
remembering all the Buddha's sermons.
"Thus I heard it said," Ananda passed down
the Buddha's words to the generations,
flowing out around the world and through the worlds,
his hands held together in front of him,
ready to serve, selflessness his station.
   To the right, flanked by Maha Kashyapa,
an old monk, mendicant, a little gaunt;
peace, too, and surrender, service and
protection, his boon, perhaps smiling faintly,
Buddha's Flower Sermon, lingering in his mind,
Ch'an and Zen enveloping his mind and life,
successor and convener of the Sangha,
Buddha entrusting him with the dharma gate,
no words or letters, the form of the formless,
a transmission beyond remembered scripture,
experience, not creeds and letters.
So Kashyapa stood and meditated next
to Sakayamuni, right hand too raised in
"have no fear," Bodidarma his successor,
the Lotus Sutra passing to all lands.
   Next, both sides, faces in meditative bliss,
curving brows and jewels, lotus-flowered robes,
Avalokitesvara, Guan-yin, Kannon,
his, her, guiding presence, merciful,
compassionate, standing, heads leaning toward
the Buddha, their Buddha nature emanating,
drawn, sign toward its essence, curving
delicacy of detail, much as showing
the way to light, protection, compassion,
flowing toward all creation, sustaining,
enlightenment foregone, leading all toward it,

supreme sacrifice for humanity,
that all humanity might find mercy, love,
compassion, from suffering on the road of life.
Exquisite robes and sashes, coiffures, jewels,
symbols of symbols, of experience calling
all on to experience, raising, transforming,
saving all from peril, purely guiding to
the Pure Land, as if saying, "Praise, call,
intone Guan-yin, Avalokitesvara, Amitabha,
for deliverance, all may reach the Pure Land."
   Last, stand the guardians of Buddha,
Vajrapani, generals, image of the Buddha's
power, protecting him from the demons
of our nature, girded in warrior armor,
ready to defend, tread underfoot *ignaros*,
forms of the Buddha's form Guan-yin,
spreading his and her protection, care,
once holding staffs and weapons, Sun Wukong
in different forms, the Tang pantheon complete,
raised to the highest heaven, Nirvana wrought
at its best in paint and clay, artistic form
of highest form, in the heart of the cave,
the Tang cave, too, a map of the mind.
   I found myself upon my knees gazing at
the niche, the walls and statues, symbols of
another world, not this, though made of this,
pointing on, beyond, to one higher,
as on, looking up, the ceiling itself,
resplendent jewels bedecked a stupa, Buddhas
of the Lotus Sutra, welling up out of
the earth, a lotus out of the muck and mire,
the mire of this world to which we cling,
clings to us; Manjusri holding the sacred
flame of wisdom, cutting through delusion;
mandalas, medicine wheels of the East,

the ultimate beauty of the universe;
Dunhuang, "the Great Western Paradise,"
the Pure Land of Amitabha Buddha,
Buddha of Infinite Light, compassion;
Guan-yin, the guide to the Promised Land,
on the Journey to the West, "Nothing in the
world is difficult, only the mind makes it so,"
the physics of the mind and consciousness.
On that ceiling, and those walls, the image
of release, moksha, achieved in form,
experienced by those who passed this way.
Eternities went by while I kneeled.
Time before timelessness. Behind the figures,
upon the walls, Bodhisattvas gazed out,
and women, the beauty of the female,
silks and elegant coiffures, graceful gowns,
musicians playing the pipa, heavenly
music accompanying the apsaras,
flying, dancing upon the plane above.
I knew not whether I looked or closed my eyes,
meditative realm beyond this world,
form moved into formlessness, and I followed
with all my heart, into my heart,
and the heart and soul of the universe.
I wanted to kneel and sit on the floor
to the right but knew it was not my place,
twenty-five-hundred years now gone by,
my karma leading me elsewhere, to service
in a different way, and so I had to resist
the impulse, turn away, tearing my heart out,
from a longed for place of peace and rest.
I pressed my hands together, bowed again,
taming the monkey of the mind.
    And then a sound reached me in that deepest
of inward moments, a stir behind me,

as to awaken and bring me back,
lest I might have slipped over, gone forever,
oh, so gratefully, but, alas, not yet.
Sun Wukong gently, slowly, stepped toward
the door, and I knew I had to follow,
broke away my gaze, but not my soul,
taking the experience with me, memory now,
all things passing, impermanent in this
world of dross. Outside on the walkway,
Wukong looked at me, said nothing,
but held out his arm toward me.
Swallowing hard, I knew it was time to leave,
move on. Hesitating, I told Wukong,
"It was here that the minder said to me,
cutting contempt in his voice, scowling,
face contorted, 'Some of the Japanese
tourists actually worship in these caves.'"
"I know," said Wukong, kindly offering
his sustaining arm. I grasped it firmly,
as I never had before, needing his strength
and protection, my guide upon my way,
mounted the wind, cloud soaring, beyond tricks,
carried us aloft, away from that blest cave.
    From that far height, as we flew down the
Hexi Corridor, the route of the Silk Road,
this Silk Road winding through the centuries,
the path of the holy monk of the Tang Court,
I could see the Great Wall of China,
the only man-made thing visible from space,
extending on my left from Dunhuang into
the dim distance, through desert and mountains,
over gully and chasm, dried river beds,
creek and raging torrent, the Wall zigged
and zagged with the land, hieroglyph
of the Chinese soul, of its tragic history,

walling out and in, while we soared straight
as birds in flight to a far-off destination.
Only Sun Wukong knew what lay before us,
deeper into the heart of China.
I thought of the Chinese sage Mencius,
who spoke to me across the centuries,
"Heaven confers a great office by first
exercising the mind with suffering,
toil, hunger, and extreme poverty,
confounding all of one's undertakings,
stimulating the mind, hardening the nature.
Life springs from sorrow, calamity, and pain."
A Chinese Job, if ever there was one.
Slowly the land changed from dry sandy browns
to greens, embroidery of colors, our
toiling caravan of the air, wayfarers, as
those from India, so long ago in mist,
Xuanzang and others, Europeans, Muslims,
all the world traveling that route to Chang-an,
and then it hit me, that must be where
Wukong was taking me, I knew as surely
as ever I had known anything,
our destination could only be the great
Capital of Tang China, the pinnacle
of Chinese history. I looked at Wukong,
the wind ruffling his yellow silk cap,
and he pursed his lips with a trace of a
monkey grin, guiding us through billowing clouds.
    Having been to Chang-an once, I knew
what to look for, in any time or age,
its broad walls marking off the city from
the countryside, a fortress against the
invading barbarian hordes. No walls could stop
us though, at that great height, Sun Wukong,
my guide and champion. We pressed on,

and soon passed the city walls and saw
to the south, as we drew closer to the ground,
the Small Wild Goose Pagoda, flew past it,
on to the Big Wild Goose Pagoda,
landing gently, in the courtyard of the
monastery, where Xuanzang had translated,
for twenty years, the Buddhist texts that he had
brought back from India, after seventeen
years of travel through the desert wastes
and mountains of a continent,
acts of perseverance, selflessness supreme.
Letting go of Wukong's furry arm,
he grinned, flipped a saucy somersault,
said, "Sage Traveler, the city of Chang-an,"
and was gone before I could say a word,
thank him for his loyalty to me, bringing
me, too, so far, along an ethereal route,
from Bagan to Dunhuang, to Chang-an,
before the brick pagoda that Emperor Taizong
built to house the Buddhist scriptures for
Xuanzang and all the Chinese empire.
Alone, alone, I found myself alone,
as I gazed up from that courtyard of stone
and white-washed walls, over tiled roof-tops,
to the many-storied pagoda, image,
symbol, reaching into the sky, astonished,
in awe, with no thought of what lay ahead.
    Behind me, a voice in the early evening,
"So you are the traveler from the moon,
and I thought I had traveled long and far."
I turned to find an elderly gentleman,
deftly bowing, in a simple scholar's robe
and hat, thin and with a beard of gray,
his arms folded in his sleeves. I knew
in an instant, from the moonlight, he was

Du Fu, China's greatest poet. From Tang,
to Tang, Wukong had brought me. I bowed, respectfully,
holding for a moment, keeping my head down,
and then arighting, looking at him, saying,
"As you knew, 'Always there have been travelers.'"
He caught it, looked at me, as I at him,
my master, always in my highest esteem.
Choking a bit, I managed to add,
"I, too, struggle to accept the journey.
If you would guide me further on the way,
I would be most grateful," almost in tears.
Flowers fragrant in that garden around us.
"Come," he gestured, leading me through the courtyard
and up some steps, a threshold, doorways,
and we were there, at the entrance of
the Big Wild Goose Pagoda,
"The Temple of Kindness and Mercy."
   Quietly, we "climbed the many stairs,"
echoing steps around us, as we ascended.
At the top of the pagoda, we walked
into a small room, open, with arched,
curved ceilings, bays out to each window,
facing the directions of the compass.
"In my time, this was the top of the sky.
Nothing now, for 'Xi'an,' Western towers
rising everywhere," with a reserved smile.
He stepped to the eastern window. Looking out,
he said to me, "Every time has its duty.
One feels care and worry for it. I was
driven by the troublesome times.
How to advise and guide aright the emperor,
was all my thought, loyalty, and duty,
humane thought and action, through my poems
in the end. Retirement from the world,
I had to put it off. Abbot Zan understood.

This tower shows the power of the Buddha.
Intricate the weavings of this world.
We seek to understand, penetrate depths.
All one can say is 'Why should I lament?'
The weapons of my day were nothing.
Chang-an thought it had an impregnable defense.
All was swept away. A few pagodas.
Our office is like that of a monk,
but we poets cannot get free of the yoke,
and so I left this place, as you, too, must.
Look, wild geese streaming from the east,"
a sadness in his voice. "A place that suits,
not quite an earthly place." He fell silent.
    After a pause, I said, "In Xi'an I saw
abandoned people suffering on the sidewalk,
others just passed them by, cold hearts hardened to
the sight, like everywhere. All human duty lost.
My country, too, to speak in proportion.
Yet times can be worse; fear fits the modern world.
Cruel regimes crushing hundreds of millions.
They sell the guts of the executed,
sometimes to foreigners, whoever can pay.
Herded millions into prison camps, slave labor,
'Reform through labor,' they call it.
Rolled over the people with tanks of steel.
Trampling filial piety, destroyed the family.
Many no longer know their ancestors,
lost, floating, on the sea of revolution.
The poor are so oppressed, I can find no words
to describe it. I clutch my head wondering
how to convey it. Lhasa and Tibet
have almost been wiped from the face of the Earth.
The suffering of China knows no bounds.
I don't know that I'm capable of it.
I, too, am growing older, my hair gray,

the young man who dreamed of an epic poem,
lost to the swirling clouds of time and space,
my health revealing signs of age, mortality.
I worry when I look into the mirror.
How to make a living, beyond me too,
wandering, literary merit and fame
two different things, as you said, opposed.
I worry I've waited too long, spent too much time
reading and studying, knowing a young man
could never write a universal epic,
endless notes. Despair pulls me down.
Duty pulls me back up, telling me to push on.
I know it's not about me, but their suffering,
terror, at how much worse it could, might, will be."
   Du Fu looked at me, gray hair, wizened head,
thin, a cotton robe, reprimand in his eyes,
I feared. I tried to change the subject,
bringing him the news, I thought, would interest him.
"In Sichuan, an ancient culture has been found,
in Sanxingdui, one that was not known
in your day. It had no written script,
but marvelous bronzes, somewhat like Shang,
yet dominated, probably, in its way,
by some strongman, worshiped, more or less.
Peoples need to find their own forms, or imposed.
Whether primitive dictators or emperors,
kings or Politburos, committees,
the 'Great Leader' oppresses about the same.
The Marxists have proven the worst in all
of human history. Insatiable lust for blood.
Only university professors in my country
continue to worship at their sanguine shrines.
They always claim it's 'for the people,'
but never get around to asking them
what they want. Duty and heaven forgotten.

They take care of themselves, like despots everywhere.
Well," I added, sighing, "after the corruption
of Confucianism, the suffering of the people
opened the way for Mao, swallowing
all the nonsense and madness of Europe.
A new form of government allows the people
to rule themselves, a little, at least,
long evolving and tested in the West,
though flagging of late, needing restoration.
Not perfect but the best we've ever had,
despite evidence of senators taking bribes,
'campaign contributions,' they call them,
greasing their dirty palms, the courts corrupted.
Nonetheless, humanity at times rising,
against oligarchy, corporate plutocracy.
Plato's dire warnings all too real.
Comparatively, though, at least, more
balance among its branches, yin and yang,
each guarding each, against the other's excess,
in theory, uplifting the people, trying,
raising them from punishing poverty.
Much of the world has now developed
some form of this new government,
hobbling along like an infirm patient,
one that fits their customs and traditions.
China, though, lags behind, with many, teetering
on chaos, another An Lushan Rebellion,
moderation and *Ti'en*, 'heaven,' lost.
Such convulsions in the offing for China.
There must be a peaceful way for China too.
Many Chinese think so, though oppressed, cowed.
Many hope that this new form of rule can be
applied to the entire world, all leaders
sitting down together, setting the world right,
cleansing the world of the weapons of blood,

destroying them, forever, never to be
used again, beating, hammering the swords
of war into farm tools and ploughshares,
peace come round For All Mankind, humanity."
  New energy surged into Du Fu,
flushing his face with life and vigor.
"A great blessing your age has found, despite
its flaws. Chaos is the scourge of man.
Duty requires you to do all you can
to protect and preserve good rule,
prevent the horrors that sweep a land
when true rule is lost. Never cease your efforts.
Forget the small-minded poetasters
and pedants of your time, alienated, lost
in self and sophistry. Think of the people.
Warring states destroy the human life of all,
drag down every human thing to violence,
bloodshed, crush the tender flowers,
a hundred flowers, bleached bones along the roads
in ditches and deserts, wasteland everywhere.
Recall what the Chinese poet in your time,
Ai Qing wrote, 'You who are loyal to time,
please bring to mankind your message of comfort,
hurry, before the night is over, tell all,
that what they have been waiting for is coming.'
Rise above the dread weight of despair."
Du Fu stepped back slightly, to the side, adding,
"I will meet you again on the moon.
And I shall bring all the Chinese poets."
He looked at me, and I at him.
Nobility and wisdom shining from his face,
and then with a courteous bow he turned,
leading down the many stairs, like Fenghuang
down from heaven, back to the courtyard,
nodding again, as did I, turned and walked

away through the garden of trees and flowers.
And I, I again was alone, alone,
in a different city and a different time,
remote, pondering all that I had been through,
reflecting on all that Du Fu had taught.
As long as humanity lasts and people
seek what is human, Du Fu shall guide the way.
   I looked at a red peach blossom tree,
then a willow, thought of the poet Wu Wei,
on the mountain, outside Chang-an, his journey
into peace, willow branches bent in wreaths,
farewell gifts to travelers on the Silk Road,
"Soon you will be part of the past,"
and the Book of Songs came to mind, poems from
the heart of early time, clear and pure, Ch'u
and Han, Ts'ao Chih, "Roaming Immortal,"
Juan Chi and Pao Chao's melancholy,
Ta'o Chien flowing out of Peach Spring Fountain,
Shih-te under a moon that never waned,
Han-shan in the moonlight of Cold Mountain,
while Li Po drank a full cup under the moon,
Chen Tzu-ang, in the Dao still much to learn.
Lost in reverie, I awoke to find,
out of the mountain mist, one had descended
down to me outside the Dayan Monastery,
Bai Juyi, an agéd sage, dressed in
a flowing robe of striking design, embroidered
edge of celestial pattern, silken rustle,
long beard contrasting with his scholar's hat,
walking toward me, through a cultivated path,
beneath the pagoda, stopping short of me,
bowed slightly, saying, "I've come to take you
to the Land of the Rising Sun,
where my poems had found their way in my own time,
but first we must make pilgrimage to Mt Tai,

a mountain close to China's heart and Li Po.
He savored Laozi's Way, the Daoist Path."
As I rose to greet him, bowing in return,
he stepped closer, holding out his arm,
the long sleeve trailing halfway to the ground.
Without a word, I grasped my master's arm,
felt strength, renewed, hope returned, anticipation
grew within. We soared above those grounds,
leaving the Big Wild Goose Pagoda
far behind, heading east, across the
Great Northern Chinese Plateau, east,
he said, toward Tai-shan, the Great Mountain,
"Leading Peaceful Mountain," where for over
three thousand years the Chinese had made
pilgrimage, and I now made mine,
with Bai Juyi's robes sailing behind us,
distance and time swirling in their furls, passed by,
leading us on a journey into renewal.
    Bai Juyi glanced at me and said, "As out of
the head of Pangu, the first being and creator
of the world, Mt Tai, before us.
'If Mt Tai is stable, so is the country,
so is the world.'" Peace, benevolence, blessing,
"Paying respect to a mountain" lay before us,
Mt Tai, rising from the green plain, stone stairways
leading up its mountainsides, pilgrim paths,
over which we flew, soared, past many gates,
temples, monuments and inscriptions
carved into the living rock of Tai-shan.
    On Jade Emperor Peak, Bai Juyi gently
alighted, in front of a temple, a promontory
in front of it with sharp precipices
all around, as the prow of a ship cuts
through ocean waters, it through mountain air,
while we now rode the surging mountain, facing

a great range of mountains and valleys.
Turning partly, gesturing behind us, he said,
"The Jade Emperor's Temple of the Princess
of the Azure Clouds, his daughter."
And I could see women and men, young and old,
dressed variously in silk and brocade,
plain black cotton and weaves, gracefully pace
through rhythmic movements of tai-chi, scooping the
azure clouds, parting the wild horse's mane,
white crane spreading its wings, playing the lute,
carrying the tiger over the mountain.
Bai Juyi gave me a few minutes to take it
all in, to try to absorb and understand.
"All of China's heart is on this mountain,
all its history recorded, from Paleolithic times
to Neolithic, the early emperors paying
their respect to Mt Tai, ascending the stairs,
through the Gate of Heavenly Peace.
Confucius born not far from here, learned here,
'The world is small.' Prayers went up for a
good harvest, protection from floods and
earthquakes, all the woes of life,
the pain of pregnancy, for a good birth,
reviving, submitting to the will of heaven,
Ti'en, the teachings of Confucius, Buddha,
and the Eight Immortals, here, somewhere,
one holding a peach, the Great Mother
of the West, perhaps in the clouds.
Laozi, too, at this azure Daoist temple.
It's not about the clothes but the heart,
not embroidered robes of silk, boots, jade dusters
made from a Yak's tail, jasper pools, star caps
and rich brocades; more than silk sashes
tied about the waist, jade-heaven gods,
Daoists playing strings and pipes, tablets of jade.

If you have the Dao in your heart, you are a
man of the Dao, though dressed in a blue
cotton shirt, with a simple black-cornered hat,
white leggings and black boots. Clothes don't carry
the meaning. To carry the Dao in the heart
is the meaning. Many people wear robes
but that doesn't mean they fill them.
The nourishing Dao, the uncarved block,
action in inaction, our duty to serve,
fulfill our duty, serve mankind, leave others
full of joy, the flow of the universe,
balanced, yin and yang behind the natural
order, Ch'i, breath, spirit, Dao, Path, the Way,
the Way of Life, cultivate the three jewels,
compassion, moderation, humility.
Soft flowing water forged and sculpted
these mountains, moved earth and stone, living
in accordance with nature, in harmony
with the universe, receptive, everything
seen as it is, without preconceptions, illusions,
the pure experience of this life and world.
'The Way that can be described is not the true Way.'"
    Quietly, Bai Juyi stepped back from me,
his robes furling in the morning breeze.
The azure clouds were behind him,
the Jade Emperor's daughter, and I thought
of Guan-yin in the Sea of Wisdom Temple,
at the Summer Palace, remembering I had
seen her, north of Beijing, years ago,
holding in her left hand an elegant vase,
in her right, a willow branch, waving,
sprinkling her sweet dew, saving mankind
from suffering. The nectar of compassion
and wisdom, a large halo behind her,
the moonlight of her beauty, the spiritual aura

of her being, as upon Sun Wukong,
Xuanzang, on the people of this land, or
in "water moon" position, right knee raised,
exquisite beauty in meditation.
Outside, where they could reach on the temple,
Revolutionary Guards knocked off the faces
of the ceramic Buddhas surrounding her,
as they did in Tibet, destroying
thousands of monasteries and temples,
and the monasteries of the Wu Dang
masters, and so many more, any form
of transcendence, mad revenge, it seems, for the
reverence so many earlier generations had held.
O Three Vinegar Drinkers, where are you now?
Everywhere blackness flecked with specks of light.
Help us find your harmony anew, the Dao.
Make our rituals harmonize with life today.
Moments that seemed an eternity passed,
while I gazed at the mountains and valleys,
the azure clouds above, in awe and humility,
at the vast sweep of time and space,
thinking of the many millions who had come
on pilgrimage to Mt Tai. Waking me
from my dreams, Bai Juyi moved back
towards me, held out his arm, sleeve furling.
We soared into the azure clouds, toward
the east, toward the Land of the Rising Sun.

    As we flew the mountains fell far below,
blending into a green patchwork of fields,
while in the east I could see a vast expanse
of blue, and before long, far below, what might
have been an island, causing me to turn to
Bai Juyi, questioning our destination.
Dismissing my look with a shake of his head,
he replied, "The Kingdom of Silla. Yamato

is our goal, what you call Japan."
At his words, a thrill ran through me, recalling
his earlier allusion to Japan.
So much went through my mind, memories,
as Bai Juyi sailed on, another vast sea,
then land coming in view, stretching as far
as one could see, even at that great height,
from south to north. Bai Juyi pushed on,
over the shore, deep into the interior,
lowering closer to the ground, until a
great lake came into view, millions of years old,
over two hundred and fifty million,
covering a wide piece of the island,
Lake Biwa, Kyoto and Nara to the east.
And to my surprise, Bai Juyi did not
fly on, but gently set us down on the
south side of Lake Biwa, on a mountainside,
in a clearing, overlooking a city
and the lake, bowing to me, as I to him,
and then he was gone, back into the air,
returning to the Pure Land of the West.
   Alone, in another forest clearing,
I looked across the city to Lake Biwa,
wondering why I was here, though I knew
I was once again in modern Japan,
thought of Kawabata, Tanizaki, Mishima,
their nostalgia for the world gone by,
the *Manyoshu*, ten thousand leaves of poetry,
the ancient poets, Hitomaro, his love
for his wife deeper than the miru-growing ocean,
all those poets, and those of the *Kokinshu*,
Ono Komachi, her withering flowers,
Murasaki Shikibu, her shining Genji,
life but a ten-foot square hut, floating by,
falling off, fading, into Kikkaku, Issa,

the master's student a dim reflection,
Socho and Sogi, Buson and Boncho,
Sora and Ryokan, Hokushi and Shiki,
Hagiwara, a sick face howling at the moon,
born and died in Maebashi where I lived;
Tamura, everything falling over a cliff.
   Out of the trees, an unexpected sight,
a man in a traditional black robe
and obi, headed toward me, a simple hat
on his shaven head, leaning on a bamboo staff.
Standing at a distance, he bowed, holding it
for a moment, as did I, even longer,
in respect for my master, sensei, Basho, poet
of many journeys throughout Japan.
He stepped closer to me, looking down
at the city, where he was buried, and said,
"My spirit has to come up here every
once in a while to refresh itself,
you understand," smiling kindly with amusement.
"The view of Lake Biwa isn't what it used to be."
I asked him, "This must be the mountain
you crossed on your way to Otsu?"
"Yes, to and from Kyoto, and the shrine at
Ise, journeys and wanderings, long ago."
And I, seizing the moment, seeking help,
"Sensei, my journey is all over the world,
and even to the moon and back. Arduous.
How can I go on? Find my way? Endure
these trials?" A long silence ensued,
while I studied the face that looked at me
without any emotion, restrained, composed,
yet thoughtful behind the eyes. And then he said,
"While you know you cannot walk in others'
footprints, seek what they sought and you will be
all right. Listen to the wind in the trees,

the cicadas, the birds of the sky and woods
and fields, frogs in ancient ponds. From them,
you will hear the far ancient sound that calls us,
always on, that can revive and inspire,
sustain, no matter how deep the despair.
Sadness is a master who will teach his lesson
if we will listen and wait for joy and beauty.
Road weary, turn to what lies beyond the road,
the journey is the goal, metaphor of mind,
mind metaphor," shifting on his staff.
    I mused and reflected on his words, replied,
"Sensei, you harmonized four different sects,
sleeping as one, under the bright moon.
I have nine to deal with. An awesome task.
So often I want to roll over and die,
give up, give in to the old complaint,
dig a hole and crawl in, pulling the dirt
over my head, like Mitsusaboro."
He looked at me without saying anything.
Then, "I know the world has changed in your time.
We Japanese have been through severe ordeals.
All the world, upheaval after upheaval.
The poet must tread the way for others.
Ronin of ronins, you have a master,
a moon full of them, whom you have not failed
to serve. Rise, go forward, like *koinobori*,
streaming carp kites, press against the wind."
I bit my lip and nodded repeatedly.
Unable to suppress further thoughts,
"So many of the young no longer believe
in a transcendental purpose to life,
think of themselves only as animals,
lost the scent of the spirit, dark cynicism
and Nihilism undermining everything,
afraid to join together in marriage,

build a life together, have children
and raise them, look to the future with hope,
instead of fear. In much of the world,
this has happened, is in the time and air.
A shallow culture undermines everything."
Dusk began to show traces in the sky,
and the moon appeared above the ridge.
Basho took a long time to reply,
"Not far from here are the ruins of the
ancient capital of Omi. Like the
cherry blossoms of my own hermitage,
like those that Tadanori sleeps under,
in the night, the petals his eternal host,
all things pass. Nothing is permanent in
this floating world, yours or mine. A breeze,
and the branches sway, their petals flutter
to the valley floor, like snow, covering
the ground, wayfarers treading upon them,"
lowering his voice and eyes with a glance.
We nodded in heartfelt agreement.
Death, a breath away, a moment and we're gone.
He continued, "I will bring all the poets.
All will meet you on the moon, join in,
attend the Parliament of Poets.
Our sensei, Saigyo, will return you to
his great metaphor, the moon." Turning,
Basho faced the edge of the woods, from which
a figure emerged, an old man in a
humble monk's robe, master and students,
bowing respectfully to one another.
Basho faded as a shade upon the wind,
while I, a shade in the making, remained,
lingered on with another spirit master,
who waited for me to join him, at a

distance, in moonlight, now shimmering
on Lake Biwa, evening fading into night.
   From five centuries before Basho,
Saigyo signaled me to follow him.
Through the upheavals of the Heike clans,
he seemed to lead, into the edge of the woods,
where a path, marked by a Torii, went up
the hill, into trees, lichen and green moss,
stone steps and pine needles, cypress, into
deep solitude, the serenity of nature,
mystery, kami, awe primordial. Far up
the stairs, I could see a shrine, but instead of
climbing all the way, Saigyo turned off the steps,
seating himself in the zazen position,
folded legs, beside the path, on a rock,
looking up past me through the trees, to the moon,
briefly pointing at it with a finger; once
the moon is recognized forget the finger.
Far below, we could see the moonlight gleaming
on Lake Biwa. Without a word, on the rise
of the forest floor, Saigyo motioned to me
to sit beside him, on another rock.
He then closed his eyes, his hands in mudra,
and I could tell he had entered a deep state
of meditation and peace, mind beyond,
detached, and so I, too, closed my eyes, followed
his example, as best I could, until I felt
that in zazen we entered a state of
deeper consciousness, traveling as it were,
in the mind's eye, its inner regions profound,
beyond the ground and forest, the mountainside
below, full moon glowing on Lake Biwa,
my eyes now open in astonishment,
his spirit guiding mine beyond this world,
through time, through space, light upon light,

infinite light, physics of the mind,
consciousness physics, physics consciousness,
beyond physiology into the spirit of light,
wrapped in the physics of all energy,
the Spirit, All in all, in all matter.
Moonbeams our guiding vessel, we traveled
across a quarter million miles, serenely,
in inner repose, our goal and reality,
Saigyo's great metaphor, looming before us,
moon mirroring mind, mind mirroring moon,
peace and bliss, a state beyond, the world left
far behind, farther than the ruins of Omi,
transported through satori, realm of light,
to disk of light, guiding symbol in the sky.

BOOK VII

THE ARGUMENT

Rising from zazen on the lunar platform, the Persona speaks
with Job on an ash heap of moon dust. The Hebrew poets of
Andalusia widen the perspective, with Hanagid directing
Yehuda Halevi to guide him below to Mt Carmel and Elijah's
slaughter of the prophets of Baal. Dante lifts the Poet from that
scene of horror, flying up the boot of Italy, into Europe.

O Divine Light, that never stops shining,
    beyond our atmosphere, Eternal Radiance,
    though we may be oblivious of thee,
sustain us with thy rays of warmth and light,
sustenance unseen, heating our earthly realm,
with beams, beyond our ken, but not our need.
I ask thee once again to lift me up
like a drooping plant shut off from thee,
to carry further forth this epic song,
whose glory, if ever won, belongs to thee.
Thou seest my need and frailty.
Mercy and compassion I crave of thee,
not merely for myself but all humanity.
Let us not destroy ourselves. Help us find
a new vision that we may humbly serve,
restore the cosmic order now, a wider
harmony in tune with thee, your global realm.
If any inkling I may catch of that
from thy bounteous grace supreme,
guide me to write words undistorted by
my earthly nature, that others may hear them too,
though a distant echo of thy glorious tones,
music of the spheres, the planetary round,
the lunar symphony of the moon.

Through dark matter, through dark energy,
Saigyo guided me by satori's brilliant light,
far beyond the Earth, supernal space,
the moon looming larger as we approached,
the Sea of Tranquility, our hope and goal,
drawing near, where I could see poets
scattered across the moonscape and around
the Lunar Module, what was left of it,
from long ago, when Armstrong and Aldrin
ascended to rendezvous with Collins,
wrapped in golden foil, shining in the light.
Saigyo gently set us down, in zazen,
upon the flattop surface of the LM,
poets moving toward it from all directions.
I closed my eyes and centered on the Being
who had brought us far on such a journey,
the will that guides us all and the heavens,
lingering in silent contemplation of
the Divine Essence beyond understanding,
but not beyond experience. Slowly I returned
to where I was, again on the moon,
with poets from every land and age,
recalling the promises of my masters
to bring even more bards and poets,
fulfilled, it seemed, before my very eyes,
by them all, Du Fu and Vyasa, others,
Korean Kwangdok with his prayer on the Moon.
    Saigyo relaxed from his position of zazen,
and I followed his example, unfolding
my legs, and sitting comfortably, looking
out over the moonscape, poets crowding
close around. I felt elated with a deep,
indescribable sense of peace and contentment.
Then with a clanking of armor, Rocinante
hobbled forward with her knight, Cervantes,
shaking his lance in the airless space,

holding forth loudly so all could hear,
"He returns! The Poet of the Moon!
We've agreed his journey has only begun.
He must visit the lands of exclusive truth.
Jerusalem, Andalusia, Europe,
England and Russia, on to the Saracens.
Nothing else will do! We've not stood by idly
up here while he's been gone. Thus the way
it should be," the old nag stepping sideways,
shaking his vizor, the brilliant white sunlight
glinting even from its dull metal.
All the poets on the plain cheered as one,
in acclamation, sending a shiver through
my soul, a surge of excitement, wonder,
their will my deepest longing, call of duty.
Then Cervantes leveled a question at me.
"What did you find down there?" "Human beings,"
I replied, "the flawed creatures of planet Earth,
where Ta Chak sang for me the epic *Reamker*,
fulfilling his duty before the gods."
Then, perhaps as Cervantes might have feared,
dissenting voices began to protest,
tearing into one another, squabbling.
Cyrano de Bergerac thrust himself forward,
decrying, "Now just a moment! This 'Poet
of the Moon' business has gotten out of hand.
I was up here first on my *Voyage to
the Moon*. Aren't you all forgetting that?
I had quite a journey up here with my
vials of dew, lifting me from Earth."
"Oh, no!" interjected Lucian of Samosta.
"I was here first, and every honest poet
will acknowledge my trip to the moon,
A True History, if ever there was one,
written by yours truly in the second century.
Homer himself attested that I was here,

on a column of beryl, up here somewhere,
when he honored my voyage, as it were,
'Dear to the gods and favorite of heaven,
Here Lucian lived: to him alone 'twas given.
Well pleased these happy regions to explore,
and back returning, seek his native shore.'
Now where is he? He'll tell you the way it was."
Sir Gawain next broke in, to my amazement,
saying, "Gentlemen, we get your point, but
please desist. You sound like quibbling astronauts,
who did what first and deserves the honor!
This epic poem isn't about you two.
The gage has been thrown down before this poet,
and he's shown the courage to pick it up,
accepting the challenge, set out for the Green Knight.
Even if you don't like it, it's the truth.
There's no denying it. No matter what."
Samuel Johnson then spoke up, saying,
in finest received pronunciation,
though a bit counter to the prevailing mood,
"His journey to many climes stands sublime,
taking account of human life everywhere,
even though it may find much to endure
and, alas, oh so little to be enjoyed,
discoursing like angels but all living like men."
Thomas More standing beside him, added,
"My good Doctor Johnson, that may well depend
on the traveler, and his utopia. For things
will never be perfect, until human beings are."
I was determined to stay out of all that,
but Jonathan Swift almost went spastic,
signaling Johnson, taking More by the arm,
and dragging me along with them away from
the crowd and out of sight behind the LM,
looking askance back at the visionaries.
Together, we talked for some time, arguing,

Swift all hot about prognosticators,
enthusiasts, "A Tale of a Tub," two
brothers and their father's will, something about
Peter and Martin, and that kind of thing,
right out of *Gulliver's Travels*, like mine.
I'm not sure I understood it all, but it
seemed strangely familiar, so I tried to learn.
No Leviathans scuttling our tubs!
Swift emphasized the "true critics" were the worst.
Oh, he was droll about that, he was.
I wish there had been more time to tell him
about the Deconstructionists, and other
sophists, but they were adamant about
hammering into me to watch out for myself.
Then Johnson started guffawing about
toadies in academic departments, the
prejudice of factions, intrigue, and servility,
propping up their worthless monuments with
awards and adulation, destined for dust,
stacked in libraries from floor to ceiling, unread,
the unreadable banality of hacks,
or the tomes of goose-steppers droning on
about what can and can not be written today,
like Faust leading his students by the nose,
since Saint Marx, Saint Freud, or Saint Derrida,
blah, blah, blah, has now revolutionized
our understanding for all time, freeing us
from dark and benighted thoughts, as though
they represented the pinnacle of history,
telling me to flush the Augean Stables,
like Heracles, and then with Gaia's help,
seek the Golden Apples of the Hesperides.
Finally, I spoke up, "I have to go back
or they'll begin to suspect." They all laughed,
heartily, ear to ear, now agreeing.

What can I say? I owe them a lot.
Like Christopher Columbus writing to
King and Queen Ferdinand and Isabella,
I had found no monstrosities on Earth,
but many monstrous deeds, dark and dire.
So poets might conceive of glorious kingdoms,
New Jerusalems of resplendent Vision,
as if the Ideal were reality,
yet the recalcitrant material persist,
heaven become Hell, paradise lost for all.
    As we got back and I climbed on the LM,
I noticed William Shakespeare down below,
and I made so bold as to speak to him,
asking him what had long been on my mind.
Will replied, "I could never forget what they did
to my family, other people in the village,
as on a spinning Wheel of Fire,
especially. . . I, I can't speak of it,
such betrayal, but with the tongue of verse,
and urge you do the same, a language of
a visionary realm of human woe,
an airy song, of dreams and nightmare."
All were transfixed by his words, as on a cross,
Christ on the Cross, the Image of our lives.
I ventured to ask, with hesitation,
"Why did you abandon your work at the end?"
"What? I went back to the country, back to
my family life. Let the pedants play their part!
After all that feverish dreaming, I needed
healing, and returned to where I hoped to find it,
but for Judeth and her good-for-nothing rogue!"
Heaving a despairing sigh, I replied,
"Many have become theorists, parasites,
in narrow circles, talked themselves into it,
worse than the "treasure" of Polonius."

As with a rapier, he slashed his arm
through the moon air, "Forget them! Write the book!
The Muses will get it to the people.
So welcome to the moon. From here," gazing up,
"We can see all the aching, rollicking world."
    Standing on the descent module,
I felt my head beginning to spin.
Saigyo having left me, I listened to
the haranguing, and more, felt alone, stood
there viewing Cervantes upon his charger,
the tribes of the bards of the world around him.
I waved him over to me, spoke in a low voice,
"Cervantes, I felt I had no other choice.
I had to let go of my psychic tic
even though it had given me my strength
for so many years, defined the nature
of my struggle, material and spiritual.
For the good of others, I had to let go.
It would have prevented me from reaching some.
I had outgrown it. It no longer mattered."
Cervantes, Tolstoy now near him, both smiling,
mouths agape with missing and rotten teeth,
nodded in acceptance of what I had done.
Cervantes, then seizing the occasion, said,
"I was wrong about satire. There are some
things in that world fit only for its sting.
Puncture the deceptions and delusions."
Nearby Milton and Dante stood, the latter adding,
"It is best for the art to have but a crust,
so one seeks sustenance in the soul."
Milton shifted and looked askance at him.
A voice from the throng then interrupted,
"Enough! So be it! Let it begin!"
The noble poet of *Beowulf*, wrapped in
his singing robes, thrusting out his staff towards

Cervantes, with more cheers from all sides,
filling the non-existent atmosphere,
ethereal music to my ears, assertive,
challenging tones, heroic, the human spirit's
deep intent to forge on, explore all regions,
physical, and into the soul of man.
Then the shades before me began to fade,
bards and troubadours, griots and shamans,
medicine men, storytellers, receded
from view, like the stars of the universe,
blazoned out by the whiteness of the sun,
the blackest black of space illuminating
the moonscape, Cervantes' fading upon
a horn, Roland's sounding there upon the moon,
with Beowulf and the Nibelungen poets,
side by side, blowing together their defiant,
forward-charging horns, Cervantes the last
of that crew, wryly smiling down on me,
and then he, too, with his nag, was gone.
   Silent solitude, beyond worldly experience.
I stood alone on the module, all gone,
I but alone with the immensity of space,
the placid moon, eons enwrapped me,
the Earth but a tiny marble, blue-white,
like the marbles I played with as a boy,
"keepers" and "cat-eyes," we called them. I wanted
to win them all, shiny jewels, a little boy's
heart delighted in playing with brothers
and sisters and friends, determined to win.
I raised my thumb up, laughing, covered
the Earth at arm's length, thought of the astronauts,
who came up here, too, searching for truth,
in a different form, but still the same, all truth
one though we seek it in various ways,
the resonating mystery challenging all

to make of it what they can, human
to fail and fall back on shibboleths,
so I thought, the marble concealed by
my thumb, alone on that sea-less Sea of
Tranquility, far from the tumultuous
Earth and all its woes, its many evils
convulsing humankind, wracked between
fluctuating suffering and joy. A jewel
in the universe. What does it mean to be
alone, alone in the universe, Unknown?
    Lowering my arm, I was surprised to see
a figure, alone, alone as Daniel in
the lion's den, far out on the moonscape,
sitting on the plain, too far to see clearly,
and so I climbed down from the LM, left foot
first, "one small step for a man," and walked
towards him, springing really, along, easily
in the one-sixth gravity of the moon,
like a kangaroo or rabbit hopping,
toward some master apparently come to take
me further on my journey, sent by the
Parliament of Poets, wherever they went.
Through the powdery moon dust I bounced,
a long way out into the Sea of Tranquility.
I had not realized how far at first,
distance so deceptive on the moon,
without any landmarks to judge by,
a journey in itself, like life itself.
Suddenly, company caught up with me,
hailing me from behind, causing me to turn
round, to discover Melville and Whitman.
We stood in the moon dust and barren plain,
where we spoke, for some time, in low voices,
they glancing back, making sure no one followed.
I really fought and didn't want to listen,

felt it was a long way to the moon just
to hear what they had to say, bitter words.
"You wanted to stand next to Homer and
Virgil, Dante and Milton, didn't you?
Did you think it would cost you nothing?
You wouldn't have to pay a price, earn it?"
Angry, I struggled not to lose control.
"That's the way it is," Melville said, breaking
the bad news to me. Whitman stood still, glumly.
"And no reward for it, not in that world."
Melville stood firm, staring at me as I fled,
walking away, leaving them both standing there.
I just couldn't endure anymore of it,
so I stomped off, and went out toward Job,
boiling inside, angry as hell, tight-fisted,
clouds of moon dust swirling up around my knees,
thinking of the Rebbe who said, "God can be
found even in anger." I was ready for Him,
ready to wrestle the angel to the ground.
   Once I had drawn closer, I recognized
Job from William Blake's painting, as it were,
the Hebrew poet, if not prophet,
man of patient suffering, on an ash heap,
in sack cloth, sitting in the moon dust,
boils and sores now healed, but a serious
demeanor on his face, severely chastened,
it seemed, by all that Yahweh had visited
upon him, not much mercy shown Job
in the battle with the accuser, nay-sayer,
God going all out to prove a point.
I could commiserate in my heart with Job,
long already my master and guide,
solace, if nothing else, left me counting
my blessings. Life can always be worse, though,
being human, it often seems pretty bad.

And then Job laid into me, "You've never
known suffering. Nothing but whining and
belly-aching, pampered Americans!
All you 'modern' people are the same.
God owes you nothing! Damn backsliders!
You're lucky he doesn't wipe you off
the face of the Earth and have done with you.
Look up there," he shouted at me, "What do
you see?" Shocked, and in fear and trembling,
I peered up at the Earth, now somehow closer
to the horizon, large and glorious in all
its color against the pure blackness of space,
the inscrutable whiteness turned inside out.
I found to my surprise that my gaze could
penetrate a quarter of a million miles,
looking down on the Earth like Menippus,
until I could see something moving upon
the surface of the planet, a mass of ants
crawling upon an anthill, drones,
busy with their feverish activity,
quarreling and fighting among themselves,
stinging, robbing, deceiving one another.
I gasped in recognition, stunned horror,
man, the foulest, creeping, crawling slime
that ever moved upon the face of the Earth.
I shook violently in fright, looking
back at Job, whose fiery eyes bore down on me.
"Eliphaz and his kind," said Job.
"Miserable comforters are they all.
They stink all the way across the universe.
'The Lord our God is One Lord,
and thou shalt love the Lord with all thine heart,
and with all thy soul, and with all thy might.'
Thou shalt not curse God and die but keep
and follow His commandments and covenant,
though no man on Earth remember what they are,

all forgetting Abraham and His Oneness.
Not sacrifices and deadening rituals,
but the sacrifice of the heart and soul.
Deeds, not words, you ignorant, would-be poet!
Your age doesn't understand poetry.
Get those idiotic theories out of your head.
'Do unto others as you'd have them do
unto you.' Are you listening? Integrity!"
Holding my head down, nearly to my chest,
I shuddered under the whirlwind of his words,
knowing some of them by heart, painfully
aware that I had never lived up to them,
but hoped, somehow, I might, longed to,
having broken all of the Ten Commandments,
like so many human beings on Earth,
is my lame and self-serving excuse.
How could I respond to his reprimands?
Although upon the moon, I felt myself
but one of the things upon the Earth.
Oh, those human beings and their beliefs.
And then Job let sail, "Don't just hear by the ear.
There is a glory in this universe,
beyond us all. Tell mankind. Prove your eye
hath seen." Deep within, I sensed the truth
of his searing words, tearing me down,
yet knew their purpose was to lift me up,
giving me new-found strength to forge on.
I slowly raised my head and looked at him,
fiery Old Testament eyes blazoned back at me,
softened, accepted, followed their own advice.
Time, the mystery of it, what it means
for human beings, hung upon the moonscape
between us, Sustaining Presence, guiding man,
mellowed and left us once again alone.
    And then I hazarded, "You stood up to Him,
once over some compelling Auschwitz of the soul."

Job replied, "That's blasphemy even I shrink from
saying to His face. We're not letting Him off.
Our sins were nothing compared to His.
He let all those men and women, young and old,
suffer and die, grievously, needlessly.
He's the most grievous sinner. No doubt about that.
Don't even suggest the Holy One incinerated
us for some reason, let alone that one.
Nothing we ever did could justify that,
though he stood by and allowed millions to die."
"Didn't you teach man exclusivity?
The 'chosen people,' all that hubris?
Set the ball rolling to the crematory?"
"Now hold on, I'm the one lecturing here."
"And I'm the one who's supposed to straighten out
the world. If it means I have to deal with you
and the Jews, so be it. I'm not backing off."
Largely ignoring me, he continued on,
"More like 'chosen' to suffer and die like dogs.
Harassed and hounded everywhere we went,
a scapegoat for all humanity. Adonai
owes us some mercy, as far as I'm concerned,
though I admit not enough of that for his
people has been forthcoming in your modern world.
So much for God. But where was man?
Why didn't the 'Christian' nations do something.
For decades they all conspired to prepare
the way for the slaughter. Where were they?"
"Guiltless, are you? Going easy on yourselves?
What about Peor and..." I shot back at him.
(Since he didn't pull any punches with me,
I wasn't going to cut him any slack.)
Off guard again, stammering, Job replied,
"All... all right, we made a few mistakes with the
Canaanites, but it only proves my point,"
shaking indignantly. "We're human like

everybody else. Besides, God wanted us
to have the Promised Land." I guffawed,
"There's no doubt about the former, but does
the latter ever sound familiar, as though
you're the only holy people on Earth."
"Where in the hell was humanity when
we needed to be on the receiving end?
Your own hearts are black as coal in Hell."
"So why are you still on your knees up here?
Begging for the mercy you think you deserved?"
Really mad now, Job let me have it,
"Buddy, you and your generation ought
to be doing a whole lot more of it,
as you're gunna find out, if history
is any indicator of collapse and ruin.
As ignorant and arrogant as your
leaders are, you're bound for tragedy,
like Oedipus, my companion in pain,
both eyes plucked out, blood and gore streaming down.
Many entered the gas chambers with the
Shema Israel on their lips, in their hearts."
"A lot of good it did them is the lament
of millions of modern Jews, let alone goyim."
"You don't know that. Why doesn't your age
acknowledge and respect that very fact?
That's an expression of your own disbelief,
the death-wish decadence of modernity.
Souls stood under bare barrack bulbs praying,
in the dark and moaning pain of grief,
right until the end, whatever it was,
the crematory, a bullet in the head,
or starvation until your army showed up."
"Well, are you sure it's Yahweh we're dealing
with and not Ahriman or Shiva?
Job shrugged, "Who knows. There could be some connection.
Given our experience, we can't rule it out.

Why is a goy like you worrying about the Jews?
What are we to you? Why aren't you out making
bushels of money like everybody else?
Even the astronauts came up here for things,
moon rocks, not ideas and poetry!
'No percentage in that!' to quote your master."
   Job stood up, gazing at me, then gestured
toward the module, where now stood several
poets looking our way. "They're waiting for you.
Remember, you can say anything to God
as long as it's in defense of his creation.
But don't tempt God or take him for granted.
You can't hide your heart from the Holy One.
He can use you as much as anybody else.
Who do you think you are? Why shouldn't he?
You serve the test as well as anybody.
No one travels through the world unscathed.
Where's all that radiant acquiescence now?
I'm not seeing much of it after Melville.
You're a hypocrite like every human being.
You want to go through what I have?
Consider yourself lucky. Damn ingrate.
Now find a way to reach humanity."
"Job, I don't want to go back down there."
"You have to. It's where you still belong.
You haven't earned the right to stay amongst us.
That, or hide your light under a bushel,
stand self-accused and shame-faced before Him."
With a start and a shudder, I looked at Job.
Pulling myself together, not daring
to say anything, I turned, brooding, and shuffled
back through moon dust toward the lunar lander.
   As I reached the group of poets, looking
not unlike Job, hailing me in Hebrew accents,
mellowed with a Spanish tinge, I began
to realize the meaning of that flavor.

Here were some Jewish poets of Andaluz,
their robes a little Moorish as well.
"Has Job prepared you for us," shouted one,
as I drew nearer to them, Hanagid, the
great poet and general, princely vizier
for the Moorish invaders, in charge even
on the moon. "Ready now to return to Earth?"
Fumbling for an answer, befuddled,
I struggled for words, while he laughed,
turning to his left, introducing others.
"We've all come. We heard the command,
and I saw to it that all marshaled here,
Solomon Ibn Gabriol, Abraham and
Moses Ibn Ezra, Rabbi Jochanan,
Judah Al-Harizi, Isaac Ibn Giat,
and Yahuda Halevi, and more from
Andaluz, the poets of Valencia, Tudela,
Sargassoa, fate-laden Grenada.
We all are here upon the moon,
the Twelve Tribes of Israel, as you see."
Sizing me up during his introduction,
I sensed his eyes penetrating to my core,
as though I were one of his men he was
about to send out against a Christian horde
from Seville. I felt a little insecure,
and then he stepped back, casting a glance
at Moses Ibn Ezra, who moved aside,
saying, while looking out over the moonscape,
where Job had been, now gone, vanished,
"All the days of man's life move but towards
the grave, what we all reached long ago.
That you walk with two legs upon this moon
must be the will of God, in some way
beyond our understanding. A little
journey, and you arrive where we are,
though you lie at rest, safe as one aboard ship,

flying across a sea, as this moon flies
across the immensity of space.
Life will pull you up short, gravestones crumbling
with the rest, as the names of your ancestors
in All Saints Churchyard, unreadable, worn
with the rain of time, eroding away
the slaves and masters, the high and low,
and every emotion they ever felt."
Interrupting, Gabriol, smiling, said,
"Trying to cheer him up, after Job, are you?"
Pushing forward with humor first in his voice,
Gabriol intoned, "Though we may limp through life,
in the serenity of the morning, He is
our rock and tower, lay prayers before Him,
though day and night, mixed with clay.
His eyes see the thoughts within.
What else can the heart or tongue do,
the spirit within, but raise a song
to one who is pleased, praise Him, while the
divine soul is in us. All creation,
above and below, witnesses," glancing
out toward the Earthrise on the horizon,
"and declares the oneness of the Lord,
his name is one, paths innumerable,
all resolved in one, God, king, alone.
Hearts ponder the created world, all measured
in weight and number, all save him, beyond.
Here above and down below, signs of Him,
north and west, east and south, here where direction
is beyond the poles, sky and earth,
all from One Master, alone.
From Him emanates the entire world.
He remains, the rest shall perish,
all creation glorifying Him, from
beginning to end. The Father is One."
Gabriol gently stepped away, while Hanagid

said to Halevi, "It is time. You alone
among us traveled from Andaluz to
the Holy Land. Take him down that he might
learn what mankind must now know.
It is the will of the Lord." The poet of
Tudela and Grenada, Seville and Cordoba,
he who sang of return, and made the return,
through Egypt, back to the land of his fathers,
stepped forward, raised his arm toward me.
Looking at him squarely in the eyes,
I seized his arm, as my integrity,
felt carried aloft from the moon once more,
led heavenward by a Wandering Jew.
    The marble in the sky grew larger, until
it filled our view, aurora borealis
flickering and weaving erratically, and
half the Earth webbed together with swaths of light,
as we burned through the enclosing atmosphere,
multicolored lights surrounding us, flashing,
Israel my shield and defense.
I could see the Mediterranean and Red Sea,
as we flew toward Zion, over Jerusalem,
"glimpsing Jerusalem's dust," Halevi
ever lowering to a mountain, coming
into view, settling down on its side,
a green valley below, dry air, fields and rock.
"Mt Carmel," he said to me, gazing below,
"The valley of Jezreel and the brook Kishon."
I looked at him, my mouth agape, wondering
why, of all places, he had brought me there,
searching my memory of the Bible,
for some clue, the reason I stood on a
modest mountain, one side out to the sea,
the other a fertile valley and brook.
Like Moses I looked across the valley,
refined in the furnace of affliction,

not sure that I would ever cross over
to the Promised Land of milk and honey,
though I felt blessed to lay my eyes upon it.
And then Halevi turned and pointed toward
a clearing where a crowd of people gathered,
jostling, striving about, loud shouts and
noise rising above Mt Carmel.
"Follow me," said Halevi, striding quickly
toward a stand of scrubby trees,
I behind, struggling to keep up,
over rocks and undergrowth, wondering where
now, afraid to be left behind without
my guide, far away, in what time I knew not,
unsure of my safety, near such tumult.
   We arrived at the edge of where the people were,
a mixed multitude, it seemed, wound up to
a height of emotion, judging by the shouting
and high pitch of voices, fiery and feverish.
I instinctively drew closer to Halevi,
seeking protection from him delegated
to the task by the Parliament on the moon.
I queried him with a glance. He replied,
"Watch. Listen. You'll understand," turning back to
the scene from our concealment behind a rock.
A shout went up, "What more do we need
to see? Yahweh's fireball has consumed
the burnt sacrifice. All the prophets of Baal
couldn't do that, all their dancing and prancing,
leaping upon their pagan altar, did nothing.
'O Baal, answer us!' got no answer.
Well, I say, we'll give 'em one now!
Send the Phoenician whoremongers where they belong!
There's only one way to purify the land.
O Israel, no more of two opinions.
The whole debate has been settled for all time.
Right here on Mt Carmel, by God!

Jezebel cut off our prophets and showed
not a one the slightest shred of mercy.
Obadiah saved our remnant, hiding in caves,
gave them bread and water, servant of the Lord,
and now what could be clearer?
What has Elijah taught us if not that?
Hear, O Israel, turn aside from Baalim,
draw close again to Yahweh, and his commandments,
written upon the tablet of the heart,
follow them, not mere words but a living ethic.
It's the will of the Lord. We've got to get
serious with the Canaanites and their gods.
So don't balk at it and whine and protest,
as you always do in your squeamish,
wishy-washy way. It's time for backbone
and action. It's obvious Baal is not the God,
so stop following him." He paused for a
long time, looking over the people, the crowd
standing still, murmuring amongst themselves,
fixed on every vehement word of his.
Not a single soul answered him back.
And then he added, "No living together with them.
We've got to slaughter off all of them."
Shocked, I began to understand, remember,
shuddering inside, and feeling scared at
what seemed to be happening right before my eyes.
I wasn't sure where Elijah was, busy
someplace I supposed, the speaker in his stead.
And then somebody else did speak up, saying,
"Elijah's the only prophet we've got left.
How long do you imagine we should wait?
It can't go on like this anymore.
Yahweh wants us to have all of Canaan.
Nothing could be clearer. The Canaanites don't belong.
It's time to clean the house of the Lord."
"Yeah! Yeah!" could be heard throughout the mob,

as he continued, "Now remember, what you
said when you fell upon your faces, 'Yahweh
is the God.' And that requires action.
One leads to the other, it does. Sure enough.
And that's why Elijah ordered to take
the prophets of Baal, the four hundred and fifty,
along with Baal's Prophets of the Grove,
and not let a one of them escape.
Don't start backsliding already, right away.
Ahab's going along with it, isn't he?
He saw the ball of fire burning up
the bullock on the altar. Think of it.
All that water, so it seemed, barrels of
water poured over the wood, saturating it,
and then the raging blaze, swirling above,
stone on stone, the altar consuming
all of the bull and rock and bone.
Only Yahweh could have done that!
O people of God, the one true Lord!
Follow him from the top of Mt Carmel!
Elijah leads the way to the brook Kishon."
The people answered him not a word.
    Helevi grasped my arm above the elbow,
kindly but firmly, as waking one from
a nightmare, my gaze locked upon the scene,
obsessed with some eternal revelation,
a pageant set before my eyes, a story
I could not leave off, some dreadful meaning
I was intent on facing, no matter what.
I asked my guide and trusted poet,
"What is it about this mountain that leads
to such arrogance, such oppression?"
And he, "It's not the mountain's fault, but
the men. They are but what they think, poor things.
Come," throwing his cloak over his left shoulder,
leading to the right, back into the brush,

around the people and down the mountain.
I followed, dazed, in half nightmare, half dream,
until we stepped out on gentle foothills
and a plain, a green valley and brook ahead.
I began to fear, sensed, knew, what sight
my master might reveal to my eyes.
His robes furled in the frenzy of his pace.
Heaviness began to weigh upon my heart.
Confusion, a struggle in my soul, for
the story of Elijah, servant of
the Lord, I had always loved, champion
of Israel, against the pagan horde.
The first of his noble race to return,
what was Halevi trying to teach me?
Master of Andaluz, the Wandering Jew,
who made it back to the land of his fathers,
centuries before most of the tribe,
escaping the Muslim conquerors of Spain.
    All these thoughts and more crowded through my mind,
as he hurried me along, and then we rose
over a small hill and through some brush,
and could hear a gurgling of water
in the brook, unseen through embankment trees.
Over his shoulder, Halevi cast a look
back to me, expressionless, grim.
Breaking through the branches, we were suddenly
upon the bank. Halevi moved aside,
allowing me to take in all the view.
The shock of what I saw gripped me as if
it were a griffon tearing me apart
with its jaws and claws, devouring
the last human morsel of my inmost soul,
like the Piasa bird, devourer of men.
For all before me was the brook Kishon.
From left to right, I surveyed all the scene,
green and sparkling, all the more beautiful

for the dry and dusty desert of the land,
but now strewn along its banks, fallen into it,
partly or wholly, floating here and there,
bodies everywhere everywhere everywhere,
human corpses, slashed and hewn, blood splattered,
cruelly slashed and gouged, gory, bloody wounds,
covered already with bugs and flies,
no longer a beautiful green marble
beheld in vision as from the moon,
a glory suspended in the universe,
but a dark and violent abode of horror,
the prophets of Baal human no more,
but rendered things, mere dead animals
in a factory of death, wanton destruction,
left to rot where they fell, not even incinerated,
cut down by them so certain they held the truth,
fierce for its triumph and victory,
at any cost, even their own humanity,
taken into the valley and slaughtered,
the Golden Rule of Leviticus not for them.
I shook and sobbed in disbelief, horror,
not prepared, despite all that I had heard,
for such a ghastly sight, hundreds and hundreds
of men, not even dumped into a mass grave,
unburied, unconsecrated in any way,
there upon the Biblical brook Kishon.
Falling upon my knees, welling up in me,
"O God, save us from such holocaust,
mass slaughter, dread premonition,
visited upon future generations.
Save us, O Lord, from thy vengeance,
in thy mercy, spare us, all the little ones.
Stop this fanaticism, return us to oneness,
the danger still upon the face of the Earth,
the stream of civilization clogged with bodies."
I shook again and convulsed, vomiting,

until I ran into the bushes,
alone, retching over the horror in my guts.
    Much time passed. I felt somewhat recovered,
though not reconciled to what I had seen,
and thought of Halevi, feeling his presence,
in the trees, beyond me. To my surprise,
it wasn't him, but someone else, unknown,
in a rose-colored robe of a different style,
wearing an odd kind of head piece, a face
with a long aquiline nose, reassuringly
standing a comfortable distance away.
He held out his arm to me, and then I knew,
a new master had come to rescue me
from the horror of that land. Fortified
by the thought of escape, I stepped boldly
towards him and grasped his proffered arm
with all my heart, conveying implicit trust
and confidence as it dawned on me who he was,
my master, Dante Alighieri, poet of
the soul's long journey through the Gates of Hell,
to Purgatory and Paradise, sweet bliss,
that high heaven of the universe,
where God's glorious angels sing his praise,
eternally, revolving with the music of
the spheres, hosannas to him forever
and ever, the Rose window of eternity.
I clutched his arm in fervent gratitude
that he had come to deliver me from that spot,
choked with clotted blood and gore and woe.
He rose and I rose with him in vision
of glory, intoxicated with the scent
of the divine, as of a starry rose bloom,
Rose window of the universe, gazed upon,
trusting he took me somewhere intended,
carrying, like Petrarch, a *Secretum*,
a destined voyage upon my pilgrim way,

back to God, my life's own journey,
a test and trial still not complete,
but bound in hope that my masters might teach
me aright the path to tread, not for myself,
but that all mankind might hear a mighty song,
worthy of them, worthy of the traditions
of the past, visionaries who sang for
their peoples, all humanity, that they might
rise to greater heights of self-sacrifice, love,
see and know one another not as things,
but souls, equally divine, humane, reflections
and dew drops of Him, glorious Father,
before Whom mercy and forgiveness, love,
tolerance of one another, is the surest proof
that we seek and serve Him now, now in our
time, not the dark and horrible dungeons
of the past, pits of torture and death,
every nation forcing on others their view
of monotone truth, shades of unspeakable evil.
Such the surging emotions inside me,
as Dante and I soared above Mt Carmel
and Canaan, out over the Mediterranean's
clear blue sea of ancient seafarers beyond
number, Egyptians, Phoenicians, Virgil's
voyage of Aeneas, Homer's Odysseus,
seen from above, an epic of the Earth,
until, far below, the Italian boot,
and all her majestic, triumphant history,
yet all so often besotted, too, with blood.
Even so, we flew north, passing over Rome,
where Dante, to my surprise, did not land,
but flew on, past the snowy Alps far below,
shrinking glaciers and valleys green,
on into France, the heart and soul of Europe,
swirling clouds of time and place, rising up,
the long migrations of humanity.

BOOK VIII

THE ARGUMENT

Dante guides the Persona to Chartres Cathedral. Through the labyrinth, the Queen of Heaven. Europe, a hallowed tale, in colored glass. Erasmus returns to London, with the Poet, to outside Westminster Abbey. Browning's poem "Christmas Eve" opens the door. Tennyson, a cordial reception and then a dressing down. The Federation of the World. Blake and Milton stroll over from St. Margaret's Church. Milton guides the Poet of the Moon to what Blake called, so rightly, "Englands green & pleasant land." A simple parish church, surrounding graves, a church perhaps Thomas Hardy had restored, in need again of his services. A prayer. And the Lady of the Lake. Excalibur. Arthur returns. An inscription on the shining blade. Wainamoinen, along with Sigurd, Beowulf, and the Valkyries, lift the Poet from the isle of green to a grove of green, turning toward early fall, as through a swirling tunnel of time, to a birch bench. Yasnaya Polyana. Tolstoy, along the path, discusses his beliefs, mourns his mistakes, grieves for Russia's collapse into the crevasse. Two young poets swept away into the Gulag emerge to carry the Persona from Russia, with Hadji Murad, heading south.

As on a journey across a great lake,
we can find ourselves confronted with fierce winds,
Aeolus blowing in our face, raging,
driving the waves, rocking our little canoe,
rolling, crests lapping up to the gunnels,
overloaded with the things of life,
its many burdens and commitments,
often for others, but seemingly taking
us off course, making shore all the harder
to attain, even so, it seemed my life,
at that far height, despite my grasping
Dante's wrist, I worried, had lost its way,

on one more voyage, leading nowhere,
upheaval filling my chest with doubt
and fear, that it might only be in my head,
a solipsistic dream, a delusion born of self,
deception sinking all my hopes and prayers
that God might deign to grant that I might write
and raise a new and lofty song of praise,
in this age, the Global Age, to His glory,
somehow help to guide mankind back to Him.
    "O Homer, Virgil, Dante, Milton, aid me!"
I exclaimed, illogically, in Dante's case,
on the verge of tears, more from these thoughts
than the whipping wind, the Florentine turning
toward me, with amusement on his face,
seeming to understand my inmost thoughts,
piercing my soul, healing and uplifting me
back from despair, fortifying me to trust
and sail on with him, my guide, heaven sent,
could but lead me on the path aright.
And I became aware that we were lowering
over fields, abundant harvests, all around,
golden wheat and crops, a fertile land,
and across the terrain, on the horizon,
a tall cathedral stood, two towers,
spires rising to the sky, while we flew on,
towards them, until Dante gently set us down
in front of them, two spires, ornately
embellished upon the left, a simple beauty
rising on the right, its square base blending
smoothly into an octagonal cone,
pointing up to the air and beyond,
exquisite metaphors, granite's finest,
elevating the soul in the very act
of inspiring one to lift the gaze heavenward.
And so I stood, enthralled by a granite metaphor,

an image of my own heart's longing,
the Cathedral of Notre Dame at Chartres,
the perfection of the art, glorification
of the Queen of Heaven, Mother of God.
I already wanted to fall to my knees,
as at Bernard's or Waverley Abbey,
but Dante led me on by stepping toward
the great entry, the Royal Portal, drawing
me with him by his example, slowly
toward the three twelfth-century doors,
Christ seated, enthroned in an oval nimbus,
at the center raising his hand, in blessing,
surrounded by apostles, evangelists,
the prophets and kings and queens, princes,
saints in Byzantine attire, glorifying
and waiting in attendance, attesting
to his celestial majesty, Lord Supreme,
Divine Ruler of Heaven and Earth.
   Next to Christ, the Queen of Heaven, Our Lady
of Chartres, Mary, sits upon her throne,
gentle and gracious, mercy and majesty,
the Holy Virgin, she reigns here,
this cathedral her homage, her court, where
all wait upon her, she at one with her Son
and His Church, she recipient of the
Annunciation, Gabriel's, the Arch-angel's
goal and desire, upon her the blessing
of Visitation, crowned in all her glory,
the Nativity and Infant, Joseph
and the three shepherds standing by,
her superiority proven by the possession
of all the liberal arts, attested by
Aristotle and Pythagoras, Euclid,
Ptolemy and Cicero, attending
the most blessed of all women,

of all men of thought, pagan or Christian,
Mary, and her Child, reigning as One.
   Dante devoutly bowed toward the south door,
of the three, Mary's door, and walked through,
past the pillared saints and kings and queens.
I followed, a mere peasant and servant,
enthralled, with no thought of turning back.
I found myself in a vestibule,
with passages leading to the twin towers,
on either side, the great nave before me,
opening far into the cavern of the cathedral.
Dante stood for a while looking reverently
toward the high altar; made the sign of
the cross, as did I, without a word, stepping
further into the nave together.
As my eyes adjusted to the interior,
I perceived above and around me
a glorious light flowing in through the
Rose window above, lancet windows below,
those along the nave and far above in
the clerestory, high up in the vaulted
ceiling that seemed to rise heavenward,
almost forever, before closing their form
as two rising hands pressed together in prayer.
Almost breathless, I stepped ahead, until
my glance noticed on the floor in front of me
a wide, remarkable design, a labyrinth,
filling the nave, from side to side, deep into
the cathedral, the Christian medicine wheel,
ancient Europe, I knew, the way of life,
my life, symbol, emblem of the soul,
metaphor of my long journey home,
led by all the poets to the land Divine.
Deep in my soul I felt a rising surge
overwhelming me, throwing me to my knees,

entering therein, into the labyrinth.
Moving upon my knees, seeking the mercy
and blessing of Mary, pilgrim I prayed,
as I inched forward, through the winding
path of eleven folding levels, wrapping
round and round, toward the center,
the rosette in the middle, even hers,
like the Rose window, the one above me,
behind, I turned to gaze up at, speechless
at its glory, beauty, blue and red light,
a dazzling jewel, cut and polished
by some medieval glassmaker, my namesake,
my ancestor, working with light and glass,
artisan of light, Christ at its center.
Light pouring down on me in the maze,
lifted, as by the pictured angels of glass,
I felt myself on another plane, swept
beyond the febrile moments of this world,
this modern world with its woeful lack of faith.
Bowing my head, I went deep into my heart,
sought Him there, and Her, and rose my head,
turning as I did to look up the nave
toward the high altar, her imperial court,
bathed in a brilliant glow of candlelight,
image of far above where Mary reigned,
mercy, forgiveness, bounteous blessings,
she in her regal dignity, high up in
even the clerestory, shone down on me,
lifting me up, as Dante's hand on my arm
guiding me up the nave, enamored,
walking, gazing at the transcendent icon,
kneeling, touching my forehead again with
the sign of the cross, lowering my eyes,
as I did when a boy, at Saint Anne's Church,

"Hail, Mary, Mother of God, pray for us sinners,
now and at the hour of our death. Amen."
  Long moments went by, till Dante stirred,
entering, around the altar, the choir aisle,
past more exquisite glass than I could absorb,
radiant light, deep inside the apse,
lined with chapels. Dante stopped in front of
Charlemagne's windows, looked up at them even
as I followed his gaze, found pictured
the Emperor Constantine and Charlemagne,
the storied lives and battles, and Roland,
striking his sword Dulendar upon the stone,
winding his horn, his heroic deeds
fending off the Saracens, restoring Spain
to Europe, to the Queen of Heaven,
to Christ's Kingdom. Blues and reds, golds and greens,
such colors I had never seen, resplendent,
coloring the epic tale. Oh Europe!
Europe, a hallowed tale in colored glass,
I mused, not quite that way again, but rise up!
Remember your noble past, what you've been
and are. Deeply pondering I stood,
till Dante nudged me to move along,
around the back to the transept, turning right.
  We stood before the northern transept,
the glorious Rose window above, Mary,
the Window of France, her high Queen,
all the nation bent its knee to her,
nobility carrying the stones with commoners,
raising Chartres to her glory. I gasped at
the beauty, while Dante, too, I could tell,
was deeply moved, even he who had seen
her in the great white Rose of heaven,
with Bernard, who had helped dedicate Chartres,
Dante's final guide of that peerless vision,

the lesson learnt, that he labored to convey,
in his great poem, I love, *The Commedia*.
Dante stepped forward once again, walked toward
the northern doors, led me out the center one,
into the harsh daylight of the afternoon.
As I stepped out I thought of Elijah,
there somewhere, looked to my left, where now he was
a frozen pillar, no longer a threat,
beyond him Job, flat on his back, suffering,
a devil above him delighting in his pain.
Shades and specters, all, it now seemed to me,
brooding, images of another time
and world, one gone by, but strangely persisting,
in our hearts and minds, ineluctable,
no matter how much we try to forget them.
   Clearing his throat, Dante said, "You've lapsed.
You should return to the Holy Mother Church.
She is merciful and will welcome you back
with open arms, heavenly consolation."
Shocked a bit, though not much, having been through
this before, I smirked scathingly back at him.
I had assumed the poets set him straight,
the modern world having moved on. Peeved, I said,
"That certainly explains why you put everyone
in Hell, whoever disagreed with you, or
for whom you nursed a grudge. Enough Inquisitions.
The world is not going back down that road.
No more of those horrors, exclusivisms
of the Dark Ages, thank you just the same.
The modern world has plenty of its own.
We don't need to go backward for more.
I thought you were sent by the Parliament
of Poets? Don't you get it yet?
Why do I have to explain it to you?
Remember, *you're* supposed to be *my* guide!"

Looking dour and scowling at me, he replied,
"All right, calm down. I was just testing you.
In the cathedral, you seemed, well, you know,
deep within, though perhaps your time seeks
a new path, even the will of God seeming
determined to move humanity along,
somewhere, what with all the furore
for centuries, I suppose," sadly trailing off.
I moved away and thought of my ancestors,
not just the Croatian Catholics but the
Huguenots, too, persecuted and driven
out of Europe, German Protestants, Irish, English,
and I, scion of Michelet, "Mickley,"
within my genes a labyrinth of faith,
reaching into Europe, deep into the past,
back to the shamans of Lascaux, Chauvet.
Dante meant well, couldn't help himself,
and then he faded upon a sounding horn,
retreating to the battlefield of yore,
leaving me on the western steps alone,
as alone as a Rembrandt self-portrait.
For some time I rolled these things through my mind,
until suddenly the door opened again
and out stepped Erasmus of Rotterdam.
Acknowledging Erasmus, I said,
"O master, father, thank you for always
being there for me. I'd have been so lonely,
but for you. I too would praise folly, but not
at all foolishly, nay, for serious reasons.
Let readers sharpen their eyes to detect
a theme that is worthy of their time.
We aim for no mere literary trifles.
Our goal is Horace's noble standard,
'Wisdom and delight.' Lead on Horatio!"
choking, nearly sobbing, fighting back tears,

despite my efforts to suppress the unexpected
emotion welling up in me. Benignly,
Erasmus said to me, "Try, my son, to let
yourself laugh at the folly of the world.
Yes, its state is seriously defective,
woeful, to the point of bitter tears,
but a hearty laugh might help you restore
your equilibrium." And so a log-jam,
of sorts, broke within me, blurting out,
"What a sad and pathetic bunch we human
beings are! Why the universe ever coughed
us up, God only knows!" Erasmus laughed,
heartily, at that, and I joined in, through tears.
"Help me, Erasmus," I said to him.
"I already have," was his honest reply.
"There is a way to revive Europe, but
you must first conquer your own doubts, move forward."
He did not embrace me, nor try to advise
me further, but simply held out his arm,
and we flew off from the Virgin's cathedral,
far above the fields, our goal to the west,
the flying Dutchman sailing through the air.
   My thoughts lingered so on Chartres,
I neglected where Erasmus flew,
until I realized we were over water,
a channel separating two land masses,
and then I knew it was the sceptered isle,
bejeweled island, green and lush, floating upon
the sea, England, home of my people, long ago,
where Erasmus himself had visited.
Looking at me, I could tell that Erasmus
understood I had realized what land it was,
but I wondered where he would take me,
to visit English friends, perhaps Thomas More?
A vast island, for so small a one,

so it seemed to me, an American, causing
me to recall my homeland, after such
a long journey, over so much of the world,
even the moon. A welcome thought, that I might
be getting closer to home, though they might not
want to own me as such, my people down
there somewhere still, I smiled, currents of history,
underground, in the veins, running clear and true.
No, not underground yet, I thought, still above it,
and high above it, even London town,
if not mistaken, there below, the River Thames,
and landmarks as I had seen them once,
from the air, too, my 737 jumbo jet,
soaring around to Heathrow. What a sight!
St Paul's Cathedral, the House of Parliament,
the real one, not a bunch of poets shooting off
their mouths on the moon, and Big Ben,
banging out mortality's relentless stride.
Erasmus set us down more smoothly than
a professionally trained airline pilot,
right in front of Westminster Abbey, near
the courtyard of St Margaret's, next to it.
    Standing at an angle to the main entrance,
I could see all the way down the side of
the cathedral to the apse, in one view.
Erasmus looked up at Westminster, crinkling
his nose in an odd way, then turned to me,
saying, "I love this land and people more
than I can say but must return to Europe.
A poet you admire shall be along soon,"
a severity on his lips, under his monkish hat.
I still felt grateful to him, leaned forward,
almost bowed, acknowledging my master,
father who had been with me so many years.
He took off. I thought, Protestant divorce,

too much free-thinking, something like that.
Yet I felt at home, as I say, but then
I'm an American, a hodge-podge hybrid
of people from everywhere on Earth, human,
as some of us have come to believe, realize.
We easily feel at home everywhere on
Mother Earth, much to the ire of some of
its inhabitants, clutching their totems,
though admittedly we have our own, local
household gods leading us astray,
like everybody else on Earth.
   And then the thought occurred to me, is someone
taking me to Westminster Abbey,
or St Margaret's Church, remembering
the latter has that delightful stain-glass
window of John Milton and William Blake,
not a more unlikely pair in some ways.
Jolly good hope for England, there is!
Ah, I'd be happy with either one of them,
I mused. That's about when Lord Tennyson
and Robert Browning strolled around the corner.
And then in fact both Blake and Milton
came striding over, arm in arm, from St Margaret's!
Something good ought to come of this, I thought.
As upon the breeze, Wordsworth's lines came to mind,
"Milton! Thou shouldst be living at this hour,
England hath need of thee," watching all so many
of her great poets entering the courtyard,
and now Matthew Arnold, and Irish Yeats,
who raised up a wild Celtic Vision.
Milton essayed, "Gentlemen, greetings, and fine
day," exchanging courtesies all around,
"And so the Poet of the Moon on Earth."
Standing next to Tennyson and Browning,
I nodded sheepishly, tongue-tied before

my betters, unable to speak, struck dumb,
trusting he knew of my journey, even more
than I, having seen him, too, on the moon,
now at a British Parliament of Poets,
a parley in which I feared I did not belong,
while they spoke softly amongst themselves,
the upper crust of literature, I among
my betters, a plebeian American,
holding my tongue, waiting expectantly
upon their words, though I could not hear
or follow, so dazed I seemed now to myself,
hiding my consternation as best I could,
awkwardly looking on. Then Browning turned
to me, waking me from near delirium,
saying, "London's not London anymore.
We've all grown used to that, begrudgingly."
I replied, "Flying in from the east, I thought
London's better than it ever was,
a world city, enriched with all humanity."
Unflappable, Browning calmly carried on,
"You've been to enough cathedrals. You know where
you should go. We've all agreed about that.
The poets up on the moon meant well,
but down here in England, with our feet firmly
planted on the ground, is another matter.
Foreign poets are always awed by
Westminster Abby, wanting to get their paltry
name in there somewhere," he guffawed,
with a dismissive look that cut me to the quick,
getting even, I supposed, for my gaffe,
and I thought unabashedly of my dream,
a high stain-glassed window, moonlight streaming
through, an English name, choked, fighting against it,
emotion overwhelming me in front of
them, while I struggled to suppress it,

swallowing hard and looking away.
Without even a trace of notice, Browning
continued, "Yes, you're a foreigner, an
American to boot, but one with some roots
running back into this isle. We've decided.
Milton shall guide you from here on your
pilgrimage through ancient and modern times,
many peoples, revealing their creeds as One."
As all that swept over me, Tennyson said,
"What are you doing for the Federation
of the World?" Such abrupt words I scarcely knew
what to say, especially when Lord Alfred
followed up with "And don't swallow any
of Auden's blather about poetry not
making anything happen. Shelley was right
about poets being the true legislators
of the world. Work harder and don't give up.
You owe it to England and the world,"
with an imperiously demanding tone.
In the face of such instruction, I scarcely
knew what to think, let alone answer back.
I thought of saying I'd been trying for
decades but no one seemed willing to listen,
like when I was a naughty little boy,
teacher made me stand in the corner,
no one could hear me whispering, speaking
into the corner, the darkness of the wall,
but suppressed it, as a limp excuse, bowing
in submission and determination,
hoping somehow to find the will power
to carry on, stiff upper lip and all that.

    Blake then spoke. "Milton shall take you to a
green garden of the land, a setting for a
cottage, outside London, in the peaceful
countryside, a village hamlet, England's

green sward. Whether York Street or High Street,"
looking knowingly at Browning, "we choose there."
Striding forward with authority, Milton,
a proud bearing held he, arm extended,
his black singing robes and locks blowing about.
I steeled myself and stepped forward, seized his
arm, while locking on his blind eyes, my master,
far-sighted, whom I could not fail, played my role
aright, summoning all the strength I had,
and we were out of there, high above,
soaring out of London, soon over a green
and pastoral countryside, the hills of Surrey
and Hampshire, where my ancestors lived,
Gray's "forefathers of the hamlet," now slept,
weathered marble stones above their heads.
So beautiful and charming was the view,
villages and farms, copses, woodlands, bejeweled
the landscape spreading out below, and after
some time we approached lower to a village,
nestled in the wooded hills, cottages and gardens,
an inn, a parish church, the tower rising
above it all. Milton put us down in front
of the stone church, at the gate, without a word,
a Puritan, stepping aside, nodding me,
to go ahead, alone. I looked about,
gravestones all around the deserted church,
an ancient tower of stone, a work of masonry,
repaired, restored perhaps by Thomas Hardy,
it could have been, I say, and in need again.
I opened the gate and walked through, reading
the names of the departed on headstones,
Abbot, Adams, Druper, Taylor, Keen, Weston,
Sarah, wife of William, "a wife most kind,
a mother dear, in peace she lived, in love
she died, her life was craved, but God denied."

Time and lichen erasing the names of most,
where all had passed through and on from this world.
Far back of the church, what looked like a lake,
a slight morning mist still upon the water,
down the hill, a treed lane along the way.
I walked to the wooden door and entered in,
a little parish church, old, a musty smell,
like time itself, agéd, scented by the stones
of the walls, evoking generations.
Once past the benches, pews lined the aisle,
where I walked midway, and then sat down,
looking forward to the altar, all alone.
A humble church, where many souls had prayed,
sought the will of God, far from elegance,
pomp, and the pretension of cathedrals,
intrigues, and affairs of state, souls turned to God,
searching and sacrificing self, the vanity
of vanities, we human beings chase.
I bowed my head and asked Him for His help.
Guide me to find a vision, with worthy words.
Make me a vessel, Lord, even one
raised to your glory, though I'm unfit,
suffuse it, for the good of others.
Bring back those merely "randy for antique,"
in the throes of Freud and Marx, Nietzsche, Sartre,
all the bats of night, turn it inside out,
back to your light. Words gave way to inner
prayer, communion beyond words and syllables,
heart communed with what it did not understand,
but sought, as generations sought, in humble
churches, a human village all about,
filled with human beings and their human ways,
for a time, precious moments, turning,
drawn to that sacred spot, symbol of life.
I shuddered, trembled, like Plato, felt a

Presence beyond, awe flowing over me,
and then returned, slowly, to where I was,
in an old dilapidated church,
abandoned by much of the population,
needing once again repair, restoration.
   I sat awhile, reflecting, thought again of
Hardy, other English writers and poets,
Bunyan and Langland, and Everyman,
felt them, through time, almost sitting with me too,
George Herbert and Henry Vaughan, Oliver
Goldsmith, Thomas Traherne, chroniclers
of my village people, parishioners
of little churches much like this one,
voices against the corruptions of wealth
and luxury, the aristocracy, full of pride,
aristocrats of depravity, arrogance,
exploiting the humble village people;
Thomas Gray's Welsh bard standing on the rock,
raging down upon the ruthless king,
"We bards do curse the cruel, weave the warp and woof,"
cut the winding sheet of oppression;
hail the return of Arthur, just king of
Britannia's line, so great Taliesin sang,
for alas, English kings were not always just.
Like the heroes of the Battle of Maldon,
wayfarers and seafarers, ocean of life,
sage and prophet ride the waves of poetry,
the waves of life, rising and surging.
   And after a while I rose from the pew,
made my way back to Milton, who without
a word led me past the gravestones, where stood
a young soldier, dressed in a World War I
uniform, a gas mask dangling from his neck,
addressing us, "Boys, it was the gas. Don't
let them forget us. I tried to write it down.

And remember ol' F. Glaysher who died
in the trenches with me, his name on the
monument of All Saints Church in Headley.
Your namesake, as it were, cannon fodder,
for arrogant fools who thought they ran history."
Stunned, I couldn't respond, and Milton taking
me by the arm, led on, down the lane, through
the trees, nearly a forest in places,
lingering druids, a skald, Queen Mab, fairy folk,
exulting in a Celtic Morris dance,
as we passed, and a ruined wall,
Roman, perhaps, with ancient cobblestone,
soldiers garrisoned in a barbarous land.
The last trace of mist still hanging on the lake,
grass and trees down to the edge of the water.
Milton stayed in a clearing above the lake,
gesturing me on, reaching the bank, moist air.
As I looked around, Milton seemed to become
another man, a different kind of sage,
his cloak changing into gray, a rough home-spun,
bearded, and then rising from the lake an arm,
"clothed in white samite, mystic, wonderful."
I caught my breath, wondering if I had gone mad,
but given everything else, I went with it.
In a blinding flash of light the sword passed,
I now realized, into Merlin's firm hand,
swinging it three times around his head,
drawing near, turning the shining blade to me,
so I could read the gleaming inscription,
"We are not afraid." A thrush could then be heard,
high in a tree, a trilling ecstatic sound.
Standing there, I could but think he knew some
blessèd hope of which I was unaware.
Arthur has returned, I thought, Excalibur,
forged in Avalon, chimeras upon

its golden hilt, jeweled, dreadful to look upon,
taken out of the stone, out of Sigurd's tree.
The song of the thrush continued to pierce
the calm air, resonating over the lake.
Gone, Merlin, the sword, taking it somewhere.
"That island England breeds valiant men."
And I, I was all alone, like Virgil's hero,
a man apart, devoted to his mission,
thought of William Wordsworth, speaking to me,
finding in his words much needed encouragement,
"If thou indeed derive thy light from Heaven,
Then, to the measure of that heaven-born light,
Shine, Poet! in thy place, and be content."

  Long time I stood by the lake marveling,
head spinning, time in flux, abeyance, until,
by the path, up the hill, away from the water,
movement in the woods caught my eye.
Three imposing figures coming my way.
Two were warriors of an ancient time,
dressed for battle, Viking, or something like it,
formidable swords and weapons at their sides.
The other walked slightly ahead of them,
an older man, long flowing beard and hair,
white as the purest snow of the north,
carrying a wooden staff, marking the ground.
I had not seen their like on my journeys,
and would have felt apprehensive but for
the calm demeanor of the sage.
Reaching about fifteen feet from me, they stopped.
The old one spoke. "I am Wainamoinen,
poet of Kavela, the land of Finns.
We have been sent to convey you to the north."
Looking aside at his companions, he said,
"You need not fear Sigfried and Beowulf.
You're not a foe." At which I couldn't help

laughing a little in relief, stammering,
"Fortunately not," all sharing a hearty laugh,
a sense of companionship emerging.
Wainamoinen drew closer to me, stretched
forth his arm. With my eyes fixed on his,
I moved forward and held it above the wrist.
We rose above the Lake of the Lady.
Soon the entire isle was far below,
as we flew north, over the Orkney Islands,
passing across the sea and land again,
streaming angels joining the four of us,
beautiful women, goddesses, Valkeries,
Sigfried called them, breasts bared to the wind,
while Beowulf and Sigfried, in a Viking ship,
followed behind, not so much in escort,
as in hot pursuit of the Valkyries.
I had to remind myself to hold on
to Wainamoinen's arm, not reach for them,
in all chivalry wanting to keep them warm,
Eve's delicious apples bared to the wind,
so beautiful, men would die for the chance
to hold them in their arms. Glorious song
poured forth from them as they flew, one saying
to me, "Namesake of the peaceful ruler,
travel on through the night, back to the moon.
We shall come for you when it's time,"
waking me from momentary fantasies,
back to passing clouds sprinkled in the sky,
giving way to dusk and a setting sun,
farms and forests far below, alder trees,
soughing pines and junipers, aspens,
sacred birch, through the blue night, shining stars.
    And I wondered to what great cathedral
or ancient holy site they were taking me,
champions from the forests of the past.

With morning light, great eagles appeared,
flanking Wainamoinen with their wings,
pressing further into the northern woodlands.
And then Wainamoinen looked aside at me,
and I realized we were descending, closer
to the trees, now fields, and soon a large house,
beyond which we landed, on a forest path.
The Valkeries banked back up into the sky
and from men's eyes returned whence they came.
Sad I felt, to see them leave, so beautiful.
Wainamoinen said, "A sacred grove of birch,
chosen by the Parliament of the moon.
I take the golden moonlight to Kavela,"
his white hair and beard furling in the breeze,
staff firmly grasped and planted on the ground.
"I must go quickly to the people of Suomi,
who need my coming and watch for me at dawn,
take them word of the Poet of the Moon."
Sigfried and Beowulf raised their swords,
as though pledging fealty, in farewell.
Wainamoinen raised his staff, looked north,
and with the breeze they were gone over the trees.
    After that awesome journey, I stood awhile
recovering, but no one happened along,
so I followed the path, lined with birches,
a canopy of woodland trees, a tunnel
of forest green, filled with filtered light
and early fall leaves, providing me with a
pleasant, restorative walk, close again
with nature, all her earthy smells wafting
on a gentle morning breeze. Far down nature's
tunnel, I could see a human form, a man,
whom I could tell was old, very old,
partly bald, with a long beard, dressed in simple
peasant garb, a Russian serf he seemed.

As I drew near, I saw him sit down
on a birchwood bench, built alongside
the trail. Brooding, he sat there, barely
taking notice of me as I approached.
To my surprise, he was Leo Tolstoy!
I, too, now a pilgrim to Yasnaya Polyana!
The destination once of much the world.
Glancing at me, he said, "Sit. We'll talk. So you're
the Poet from the Moon. Many of us
beat you there first. And don't forget it.
Art was founded on the moon. Long before science.
You have to write about that. As I did.
Stop wasting your time on so many other things.
Only you have the sensibility
and must bear it for the good of the people.
Don't expect them to understand or agree.
Most of them never do and won't, but a few.
They'll hear the echo of that far-off song,
music of the spheres, memory of that rarest
experience, since we all have, within,
a gift, the grace of God, as once here,
on this path, I..." and then he broke off, silent
for a while. Looking back more sternly at me,
"It doesn't matter that the role of art
has been lost in your time. It is in the heart
of man, waiting always for the poet
who can give it form, express it in words.
Your poverty is a blessing. If only
I had had it instead of this damn estate!
Forget the sorcery and humbug, crude rites.
Remember, they excommunicated me.
One of the most pious Russians that ever lived!
Of course I renounced the corrupted church.
They had renounced Christ! The organizations
always do, all of them grab for power, money.

Constantine showed them how, wolf in sheep's clothing.
But the power of conscience, and the pen,
her faithful servant, mightier than the sword,
or all the lying tongues of Christendom,
can win out, in the end, if you serve truth,
as you see it, humble human poet
though you be. The test that confronts us all.
Nothing else is asked of us. Sift the wheat
from the chaff, as Christ taught. The crafty lies
of church doctrine mean nothing. Superstitions
and debasements, burying Christ's teachings,
hiding them from the people of the world.
On this, Dostoyevsky and I could agree.
Ah, the fables, incomprehensible stupidities,
not mysteries. Well, that's the way it's always done,
calculating the masses will stumble along.
The people always need a new vision.
You will achieve yours. Don't give up. Push on.
Work. Trust in the Divine Being.
One soul alone, with God's help, can move mountains.
You have been born to raise this song. Now sing it,
like the soughing of the wind in the birch trees.
It seems hopeless, the world so very hopeless,
and, yes, it is hopeless, but while we can hope,
we are human, and our duty is to give
hope to the hopeless, love to the loveless,
sustenance to the poor. Follow Christ's Example,
forward to the future of the human race.
Every generation must find their hope,
make their hope. Poets and writers play their part.
The world is awaiting your song, though it
knows it not, and will prove it by recognizing
it as its own song. Then you will feel the
fulfillment you've never had, know it
to be one with the ancient pledge you made.

Look at me. The crevasse opened up and
swallowed everything. Poor Mother Russia!
I grieve with all my heart. I know I was
wrong on many things, but not that the collapse
was coming. I tried to warn them. Even
as anarchy also led me astray.
I admit it that even a free-thinker,
such as myself, ended up too literal
about the Bible, me, the heretic.
But about love I was never wrong.
Cling to love. It is the Golden Rule of
God Himself, the ancients, the truest gold,
the only worth having, giving life to all.
Up there, from the moon, I would think you should
be able to see it clearly. God's love
encircling humanity, the teaching
written on The Green Stick, ready ever
to sprout anew, afresh for humanity."
Reaching into a pocket, pulling it out,
pressing it into my hands, Tolstoy's eyes
penetrated into mine, piercing my soul.
"Take it to the moon. That is where it belongs.
That all humanity may learn its secret,
that when men lift their eyes to view the globe,
they might recognize the symbol of their hope.
On the other side of the crevasse,
raise again this song. Beg God for His help!
All we writers are here to help you.
You know that. 'Trust Thy Self,' the ancient
Greek way, and yes, you'll err, but as long as
you fight for man, the Muses and the gods
shall guide you, stand beside you, defend you.
Time shall sift you, the dross from the pure metal.
You mustn't let yourself despair,
but carry The Green Stick to the moon.

This is your duty. God has charged you with it.
I charge you with it. It is your test.
Sacrifice everything for such service.
Cherish the blessings you've been given.
Once in a blue moon, in a millennium,
the gods call a poet before the people,
to make and raise for them an epic song,
help them rise to a higher consciousness.
Don't fail to value the gift you've been given.
What greater vision than this? What is human,
shared by all. Those who claim they have the sole truth
of all history seek to deceive others,
to enrich themselves, not serve the people.
I told them I didn't believe my truth
to be the one, indubitable truth,
for all time, but they wouldn't listen,
didn't understand, or want to understand.
For some, that's the way it always is.
I spoke for my own life, standing before death.
Do the same. Don't worry about those who
want to tear you to pieces. The sincere
and honest will understand. They always do.
You have to let go. It's not about you.
And so, all I have are platitudes,
and you've come all this way for that, like so
many fools!" Laughing gently, and smiling,
Tolstoy leaned back against the bench, looked down
the path into nature's tunnel of leaves.
My master's words reverberated deep,
their wisdom fresh as the breeze, laden with
the morning scent of the woods, green paths,
resonating into profound simplicity.
No abstract theory of the lecture hall,
but love of God, our Creator, Mystery,
beyond our human ken, calling us,

testing our mettle on the field of life,
where we can become greater than our self,
straining to become our true Self.
We sat quietly together for a time,
each with his own thoughts and meditations.
And then Tolstoy stood up, looked toward the house,
the path, and I knew it was time to part,
however painful for me, so much else
I might have asked, talked about with him.
We gazed at each other, deeply it seemed,
and without a word Tolstoy walked away,
leaving me by the timeless forest bench,
a simple and true work of craftsmanship.
My emotions surged again within me,
to watch him walk away out of sight,
while I struggled inside, to accept it all,
pondering The Green Stick, still in my hands,
putting it inside my breast pocket.
Walking into the tunnel of time,
leaves swirling upon the gusts of wind,
drawing me in, down the path once more,
I found myself accompanied by two young
poets, poor Russians, they said, roughly dressed,
greeting and telling me they had been in
Moscow's Lubyanka Prison, swept into
the Gulag, cruelly murdered, buried in
a mass grave, two more names and photographs,
filed away, the killing machine grinding
through millions. Their cold, matter-of-fact tone
sent shudders of horror and revulsion
through me, though I didn't fear them,
but what we human beings can become.
And then another man joined us. As we walked
farther into the tunnel, they introduced him
as Hadji Murad, whom Tolstoy wrote about,

a Muslim mystic of Chechnya, who
knew the way to the border, would escort us,
Hadji Murad, betrayed, beheaded by
the Tsar, extended his arm to me.
I took it, brother grasping brother's proffered arm,
a beautiful thistle coming to mind.
Without a word, we were flying south,
over the Russian steppes, below the radar.

BOOK IX

THE ARGUMENT

A house in Konya, Turkey, ancient Iconium, where St. Paul preached the Gospel. Around and around. Ethereal music and chanting. Another world. Rumi longing for the Beloved, the scent of her tresses, through fields of flowers to a riverbank of reeds. Attar and a soaring flock of birds fly the Persona from the plain of Konya, that Valley of Search, to another plane, through Seven Valleys of the Soul, down into India and the plain of Agra, leaving the Poet in Emperor Akbar's city of Fatehpur Sikri, before the Ibadat Khana, the House of Worship, on the Pachisi Courtyard. Akbar's court poet Faizi receives the Persona, along with many mystic poets and Sufis of India. Persuaded by Tagore, given the trials of the time, Rahman Baba, an Afghan Pashtun, comes down from his mountain village to confer with the Poet of the Moon. Evoking the majesty of human history, Lord Alfred Tennyson extols Akbar's dream. The many oceans mingle. The dancing girls on the Pachisi Courtyard.

South across the farm fields of the endless steppes,
I looked over at the Gulag poets,
they at me, and then they began to turn,
flying away, to wherever they had come from,
and that was when I saw that each one had
a bloody black hole in the back of his head,
one bullet, and then thrown into a mass grave,
perhaps outside Kiev, forest or taiga,
north of the Arctic circle of the soul,
a Siberian wasteland, and they were gone,
leaving me shivering in the freezing wind.
Hadji Murad flew on, taking me with him,
over the border, through the Caucasus mountains,
looking down, deeply stirred, on Chechnya,

his home, shedding a tear on the land below,
sweeping soon across the Black Sea, into
Turkey, past Trebizond, that place of pain
and denial, beyond, onto a high plain,
vast, covered with green, as after a spring
thunderstorm, a secluded mountain retreat,
an ancient town of human habitation.
With the sun going down, we alighted
outside the town, Hadji leading me
through the winding streets, in another time,
another place, while I followed behind,
until he stopped in a lane before a house,
leaving me alone, for before I could
respond, he bowed a kindly "Salaam" and
was gone. Unsure of where I was and tiring
of my journey, arduous, I felt a pang
of despair, that it might never end,
one mystery after another, punctuated
by horrors, the human lot extreme.
What was I to make of it all, a show trial
so it seemed, at times, of the condemned.
I could but heave a sigh of hopelessness,
there before someone's doorstep, I knew not who,
or cared, but wanted to go home, back to
my own place and time, to hell with the moon,
I thought, and all my running around the world,
being dragged by forces beyond my control,
some compulsion I could not understand,
emptiness, longing. Faint lights down the street,
glowed dimly, a passerby now walked around
the corner, gawking at the stranger,
out of who knew what time, but odd, different,
standing out, not one who belonged.
Where was I, and why, pounded in my head.

And then musical instruments, drumming,
a voice singing, chanting, a hymn, a prayer,
devout, deep, poured from the full throat of
a man, within, and another appeared
at the opening door, kindly gesturing
me in, standing back, allowing me to pass,
reassuring me forward, so I stepped in,
resigned, drawn into an unfolding stage,
only God knowing where and why.
I left the agony of my heart behind,
moved on, trusting, somehow, somewhere, someone,
or something, led me on, for some reason,
some purpose beyond my petty problems, pains,
my struggles of the soul, beyond my self.
I hoped against hope, weary, but finding
the music and song beginning to lift me
a little with their melody, a Turkish blend
of drum and reed flute, a Muslim chant.
Stepping into and through an inner courtyard,
where I could see a figure twirling in
an adjacent room, around a pole, or post,
a support of the ornamental ceiling,
glancing up, an oriental scene painted in
gorgeous hue, flowing colors, geometric designs,
while along the sides of the room sat several
men and musicians, singing gently,
deeply, in harmony and antiphony,
a gloriously flowing song, richly tuned,
nothing like curs baying at the moon,
every age having plenty of those.
The twirling man went around the pole,
and I watched from the edge of the courtyard,
drawing nearer, now enthralled with the scene,
drawn into it, sensing something deeply
resonating in my own being, at my core,

like nothing else I had known on my journeys,
like a falcon in a widening gyre,
called back by the dream of the falconer,
sailing back to the arm of the king,
so the man's one foot planted firmly on the
ground, as on a strong foundation, the other
turned, pounded, danced in circles, pirouetting,
advancing forward, while he held up one hand,
the other down, dressed in a simple
black blanket, wrapped in it. Off the sands of
Arabia, I thought, a Bedouin of sorts,
some mystic dervish chanting in rapture
his love for the Beloved, and then I realized
who he was, the poet Rumi, Maulana,
master, Pir, in Konya, where St Paul had
preached the Holy Gospel so long ago,
the ancient town of Iconium.
All night was passing as in a trance,
whirled around me, I, too, enraptured,
flowing into the absorbing song of prayer,
lifting my heart with every crescendo
of his longing breast for the Beloved
of our life, left the self, all its little woes,
strived for the Self so far beyond me.
I threw my head before the Beloved.
He became my Shamsi-Din, the Friend,
solace and goal. How I longed and wept,
while the musicians played their instruments,
drum beat and reed flute, soaring strings,
oblivious of self and time, beyond time,
twirling and chanting. I followed him, upward
to the Divine, lost my self in the Self,
merged in Union, Reunion, with My Self,
One, again, at last, the arduous journey

achieved, break through the Mask, tear aside the Veil,
Veil-less, become One, am One, the Truth.
  Suddenly Maulana stopped and rested,
and so the music, silence filled the space,
the room, and the courtyard. All stood still.
And he looked at me, a look that pierced me
to the heart, a gentle gaze, Maulana saying,
a look of longing on his face, "Friend, you've come,
and Shamsi, have you found him? Have you sought him?
The shining moon is Shams, Shams the shining moon.
Brother, thou art thought itself, the rest sinew, bone."
Grasping his meaning, I replied, "I seek him still.
God willing, I shall find him on my journey.
I seem always to be some steps behind him,
far behind him even in times of duress,
an occidental age of worldly flesh,
lost orient of the abode of angels."
Still gazing intently on me, he came
into the courtyard, never taking his eyes
off me, bowed a salaam a few feet away,
and said, "Come, I'll show you where to look,"
leading me across the courtyard and out
of the house, down the lane, soon out of town.
Dawn was well upon us now. I could see
green fields of flowers, stretching around us,
rose and hyacinths, poppies and tulips,
a fragrance beyond this world, a sweetness
so enthralling I was not sure I was alive,
but in some other world, a Garden of Truth,
entered into from that courtyard at his
biding, summons, and so we strolled nearer to
the mountains, down from which a river ran,
and in every meadow on the way a song.
He took me down to the bank of the river,
and there along its side a reed bed grew,

thick and lush, the rushing water flowing by,
down from the mountains, clear and pure,
the morning sun glistening on it as it flowed.
High above I could see the daylight moon,
and thought of all the poets I met there,
and now Maulana, here by a bed of reeds.
I scarcely knew what to make of it,
the moon distinct in the morning sky of blue.
Rumi began to speak, "The reed tells
its tale, as you heard last night, longing, longing
to return to its bed here by the river,
cruelly cut, so it seems, torn from here, plucked
from its fellows, parted from the bosom
of its home. How it wails and wails, plaintive,
its song rising to heaven, raising a
resonance throughout the land, the passion of
Love Divine, like Majnun longing for Laila,
it wails and sifts through the dust of this world,
seeking her everywhere, perchance he might
find her somewhere, so the song of the reed flute,
even the one you heard, the one you hear."
And then he pulled out a pen knife and said,
"I cut this reed for you, a token of Love,
Poet of the Moon, plant it on the moon
that it might draw water from the dust
and grow, flourishing, for all people to see,
a lush bed of river reeds upon the moon."
He handed me the fresh reed, newly cut,
and I took it, morning dew still upon its
green shoot, green as the man of
mythic universal verdure, Al-Khidr.
Rumi seemed to pass to another realm,
not there with me, elsewhere, in ecstasy,
beyond time, beyond space. A gentle breeze
swayed the reeds, back and forth, back and forth.

I felt it upon my face and in my heart.
Rumi slowly came back, returned from the
Return, Reunion, and looking at me,
through stations and stages on the path,
mildly smiling, said, "Our master shall come
for you. Before too long. He knows the Way.
He led me and shall lead your steps aright."
   I acknowledged his words with a salaam,
touching my forehead with a flourish,
always quick to relish local customs,
while he moved off, back up the embankment,
over the rise toward the plain, leaving me,
wondering whom he meant? Sana'i, Hafez?
Perhaps Al-Junayd or Farid? I knew the Pir
I hoped would guide me from that bed of reeds,
take me on a far journey, the one with whom
I'd traveled for decades, raised me with a flock,
on the arc of ascent toward the Simorgh.
And then I caught the scent of his trade.
There he was at the end of the reeds, Attar,
holding out his arm, his long robe flowing down,
furling. I hurried toward him, the true
master of my heart and soul, the fragrance
of Roses pervading the air, river bank,
intoxicating me with its heady wine.
I surged toward him, startling him so,
he laughed at me, in recognition I hoped,
and in his surprise slightly lowered his arm,
frustrating my attempt to grasp his wrist,
crest fallen, my face must have appeared,
for he laughed again, raising his arm,
and soon we were soaring beyond that land,
that state, that valley, high above Konya,
from that realm, even to another realm.
We flew, surrounded by a flock of birds,

rising out of the reed beds, birds of every
kind and every shape and size, soaring,
like Chaucer's "Assembly of Fowls,"
a Parliament of Birds, or taken up like
in the great Cicero's own "Scipio's Dream,"
birds of prey and the harmless feathered kind,
the goshawk and the sperhawk, quail's foe,
but not that day; the wedded turtle true,
tercelet and cuckoo, lapwing and kite,
the faithful stork, the drake, killer of its young,
the purple finch and its liquid notes,
the parrot seeking a perch in paradise,
the partridge strutting the air with pride,
the falcon fiercely seeking its liberty,
the nightingale pouring forth in longing,
the exiled peacock searching for its home,
the ring-necked pheasant's piercing sight its goal,
the pigeon, taken away, returns,
the mourning dove cooed for its missing mate,
though weakest, the common sparrow flocked,
the nighthawk flew high and proud in camouflage,
the nuthatch that upside down hunts for bugs
in the bark, stalking now a greater prize;
the goldfinch left the achinea behind,
while quacking the wood duck rose from the water,
the blue heron, its long legs behind, stroked
its wide-spread wings forward through the air,
the lonely owls of every kind, barred and barn,
snowy, eared, great horned, boreal, and screech owls,
and all the birds I love from Michigan,
the red-wing blackbird and robin redbreast,
the warbler and downy-headed woodpeckers,
the grosbeak, yellow-bellied sapsucker,
the flamboyant red-headed woodpecker,
the loon with its wildly cackling call,

which once, with delight, I heard and watched from
a hill on Isle Royale, overlooking
a lake, its intensely echoing cry;
blue jay and bluebird, house finch and junco,
the grand bald eagle, humble crow and raven,
cormorant and osprey, greedy for prey,
the wild turkeys from my backyard,
chickadees and titmouse, "redbird" cardinal,
all the birds I love to feed and watch,
the iridescent humming bird outside
my study window, so rare and fine,
hovering over a flower, then gone,
even the common crowd of grackles,
starlings, cowbirds, and Canada geese,
like their statue in Wawa, direct in flight,
all the inhabitants of the beaches,
the spotted sand piper, the herring gull,
the great egret's white neck pointing the way,
all lifting us up from that valley of search,
seeking a trace of the traceless friend,
from every region of the globe, all flew
with us, a symphony of melodious song,
beauteous plumage, of every range,
majestic Japanese cranes, trumpeters,
around us flocked, hundreds of thousands of birds,
up from that valley of search we flew,
seeking the Hidden Friend, like the Majnun
of Love, long suffering, leading us on,
patience and pursuit carrying us aloft
with the breezes of the air, beyond air,
accompanying us, carrying us along,
into a realm high above the valley of
Konya and the world below, my guides
the feathered flock and Attar's seasoned hand,
beyond the plain of limitations, set free,

absorbed in search of the Beloved, longing,
beyond, unearthly now, aloft, the Simorgh
of every continent our goal, I felt,
knew, deep within the garden of my soul.
Like Xenophon, up into the continent,
inward we flew, into the interior.
And even then I realized we were passing
over mountains, flying by and over,
soon other valleys, that I could see below,
a new land, ancient, and felt in my heart
an atom of pain, into the valley
of Tabriz we soared, upon that steed of pain,
plane of limitation, inexplicable mysteries,
despite myself, found I welcomed it, knowing
if there be no pain this journey would never
end. Looking aside at Attar's face, I could
tell he felt it too, pained he looked, shared its
stinging jab, we nearly writhed upon the air.
I thought of Al-Bastami, "Those favored
by God are rewarded with suffering."
Yet we sailed on into the Valley of Love,
and all that woe, oh, we human beings,
pain our daily bread, stirring up, lifting
the heart away from all our fantasies,
Al-Ghazali coming to mind, "Only God, the
Creator, can judge intentions, belief, love."
Sailing on, the hoopoe before us, she turned,
led us in a different direction, down a
backbone of mountains, into mountainous valleys,
another land, Sulaymaniyyah, refuge
of the mystic Sufis, at last the longing
of our hearts had brought us there, yielded
the fruit of despair, the Valley of Knowledge.
The fire of our hope fell to ashes,
a watchman seemed to be pursuing lovers,

from door to door, fleeing before him.
In a quiet valley, a humble house,
as in a dream of Sufis, Ibn Arabi
appeared in a vision, "All existence is One."
Flying over, we found the house, scaling
a wall with untold pain, dropping down into
the garden below, together, Attar and I,
a flock of birds all about, alighting on
rose bushes and flowers, Garden of Eden.
There we found before us, the Beloved,
holding in her hand a lamp, seeking a ring
she had lost, looking up at us with a face,
love's own, a piercing gaze of Beauty,
beyond this world. O bless the Watchman
who drove us to this spot! Had I but seen
the end in the beginning, I'd have blessed him
from the start! And there, together, Attar
and I stood, shedding tears, weeping
in that Valley of Sulaymaniyyah,
world and valley beyond this world.
"Oh Lord, bless the watchman, bless him, bless him,"
on my lips, and in my heart, deep beyond words,
he drove us, swept us before him to Her,
to knowledge of Her, after utmost anguish,
there in a garden of Sulaymaniyyah.
    Attar gestured for me to take his arm,
tearing my heart out at the thought of leaving,
and took me away again, carried with
the flock of fellow seekers, birds of every
array, we rose, the pain of flight, torn away.
We flew, all limitation left behind,
into mystery now, we soared, on to lands
before us, even Shiraz, it seemed, Hafez
nearby, ushered us into a Valley of Unity,
a sea of Oneness, a splendor of light,

in our hearts, in every meadow of that land,
a song, detachment filling us, as we
swept into the plane of Oneness. Hafez
upon my thoughts, "I hold converse nightly
with every star, desire thy moon-like face."
We quaffed the Cup of Unity, drinking deep
its Choice Wine, the Earth a pearl upon a string
of Pleiades, high in the heavens,
thy brimming Cup of Wine I prize the most.
We rode the slender back of the crescent moon,
earthshine illuminating the night side,
Unity, sweet Unity, beyond our lips to convey,
and then descended into another valley,
the Valley of Contentment, throned in the
heights of mystic meaning, swept us along,
and far below, Khorasan, Nishapur, Balkh,
the land of Tus, where Ferdowsi and Attar
called home, and the old Silk Road stretching
all the way to Dunhuang and Chang-an,
at the other end Venice and Rome.
So many lands and valleys tied together
by the caravanserai of the soul.
I could but think, "O Ferdowsi, pray for
Ahura Mazda to guide me on the way,"
struggling with the antinomies of life,
and all his sweeping vision before my eyes,
the greedy Shah reneging on his pledge.
I looked at Attar and saw him shed a tear,
a tear upon the land, as for Ferdowsi,
all those skulls piled high by the Mongols,
red tulips and poppies waving in the breeze,
valley meadows passing far below,
into the Valley of Wonderment,
we felt at every moment our wonder grow,
bewildered, by it all. What soul can understand?

God, the Exalted, hath placed these signs in men,
that none may deny the glory of his hand,
life beyond, beyond our ken, beyond reason,
little stultifying ways of knowing.
What wonder enwraps us! Labor that the
meaning of humanity might come to light.
   Somewhere in that valley, so I thought,
in these mountains, Ferdowsi's Kay Khosrow,
who like Buddha left this world, gave up
his power and disappeared, bewildering
wonderment lifting him to another realm,
Khorasan, the crossroads of the worlds.
All the Sufis pouring through these gates,
home, too, of Hajj Bektash, his Order of Sufis
serving the Ottomans, all the way to
Bosnia, open, holding women equal,
revering education, separation
of mosque and state, all the Sufi Orders
of the Muslim world, Bektashi and Alevi,
Jilani and Khaladi, Yasawi and Haleviti,
Chishti in India, Malawi in Africa,
Naqshbandi, hosts of an important guest,
believing Unity resides in perception,
in experience, not Being, man but a drop
out of the cosmic Ocean of Being;
love of the Beloved calling for discretion.
Yasawi, leave the ship, plunge into the Ocean,
become one with the surging waves;
fly with Attar in the heights of Kubrawi,
Suhrawadi, illuminating the soul,
Hurufi and Badawi, all following Ali,
all the shaykhs and pirs of Sufism,
whirling in my mind, Rabiya seeking
no reward, dissolving herself in Him;
Ibn Arabi, sealing the heart in Wisdom.

In the night season, rise with the Jews and pray.
Blow the Shofar of the *Zohar*, enter the
Kabbalah of the human heart.
Like the Malami, conceal your contentment,
like the Uwaysi, seek guidance from the past.
  Attar looked at me, as though he knew
the contents of my thoughts, my wandering heart,
as I passed to that great conqueror,
Alexander, on his journey into
the soul of Asia, city after city,
stage after stage, station after station,
his mystic travel rocking the loom of time,
became even mine as we flew along,
at that ethereal height, rampart of soul,
rarified Bactria of longing, Helmand,
Kandahar, and the Khyber Pass, valleys of
mist, the rise and fall of civilizations;
Attar carried me on into the valley of
True Poverty, Absolute Nothingness,
dying from self and living in God,
where I thought, realized, these journeys
have no visible end in the world of time,
oh, thy Glory, our healing salve,
our Guide upon the Way, Master of
the Mystic Path, "Say: I am You."
God, Allah, Yahweh, Adonai, Great Mystery,
Dao, Nirvana, oh, Bodhisattva, lead us
to thy grace, the apex of consciousness,
secret of Divine Guidance, hide it,
the faintest trace would nail us to the cross;
full awareness, utter self effacement.
O Rumi of the soul, through every valley,
the Sun is the Moon, the Moon is the Sun,
move beyond this time of *fitnah*, time of strife.
Alexander swept down through the Khyber Pass,

down into the India of his soul, and we,
Attar and I, I holding firmly to his wrist,
we flew, flew on, on my journey, journey of
poets, souls summoned, commanded, through naked
wonder, past many trials and tribulations,
the death of self, walking upon the waves,
rolling, flying upon them, down into the
plain of Agra, to Fatehpur Sikri,
Emperor Akbar's city, he of the
Mystic Way, Tamerlane's heir, seeking Unity,
India's noblest ruler, seeker of Oneness.
Alighting, Attar set me down in the courtyard
of Akbar's House of Worship,
red sandstone, sculpted, ornate, jewel of India,
once flapping in the wind, like Mongol tents
of the wandering horde, crafted out of the
crumbling stone of this ephemeral world,
a momentary form against erosion.
    Of the hundreds of thousands of birds,
only thirty landed there with us.
Attar lowered his arm, causing me to release
my grip, stepped back, toward the House of Worship
and a group of people standing outside.
I stood still, surveying the new sight
that spread out before me, Fatehpur Sikri,
Akbar's Capital, long known and dreamed of,
so many years a standard in my mind,
for decades a goal of my life's journey,
did I but know, yet never understood,
dipped into again and again, savored,
yearned for, longing, as for the Beloved,
now home, come home, even so I felt,
standing there, taking it all in, so it seemed.
The glory of the place baffles wisdom,
the Panch Mahal to my right, five stories

rising high and open, where the emperor
would sit, musing on the Pachisi Courtyard,
the gardens, the Pool without Peer, walkway
bridging out onto it, allowing one to pass
over, but build no houses upon it;
like this world, metaphor of fragile existence,
yearning for home, state and station, no solace,
even a harem of five thousand women,
rare the man not to lose his soul there.
    In the early morning air, a sultry day
approaching, without a cloud in the sky,
sheer blue, I turned around to Attar and
the poets with whom he now stood. Elation
flooded over me, as I recognized
one after another, poets of my heart
and soul, friends and fellow travelers along
the Way, the journey back to Him, arduous,
but not to be denied, the call so clear,
enthralling. Attar moved to the right and
a man with long white hair and beard came our
way, Rabindranath Tagore, met again,
a second time upon my earthly journeys,
in India. And he to me, smiling softly,
"We meet again. You must really like India!
Why is it you can't keep away from here?"
I laughed at his kindly humor, East to West,
West to East, the twain met together, friends,
human, alive, real, no phantom of the mind.
(I guess I'm supposed to be "West" in
this tale, though I think I belong elsewhere,
a global world struggling to be born,
Tagore, the poets, my co-creators,
singers and dancers, on Earth and the moon.)
Still with a friendly smile, Tagore continued,
"Welcome to Akbar's House of Worship."

For a moment on the breeze, his greeting hung,
as he looked at me, then turned back toward
the other poets, gesturing for me to follow,
taking me closer to them, back into time,
that tent wrought in stone, standing before a vision,
it seemed to me, a dream, shimmering in
the Indian air. And then, no introductions
needed, they knew me and I them, old masters,
all of them, I the long-traveling, would-be
poet, arrived, at last, before their feet,
which I would have bowed and touched had there been time,
even I, I stood there, disciple, devotee
of their tutelage, in respect and reverence
for masters of the spirit, visionaries,
whose visions we still need, even more so now
than any endangered moment of the past,
our time so threatened by dreadful fanatics
of every kind, East and West, truth be told.
    Akbar's poet Faizi took the stage,
as to welcome all to the Capital,
saying, "Akbar sought Unity in all,
his sphere of wisdom and vision, Akbar Shah,
the greatest emperor since Ashoka,
the only one whose brow has opened on
the Earth like the dawn, a king whose eyes have been
lessoned by the heart, reigning here in Fatehpur,
and I and my brother Abul-Fazel
were favored to serve the emperor,
with every waking breath. I a humble
physician, raised above my station to
a higher station I could never have
dreamed of. All came here upon the Shah's decree,
Sunnis and Shia, Christians and Jews, Sikhs,
Parsis and Jains, Buddhists and Hindus,
Chishti Sufis and Carvaka atheists,

every belief. He yearned for perfection,
searched for it alone, sought Unity,
the One behind the many. Fanaticism
found no favor in his court, but only those
who quivered at the high sound of the Sitar,
as Amir Khosrow can attest, nodding
towards him, where he stood, exchanged an
acknowledging bow, his figure gracious at
mention of his name, his epic eulogies
to kingly might, "parrot of India,"
in colorful singing robes, stood among peers.
Faizi continued, "Akbar's seeking mind
penetrated all the dinning complexities
of exclusivism, its bigotries.
Here truly stands a House of Worship,
glorious throughout all the realm and world,
even unto England and Europe,
so Queen Elizabeth admired him,
unlike anyone the Earth had ever known."
    Faizi ended, stepped lightly back, giving way
to a companion by his side, Kabir, met
also once more. "O master, what a blessing,"
I thought, "to see you again, and hear your
words of wisdom that enlighten down the
corridor of centuries for all who will
listen to your song." Thus he began, "In Akbar,
India gave birth at least to one king
who saw maya all about his palace
and the world, whether mulla or priest, murshid
or pir, pandit or monk, worshiper of
fire or stone, dualism or non-dualism,
with or without qualities. Akbar plunged
into the ocean of life seeking the Essence,
not the chaff, bestowing the land for the
Golden Temple, gathering all souls to God,"

softly trailing off in humility.
And then Bulleh Shah stepped forward, adding,
"Neither a believer going to the mosque,
nor given to unbelieving ways, neither
Moses nor Pharaoh, Akbar sought the Way,
here in this one House sought the Transcendent One,
whom all have sought and must seek, all of us.
I know not who I am. Know not anyone
other than the One. This was not a shah,
but a soul voyaging home, despite the world."
Then Lalan slipped around Tulsidas,
exclaiming, "How does religion look?
I've never seen it. Some wear Hindu rosaries,
some Muslim beads. People say they've got
different religions, but do we bear the signs
of religion when we come or when we go?
This is the only House of Worship
I could ever worship in, the human heart.
Uncatchable moon shining down, unite me
with the Man of my Heart, the real adversaries
are inside us. Lalan says, a light like
Akbar can never go out. Uncatchable moon.
See the moon," he said, pointing into the blue.
   Off to the side, I noticed the poets Urfi,
Brahman, and Fasi Kashmiri, listening
to Lalan's every word, as we all were,
and with them Satya Pir, who quickened at
the mention of the moon, broke away, saying,
exultantly, "I may be a wandering
Sufi mendicant, in my tattered rags,
but I know true royalty when I meet
or hear it, and Akbar was the shah-in-shah
of the soul, as well as the earthly realm.
I revere Buddha and Kalki, Krishna
the formless, Brahman, Lord Shiva and Ganesh,

Narayana, Lord of the Heavens, Avatars.
I bow to Hari. If I've ever meditated
on Govinda, this is a House of Worship,
the pure and true refuge of man,
here in this relentless Kali Age."
And then a jostling and scuffle occurred,
in the back, Khusrow's friend, Dihlawi
moved aside, and Panapati, allowing
Sarmad, a wild looking man to break
his way through the crowd of poets.
At that moment Tagore took two quick steps
forward, gaining the attention of the
assembled poets, announcing, "I've invited
the Pashto poet Rahman Baba to leave
his mountain seclusion in Afganistan
and consult with us here, though at a
royal court, and share his guidance and wisdom.
Baba, if you would," Tagore lightly
waved in his direction, while standing aside.
All eyes turned to the Afghani master,
many wondering how Tagore had succeeded
in getting him to leave his mountain retreat.
Rahman Baba stepped forth and began,
"It is true I am not one to leave my place
in my village, and have not seen countries
up and down. But like many here I have been
to other worlds, the only world that truly counts.
Penniless, drinking water from a clay bowl,
I could not say no to healing the wounded
hearts of others, the time now so full of
wounded humanity. Humans are all
one body. Whoever tortures another,
wounds himself. In love, our healing, and Akbar's
House of Worship was a house of Divine love,
more than many realized, his head not in

the clouds, but attending to the offspring
of the Earth, grown so much wider now,
or so I hear. The stream cannot flow backward,
nor return the misspent time. Sow flowers
that your surroundings become even as
a garden. Don't sow thorns, sow love, seek love.
I don't need to look elsewhere, for my Lord
is with me in my home. The Earth hath bowed
down its head in adoration. Bright like
the sun and moon, His manifestation,
so illuminated, constant Divine attention,
the most affectionate eye of the Lord,
the firmament bent over in worship
of Him. Every tree, every shrub, stood ready
to bend before Him. Every herb and blade
of grass are a tongue to utter his praise.
Every fish in the deep praises and blesses,
every bird in the meadows and the fields,
magnifies Him. No one hath lauded Him
equal to his just desert, neither hath
anyone sufficiently sounded His praise."
Silence, and respect, hung upon his words,
as every poet stood mute, mulling
over what we had heard from the Afghan
mountain fastness of the rock of God.
Baba walked back, leaving all pondering.
    A jostling took place again to the side,
and Khusrow's friends Dihlawi and Panapati
moved over, allowing the wild man
to push his way forward, Dara Shikoh's
companion in Unity, Sarmad, a Persian Jew,
student of Christianity and Islam,
become a dervish mendicant in India,
a Muslim convert, wildly lost in the
fervor of his quest, stood there before us,

dressed like a Digambar Jain, bursting out,
"Those with deformity, He has concealed in
robes, but I, like Hallaj, bare my soul. In whatever
garb, Thou mayest come, I recognize Thee!
And attain the love of the Best Beloved!
We must seek Him even unto India!"
   Eyes went round, without a word, Tagore
taking control, all hanging on him in hope
he'd find a way to rescue the situation, saying,
"One final poet must speak. He has been here
before, to Fatehpur Sikri, comes again,
though not a Hindu or Turk, a seeker of
the Higher Pantheism, the Oneness and
Unity of God, even Lord Tennyson,
Victoria's royal bard and poet laureate,
here may he find another court a home."
And the poet who had so recently
chided me in London, he the author
of that sweet-singing song, *Idylls of the King*,
tale of King Arthur's regal Camelot,
strode calmly with self-possession to the fore.
I, an American, wondered how the
other Indians would welcome him,
but, to my uninformed surprise, he was
accorded every measure of respect,
and so I felt in my own heart for one
from whom I had learnt so much, despite his
tongue lashing. He spoke, in a serious tone,
acknowledging all assembled, near and far,
looking at Valmiki and Vyasa, from face
to face, beginning, "We all know we are here
but for a moment, called by the assembly
of the high shades upon the moon, that far height,
that symbol and reflection of all Light.
Here in India, for a brief moment,

Akbar lived up to his name, worthy of
his title and his land, built this House of Worship,
Divine Faith, Divine Movement, a symbol
for all time, a Brahmo-Samaj before
its time, the universal one of all times.
Dare we ignore his regal example?
His vision is our vision, each and every
one of us. We know it in our bones,
and we have said so for the instruction
of the Poet of the Moon, home, home
for us all, if we are true. I say that if
Britain ever achieved even one single
virtuous act in all its years in India,
even so it is true that Akbar rendered
unto all the world a lasting virtue
that must never be allowed to go unknown.
The Divine Being calls us all to witness
to the Truth, to seek Him in His majesty,
His mighty test of every soul. And even
as it appears, the Good Lord chooses not
to favor one religion over another,
so Akbar knew the self-same Spirit
animates them all. It is the Spirit that
he sought, perchance he might find it somewhere,
since East and West meet as one on the moon,
and here on Earth may strike a reflecting beam.
Poets, by whatever hands will build this
sacred Fane, I proclaim they serve Akbar's
vision, the vision of the Godhead of all."
And thus it was, my master, finished, sending
shivers through my being, his words of truth
moving me deeply. Awed, overwhelmed, I swooned,
falling to the red sandstone of the
Pachisi Courtyard, like a courtyard dancer
of long ago, losing her balance at the

sight of the regal emperor, high above,
the strain of the heat, she as humble as
Shakuntala from her rustic hermitage,
in this city of dreams, abandoned city,
left behind as by a soul abandoning
the world for the immortal life, eternal,
abandoning the ancient human riddle.
When I awoke all the poets were gone,
and I was all alone, all alone, looking
down toward the Pool without Peer.
Through the shimmering heat I thought I saw,
or perhaps thought of, Emperor Akbar's
harem of five thousand women, dancing
on the Pachisi Courtyard, while he watched
high above, an unforgivable indiscretion,
indulgence, for the Akbar of the Divine Faith,
reducing women to slaves of insatiable lust,
forced at times to dance for him stark naked.
Like Goethe's Gretchen, women used by a man.
O Jayadeva, no Krishna with Radha.
Nor the purity of Rama and Sita,
Majnun and Laila, Solomon and Sheba.
Houri, heavenly angels of paradise,
release women from the bondage of Akbar!
Before my eyes they moved, elegant, clothed,
the solidarity of the harem, women,
if each woman was not pitted against each,
feminine power and grace, womanhood,
in finest attire, proudly robed, bejeweled,
no longer servants of the flesh, but noble
and free, the Divine, the beloved woman,
creatures who dance to a different drummer.
Woman is man's mystery, man is woman's.
O Keshav Das and Vaishnava poets,
help me find the woman who is divine,

and whom a man can hold in his arms,
a man whom she can hold, want to hold,
wrapped together in love, for the little ones,
tender like lovers of many decades.
What a joy to be alive and a woman.
How right was Jane Austen, better anything
than marrying without affection.
O Krishna, if reincarnation is true,
let me come back as an Indian man.
I don't want a harem. One goddess will do.

BOOK X

THE ARGUMENT

Passage from India. Passage to the Americas. Borges opens the door. Walt Whitman captains the Persona back from the "streams of the Indus and the Ganges," "circumnavigation." Pacific blue. Octavio Paz, a shape-shifting jaguar, and Teotihuacan, the Temple of the Moon. Neruda's "The Heights of Machu Picchu." Borges, through a mirror, on the pampas, Buenos Aires. Under the Southern Cross, bitter juntas of the soul. Argentina's "disappeared." Mirror moon draws in the Poet of the Moon, onward to another continent.

In the heat a vision of a man, walking
toward me, an incongruous figure,
clearly not Indian, a dumpy cocked hat
and a flowing white beard. I moved toward him,
curious, until I could see who he was,
stopping abruptly in my tracks, surprised.
Ol' Walt Whitman, in a relaxed way, said,
"I'm here to give you passage from India.
The poets of the Americas were right.
Finally a poet worthy of the name.
Have you learnt from the Asian masters?
Drunk deep from the streams of the Indus and Ganges?
Brahma and Buddha, the mystics of the soul?"
He revealed no trace of having met before,
and I too didn't bring it up at all.
I felt pained to remember him and Melville.
"Oh Walt, you know I'm wracked with doubt.
I make no such claim. Readers must decide.
I seek only to honor the language
and the human race, wake it up a bit,
if possible, fearing the odds are against it,
help it see anew its myriad problems,

clarify its perspective once again.
In this world a little can count for a lot."
I fell silent, looking at him, hoping,
trusting he'd understand, choking inside.
He could tell he had struck a nerve, deeply,
and said nothing for a while and then stepped back,
holding out his arm, white beard and hat above.
I grasped his arm with all my heart, gentle
old homo, I had no fear of him.
We smiled at one another as we soared,
India below, wheeling, kaleidoscopic,
and I saw Ayodhya, the Temple of Ram,
and the Babri Mosque, built together, meet
and merge in one vision of the Divine Being,
his equal regard for all dharmas. And then
I saw impoverished peoples swarming across
a continent of the mind, reviled by the
indifferent wealthy whose souls had grown cold,
hardened against human cries of hunger
and pain, indigence and want, old and young,
denied the light of knowledge and learning,
cities poisoned by Western corporations,
left to suffer by their own government.
Still, we rose, passage, immediate passage,
eastward, over desert and mountain, jungle
and ocean, the Bay of Bengal, Burma
and Thailand, Myths Asiatic, Asia's fables,
stowed in our hearts and souls, Pacific blue,
spreading out before us, islands and clouds,
charting Oceania by night with the stars,
our outrigger, from island to island.
Walt followed the flight of birds, sustaining shores,
past a whirlpool of destructive debris,
grinding and choking the living species
of that vast expanse of ocean blue,

eastward, ever eastward, home from Asia,
back to, I thought, the land of my birth.
Eventually I realized we were drawing near,
approaching a wider shore, extending
as far as I could see, from our great height,
yet it was not California, but a
southern land, mountains and jungles.
Walt glanced over at me with a devilish
look in his eye, startling, unsettling me.
I began to wonder where we were going.
    Landing in a jungle clearing, he set
us down, amongst foliage like nothing
I had ever seen, bird song, heat, humidity,
smells and fragrances, all unknown.
A new world, I was in, but not the one
I called home, the United States of America,
flawed and tainted by human evil too.
Dropping my hand and turning, I asked,
"Walt, where are we? This isn't the
good ol' USA, is it?" Laughing, he said,
"Just a little south, Meso-America.
Poets' orders. They told me to leave you here
with the hideous-faced Metzli,
and every horrid idol and image.
We know you're rather worn out and want to get
back home, if not the moon, but the consensus
was you had to push on, to a few poets,
especially in South America.
A local hombre will arrive to guide you."
With that, Walt rose, and disappeared above
the canopy of dense jungle, heading
north, to the Brooklyn Bridge or New Jersey.
And I, I was again alone, with bird calls,
quetzal birds, and parrots, humming birds,
in the jungle of my heart, apprehension,

as uneasiness and fear crept over me,
a sense of the danger of the place, lurking
within, creeping through exotic undergrowth,
and then the thought that my guides had brought me
thus far, so, perhaps, here, too, they might know
better than I, that I must be safe from the
jungle animals and whatever else
stalked below the trees. Still, I peered around,
until I sighted, emerging from the
jungle, a modern man, Octavio Paz,
an eminently civilized Mexican,
poet of a world voice, from India
to Mexico, and all the West,
putting me now at ease, as he drew near.
"Hola, Gringo from the Moon. Welcome to
Mexico. I am here to guide your way,
to take you to the Pyramid of the Moon,
surrogate for Cortez, scapegoat,
come to sacrifice to appease our gods,
because obviously there's a connection."
I didn't understand what he meant. He added,
"For all the colonial sins, not
perpetrated by you, but other men.
What do we care about minute details.
Victims have rights, too, a right to get even.
But I can't get you there like this," shaking
his arms, "A little Olmec shaman help
is what we need." With that, Paz began to change
before my eyes, shape-shifting into a
sleek, black jaguar, glistening yellow eyes,
taking my unexpecting breath away,
even gasping a little, caught off-guard.
"Don't be afraid," he reassured me. "Black
jaguars served the will of all the shamans,
Mayan, Aztec, the gods of this land.

Climb up," kneeling down so that I could.
What was I to do? No place to flee to.
Man become beast, beast man, beastly man, or not.
There was no alternative before me.
I had to trust Octavio Paz, under
that sleek black fur, velvety coat.
I jumped on and clutched with my fingers as
best I could, no thick mane or fur to help.
The beast sprang forward with us, or me, upon
its back, my holding on for dear life, too scared
and amazed to think. We raced through jungle
undergrowth, as I gripped harder around his neck,
until the jaguar broke through a wall of green
and out onto a mountainside, city below,
a city of ruins and pyramids.
"Teotihuacan," Paz purred over his
shoulder at me, running across dry fields.
"Meso-American Valley of the Kings,
Avenue of the Dead, birthplace of ancient
civilizations. O gringo, do I ever
have a surprise for you," laughing, making
me squirm on his back. And then we drew
nearer and entered the outskirts of the city.
  I began to hear music of a strange
and unusual tone, coming from up ahead,
as we followed the Avenue of the Dead,
Teotihuacan's main processional, pyramids
on either side; the temples of Quetzalcoatl,
on our right; peasants and people lining
the way, in colorful native costumes
of another age, watching and chanting,
in unknown tongues, as the black jaguar bore
me on, past the Pyramid of the Sun,
past many smaller pyramids on either
side, into the Plaza of the Moon, lined

with Aztec peoples, shamans and poets,
dressed in colorful attire, watching
our arrival, as we stopped before the
Pyramid of the Moon. All the plaza
lay before us. As I dismounted, Paz
shifted his shape back into a man,
a murmur rolling through the assembled crowd,
joined by music and drums filling the air.
Dressed in quetzal feathers and turquoise
head dresses, with jade and gilded ornaments,
the Aztecs received us, bowing, lavishing
us with signs of honor and respect in
languages I could not understand,
Paz smiling and nodding toward me,
a vast crowd milling around the plaza.
And then the music changed and a group of
dancers appeared, men on one side, women
on the other, high and regal, evoking
an elevated atmosphere. Spellbound,
I watched, the women goddesses of beauty
and charm. "The People of the Sun" all around.
From our vantage at the center of the plaza,
we saw a procession enter and move
towards us, in rhythm with the music
and dancers. Dignitaries, so it seemed,
spoke with Paz, ever the diplomat for me,
drawing nearer, motioning to change into
the flamboyant robes and costume they offered,
with peaked headgear, while I, always willing
to accommodate to others' customs,
saw no reason, behind their smiling faces,
to deny their wishes, so warmly I received
their offerings and donned them. At their urging,
we joined the procession, dancing, so it seemed,
in welcoming jubilation, common humanity;

Paz joining in, smiling all the while,
a custom of elevating charm and grace.
   A priestly type brought me a beverage to drink,
which I could not refuse, being polite,
not wanting to offend, though I noticed
only I was proffered the concoction.
So it was we reeled around the plaza,
and then I realized we were ascending
the Pyramid of the Moon, up its nearly
vertical steps, soon above the cheering crowd.
At the very top, I imagined, proudly stood
the presiding king, and asked Paz, but he
assured me it would be the high priests and
their attendants, the king would stand aside,
leaving the reception to his underlings.
Teotihuacan, the glorious city of the ages,
the servants of Metzli, the moon-god, a delight,
I thought, all things now having a moon theme,
as befit the occasion, since I fancied
myself quite the voyaging astro-poet
of the imagination, the full moon above,
always above the high places of the Earth,
whether ancient Israel or wherever,
looking up at the Rabbit on the moon,
as the moon appears to contain a blemish,
dimming its surface lest it be too bright.
Standing in front of the priests, swaying, I saw
statues of Coyot, the moon goddess, Paz
translated and explained, pointing to other
statues of Metzli and then Xochipilli,
goddess of flowers and poetry,
while an attendant dressed us again in new
attire, honored us as poets from afar,
gesturing in prayer toward the god's image
and to us. Then, breaking out into a chant

of poetry, he sang, "What can put down
lasting roots in this place of change, the world?
Everything we see here is only passing.
Even the most precious creation, jade
and turquoise, end in pieces, crumbling dust.
The time will come for us all to go,
by day or night, down into mystery."
Solemnly, he ended, fitting it seemed,
all assembled on the summit of the
Pyramid of the Moon, looking out over
the panorama of the land. Magnificent
was the view, the people assembled below.
    As the high priest nodded with a bow towards
me, Paz stepped back, and the priest and his jackals
suddenly grabbed me by the arms and legs,
to my utter horror, lifting me above
their heads, carrying me to a rock altar
I now could see. "Paz!" I screamed, with all my
might, "Help! Stop! Get me out of here!" But it was
too late. Betrayed, by a fellow poet.
A surprise, indeed. A low blow. I, writhing,
contorted, rendered groggy by the potion,
stripped and held down on the eagle stone,
an attendant grasping each limb, one holding
me by the neck, my arched chest, thrust up,
the cannibal priest hovering over me,
an obsidian blade, turquoise and shell,
while I cried for mercy, in a language
they could not understand, never known before
on the Temple of the Moon, its gory rites,
my blood about to be sacrificed
like nectar for thirsty hummingbirds.
In darkest vision of darkness, he cut
and ripped from me my heart, my pound of flesh,
still alive, beating, horror overwhelming,

darkness all about, the blood-red moon above.
I saw the grisly priest pull his hand from
my chest, raising the fistful to the moon,
held out for all to see, understood him now,
heard him say, shaking my pounding heart,
"Now, O Poet of the Moon, you are ready
to speak to the nations! You are ready
to learn from the poets on the moon!"
And I fell into a deep, dark hole,
consciousness seemed gone, I was in blackness,
horror filled, spirit jaguars came for me,
jungle journeys, my body lifted to the top
of the steep steps, thrown down, falling head over
heel, to have my flesh sliced and hung on
the curing racks below, bumping down, tumbling,
banging, skidding, O horror, horror, horror,
flung down the steps of 80,000 victims,
ever falling through turquoise and azure,
descending, sank as a diver sinks when
his life line is cut, sustaining air gone,
his link to life, helpless, lost, down through
struggling bubbles and furious thrashing,
desperately trying somehow to rise,
not fall, tumbling over and over,
bouncing from one step to another,
freefalling, skipping steps to horror below,
I feared, knew now, oh too well, the hateful,
blood-thirsty human beings that we are,
no mercy, no mercy, cannibalism
lurked and awaited me below,
the lowest human depravity, man eaters,
man eaters, cheered and exulted for my flesh,
hungrily eyed my descent, terror the
ocean of my fall, and then a hand grasped
my wrist in mid-descent, arrested, wrenching pain,

and bubbling foam, shot up, led, pulled me from
the dark depths of that ocean of agony,
brutal, cruel, savage, my trial there,
pitiless, a hand came forward and placed
itself upon my chest, a transforming,
healing hand, pulled me from that fate,
gathered me on his back like a floral
garland around a jaguar warrior's neck,
and we began to rise, above the steps,
above the Temple of the Moon, leaving behind
the screaming savages to devour
some other poor soul, some other sacrificial
lamb, scapegoat, victim of gore. Nursing my wound,
carrying my burden into Mordor,
like Frodo fearing the blow was mortal,
my place now in the West, gazing at the moon,
we flew, I knew not where, nor cared, so long
as it was away from the violence of that place.
I murmured and moaned, "O humanity!"
Too great a price for any man to pay.
O friends, remember this poet in your prayers.
   Through the mist of clouds, a voice spoke out,
"Sorry about that, gringo, but the order
came down from the moon. What could I do?"
And I realized it was Paz who had saved me
from being eaten, rescued by my betrayer.
How could I feel otherwise, yet knew he had
but performed the cruel decree of Parliament,
my masters, their sober lessons, one which I'd
much have preferred to do without. Resignation,
if not repose, slowly returned, a little,
as we flew farther away from that horror,
its lasting dregs within my wounded heart.
With cautious eyes, I looked at Paz, he at me,
beyond words now. In a jungle clearing,

he left me with words I didn't care to hear,
"Gringo, remember, critique the pyramid,
always the eaters of men and women."
After all, I thought, I'm a modern man.
We eat one another in more abstract ways.
Despite my vehement pleas not to leave,
desperately trying to deter him,
he faded and was gone, and I was alone,
still begging, fearful of the jungle birds
in the trees, jungle undergrowth all around.
"Oh, no, Paz, I'll never, ever forget,"
thinking of my sacrifice, I could not
calm down nor feel at peace, sorrowing
for all the lost ones dispatched unto death,
my escape such a dreadful trauma,
that I could but bemoan for endless time.
    Out of the haze, the sound of brush, a form
approached, a South American man,
not Aztec, but a trace of the indigenous
in his face, a proud bearing, and I realized
he was Pablo Neruda, Stalin's man,
bard of Fidel Castro, lackey to despots.
I thought of Ezra Pound and Mussolini.
How could poets serve such violent tyrants?
Having just experienced the Great Terror,
I hesitated before his outstretched arm,
not quite one of my heroes, while I brooded.
Reading my mind, Neruda waved his hand,
saying, "You'll understand I've come by order
of the poets on the moon to show you the
suffering of the people of my land,
of my continent. Trust me, for the sake of
the Muse. You are safe in my care.
You too have spoken for those who are dead.
In the Republic of Letters we meet.

Gringo, take this lesson back with you to the moon.
I learnt it from old Walt and other poets.
Perhaps in concern for our brothers we can
find common ground." Not lately thinking highly
of "orders" from the moon, I wanted to cut
free and run for home, back to El Norte,
yet his words softened my newly restored heart,
and so I reached for his wrist, my eyes on his,
man to man. What could I do? We rose, jungle
falling far below, mountains, sere and green land,
flying south, farther from home. With a sigh
I wondered where, what new adventure,
the poets now ruthlessly demanded.
Resigning to my fate, I nursed my wound,
as the miles went by, a thin strip of land,
another mass of continent appeared,
vast civilizations into the dim time
of human history, pre-history, voyage
and journey, trial and suffering, dread violence,
much, I knew, was like the blood-thirsty kingdoms
of Mexico, Guatemala, Nicaragua,
not much different from the modern day, it seemed,
still built on a pyramid of tyrant kings,
crushing people down before their weight,
as we too propped up banana republics,
despots eager to serve Wall Street for coin,
poisoning the land and generations,
destroyed villages, peasants in mass graves,
rape and brutalization, poverty,
crying in the night, if not all day long.
No solace for grief inflicted on all,
each victim an individual story,
abstractions fail to convey the human pain.
I felt somehow their wound was my wound too.

I awoke from my musings to realize
we were deep inside the continent, flying
down the backbone of mountains, spread about,
the vast Andes below. The Chilean poet
glanced aside at me, lingered, and then gazed
at the horizon, valleys in the sun.
To my amazement, I saw a great condor
and an eagle rise and join us, an escort
of majestic birds, sailing in sunlight,
green below, blue above, beauty pervasive,
my soul rising on the currents of the air.
Neruda again turned towards me and said,
"The heights of Machu Picchu, a great city,
lies ahead, the River Urubamba
far below," wind streaming through his hair,
face lit by the sun like an Incan king.
And I could see an enormous complex
of buildings and terraces spread out across
a mountainback like a saddle, cradled,
a switchback of many trails leading up,
ruins of great boulders and stones, hewn and
carved together, as if by gods, not men in rags.
Far below, tales of woe unknown, but guessed,
a mountain fortress not even the Spaniards
had penetrated. Here Neruda brought me,
setting us down on the mountainside, near a
formidable ruin, a stairway leading
farther upward, past ramparts and bastions.
The air so thin and rarified I nearly
struggled for breath, almost as much from
astonishment. Neruda said to me,
"Son of Viracocha, Lord of All, I bring
you to Machu Picchu." And without delay
he turned to the stairs, leading me up the
mountainside, one at a time, laboriously,

a vast sweep of human experience surging
through me with every step, thoughts of the souls
that lived here and in the Incan lands,
Cuzco, Arauco, Tiwanaku, Chichen,
Gurani, Atahualpa, and many more,
stretched and lay behind us now, as we climbed
our way upward, past the great central Temple
of the Sun, reaching the Intihuatana,
the solar observatory, sundial
and altar, to Inti, son of Viracocha,
the highest Incan deity, the only
surviving altar of the Incans, intact,
beyond the discovery and destruction
of the merciless conquistadors, the thieves
who destroyed and stole a civilization,
mountains of gold carried off to the old world,
nothing whatsoever new about that,
changing woe for woe but little else.
I thought of Neruda's mummy of Stalin,
the mummy he paraded through the streets
and pages of his poetry, his *Canto General*,
but kept the thought to myself, lest I offend.
I was just no longer willing to take risks.
   At last we stood before the primal shape
of the Intihuatana, its granite hewn
to cast a shadow marking time, block rising
upward out of block, from the natural stone.
I gazed down the main plaza to my right
and thought of all the people that milled about
here long ago, and now we modern tourists,
looking for something, come to gawk and admire,
taking pictures to talk about back home,
"We've been there." What does this place mean to us?
What do we come looking for? What do we ask?
Ask of ourselves? And I felt sad, deeply sad,

sad for all the loss and tragedy, romanticism,
the emptiness of our time, modernity,
so called, our gods lost for tawdry rites and
substitutes, a human vision sacrificed,
like poor Incan Juanita, a mere child,
stuffed into a frozen hole on a mountain,
for a meaningless Incan ritual,
for a cruel and merciless way of life,
seeking reassurance from the elements,
misunderstood, misconceived by the priests.
What kind of ghastly creatures are we?
And in my heart, a prayer arose, standing on
the Intihuatana, "Pacha Mama,
Mother Earth, O help us now, we human beings,
so lost upon this spinning globe, poisoned
everywhere, with sludge and chemicals,
in Bhopal, Niigata, Love Canal,
the Tittabawassee River, everywhere,
around the world, beyond recounting.
With Whitman, I saw the Great Pacific
Garbage Patch, a vast region of ocean,
a floating dump of plastic trash and debris,
killing your creatures on land and sea,
all the wayward peoples in danger now,
with all the world warming, glaciers melting.
Protect us, guide us with your sustaining care,
hold us, a babe upon your nurturing arm,
feed us at your sweet breast, bring us through
tumultuous times to peace, hitch again
the glory of the Sun and Moon to Earth,
even as here, at this hitching post,
cover all creation with their radiance.
Worst of all, nuclear radiation,
cesium, iodine, strontium, tellurium,
endless plutonium and uranium,

Three Mile Island, Chernobyl, Fukushima,
gyres and gyres, oceanic gyres, widening
down the centuries of genes and birth defects.
How shall we hear the sobs of the innocent?
How shall we protect them from ourselves,
from the toxic garbage we ourselves have become?
O Mother Earth, like the Pleiades lost
in daylight, with Orion pursuing,
guide us to the Temple of the Moon,
help us find it, around here somewhere too.
Guiding, reflected light of Viracocha,
spirit of human longing, raise our sight."
Below me the valleys on either side,
the mountains, once gods, endured serenely.
High above the eagles and condors circled.
The air was the freshest I've ever breathed.
    And then Neruda stirred me from my thoughts,
led me down to the old plaza and disappeared.
And I, I was alone, yet again, on an
Incan mountaintop and deserted city.
No lords and ladies with their court.
No virgins of the mountains dancing for them,
released from their bondage, servitude, abuse.
No peasants laboring, dyeing cloth or
milling corn, weaving llama, vicuna,
and alpaca, rich with embroidery,
into colorful cloaks and ponchos.
Only ruins, more ruins, ruins all about.
I began to weep, to cry, for all I felt,
the suffering of the place, of humanity,
in every place and time, the aching human
heart, crushed below the tread of tyrants, despots,
holding out hope with one hand but striking
with the other, a few brief moments,
here and there, of civilization, something

242 THE PARLIAMENT OF POETS

like it, and then gone, again, lost, lost,
lost civilizations, civilization lost,
so fragile on this spinning, blue-green bulb,
bud, flower, again, bud and bloom for us.
   Time passed with these thoughts, pain brooding on pain,
until I noticed a figure walking my way,
from Mt Huayna, with a cane, feeling the ground.
I purposely shuffled as he approached,
to indicate my position, he saying, with dignity,
"I told them on the moon that the only way
I'd come was if Neruda cleared out first.
Glad he's gone," and then I knew he was Borges,
carrying on still his vendetta, adding,
"Paz got him right. 'A servant of fascism.'"
The irony nearly knocking me down.
Life is so complex in South America!
Alas, like everywhere on planet Earth.
I drew a deep breath, leaning back my head,
not knowing what to say, saved by his plunging on,
"Another woman come to Argentina.
That was long ago. My governess too.
She could have been. Stranger things, in this world."
I was pleased to think of my great-aunt,
in sepia, in gaucho dress and hat,
and warmly shared the moment with Borges.
Like some blind Homer or Milton, Borges
held out his arm in my general direction.
I gladly placed my trust in him, my master.
High above Machu Picchu we soared,
blind Borges, more seeing than seeing men,
steered by instinct for his native land,
his proud head elevated toward me,
as I clung to his wrist, said, "O Poet of
the Moon, you who sought the Simorgh with Attar.
What a blessing to fly in your presence.

What I would give to have you guide me to Her."
Tears welled up in his blind eyes, streaming down
his cheeks, as we flew above the mountains.
Much overcome by his words, I could but speak
the truth, and said, "We never found Her, and
I don't know the way back. It was a bounty
beyond my deserving just to pursue Her
with Attar and the hoopoe's flock of birds.
She always remained out ahead, out of sight,
but I felt her presence in my deepest soul.
I live to pass a trace of the traceless Friend."
And he, "Ah, beyond us all, beyond us all,"
above the Andes, extending forever,
mountain after mountain, valleys beyond number,
a flowing sea of green jungle, giving way
to green mansions, jungle and pampas,
pampas spreading to the endless horizon.
After that, long we flew in silence, thoughtful
meditation on the Simorgh, that Bird
among birds, in ultimate quest of Her,
the vast pampas below, until slowly,
he began to descend, rancheros, squares and
grids of fields and farms, scattered towns and cities.
Passing one, Borges set us down on the
plain, with nothing around but flat land,
stretching as far as the eye could see,
twilight now beginning to fall, giving way
to night. Stepping aside, he said, before me,
"Much farther than Barrio Norte, south of
Pergamino, where my grandfather was
driven out, as a young boy, out of the house,
to look under the canvas of a cart,
outside the family casa, full of severed
heads, the horror sending him reeling into
shock, mute, silently exiled to Uruguay,

fleeing Argentina's dirty knife-fighters.
To the south," he said, pointing with his cane,
getting it right, somehow by chance, it seemed,
"lies Buenos Aires, the other antinomy
of my and Argentina's soul, the human
drama of birth, everywhere on this planet,
struggling to be human." I followed his
gesture and gazed toward where he said the
city was, darkness coming on, southern stars
beginning to appear, unknown to me, long
a follower of stars, guide posts of my life,
like ancient mariners, in Homer's *Odyssey*,
they have been for me, too, guiding points of light,
for in other fields I've stood in surrounding
darkness, gazing above, at far heights, prospects,
O shining beacons of who and what we are.
    Quietly we stood together and kept watch
on the pampas, until I could see the dim
glow of Buenos Aires, far away, under
the stars and what must have been the Southern Cross.
Alone, alone, two lonely poets stood,
together, on the pampas, in silence and awe.
I wasn't sure at times whether he was he,
or I was I, or Alonso Quijano,
fading to Don Quixote, surreal country,
surreal continent, with a surreal history,
replete with fluctuating blood and gore,
like humanity everywhere on Earth.
Looking up, the rising moon made my head spin.
I turned to Borges, asking, "Alonso, or
should I say Pierre Menard, I know I will
have to resume my journey before long,
back to Don Quixote. What do you advise?"
Borges, like an Alexandrian librarian,
"Are you sure you've ever left him? Indeed,

you may be him, traveling incognito;
another student seeking Al-Mutasim."
Unsettled by the possibilities, I tried
to evade the subject, stammering a bit,
"I know what it means to be from a northern
suburb, for I, too, am from one outside a
forever collapsing city, in decline,
by all accounts, shaking my confidence
in civilization, like an earthquake
shaking and rumbling deep below,
churning all to rubble, liquefaction.
Nothing we human beings make seems to last.
Time giving way to time. But anyway,
the suburbs can be pleasant, while they last,
undercutting their own foundations.
Like Cervantes on his ramshackle farm,
I'm stuck with an old colonial house,
not farming, but dabbling in real estate,
not much of a businessman, as Cervantes
and Robert Frost weren't much at farming.
I hope, more of a poet, who instead of
playing golf in the morning, the casino,
or any of the typical clichés,
reads Shakespeare, Dante, and Milton,
striving for something worthwhile in the end,
though it often seems I'll never live long
enough, the dread weight of despair tugging,
dragging me down into the grave.
I grieve, grieve forever for my family,
driven out, Great-Grandmother Zink beaten
for her empty purse, a neighborhood bakery
moved repeatedly, farther out, and all those
memories of my boyhood in Cadillac Square,
in downtown Detroit, vibrant, full of life,
not fear. I am one who knows what it can mean

to live in a suburb on the edge of a
collapsing civilization, one worthless
project after another, making things worse."
   Borges looked uneasy, agitated,
shifting his stance, saying, "Consequently,
we shouldn't stay here too long, to be safe,
we'd better think about moving on soon.
The Congress is a nice idea, and truly
should exist someday, though secretly now,
that institution of the universe, ourselves.
That is to say, one always has to be on
the lookout for swords and daggers, knife-fighters."
Understanding the connection, I admitted,
"I'm only a gringo from El Norte,
though, like you, one with English roots,
a practical sensibility, if there
ever was one in this world of El Toboso.
Oh, Borges, a tale out of your own stories."
We enjoyed a good laugh together,
two hidalgos standing on the pampas.
The moon was now high in the east.
On the endless plain, north of Buenos Aires,
Borges said, "We must look up, elevate
our view, gaze far, away from our small self.
For all our travels to and from the moon, we're
not even able to draw near its essence.
High in the heavens the moon remains.
Though astronauts went there, they didn't get it.
So the moon hangs in our dreams, our reflections
on who we are, and what it all means,
reflections on this vain and dubious world,
wracked by one violent junta after another,
juntas of the raging soul, self-serving
creatures, tearing apart the flesh of others,
for their own sustenance, knife-fighters on

the pampas of the soul. If Argentina exists,
it finds unity in the rich stew of
humanity, simmering together. Savor it.
So the Congress of the World always exists.
We don't need to, and can't, create it.
That singularly modest word, the moon,
part of all antinomies under the heavens,
opposed to another junta, another Perón,
sinking boatloads of people in the sea,
dropping them from airplanes and helicopters,
burying them, dumping them into mass graves.
Man is nothing more than vain reflections.
O wavering moon, shine brighter for us all!
What can a poet do in such a world?
Dream for a dream world to create a real one,
one worthy of humanity, Argentina.
Alas, a dream world can also constitute
worlds of horror and suffering, betrayal.
Neruda showed us that, singing for Stalin.
Poverty can drive people to terrible things.
Praising murder and violence doesn't help.
The ancients understood the role of epic.
Be a voice of courage and hope.
Homer and Virgil extolled the tragic hero,
the man fighting for the city, a cause,
doomed from the very beginning, like Oedipus,
the dignity of the defeated,
like Michelangelo before the pope,
like Odysseus seeking his homecoming.
Dante, too, chose a pattern for all men,
the happiness of man before the Divine.
So the epic poet tells a tale,
following the way of the ancient shamans.
Men long to hear the tale of their time,
and only the true poet can sing that tale,

called by the gods to sacrifice his life
to the writing and service of their vision.
Only your struggling within the depths
of your own soul can make you a maker.
Then might you bring back epic to mankind."
Borges ended, stepped back, aside, to my left,
feeling with his cane, his words resonating,
while I gazed on the brilliant moon,
high above, huge, luminous moon, full moon,
mirror moon, moon mirror, of all humanity,
so it seemed, reflecting the universe,
the moon, a universal moon, an Alef,
reflected there our dream of dreams, aloft,
through dreams the Ideal become reality,
gliding through the sky, and as I looked on,
it strangely seemed to change, to become like
unto a mirror, and I saw reflected there,
in truth, all humanity, from the pampas
of Argentina, billions of faces, reflected
back to me, from this small Earth, scintillating
light, danced around the faces, through the night,
lifting my soul to a new found height,
moon again become a mirror,
mirroring quicksilver in the sky.
I saw my small self in the moon,
felt I was falling into the moon,
a mere man, poet, struggling with his soul,
with how to speak to the world, all of it,
people in every land and clime,
up raise a universal epic song.
O world, full of long-suffering and pain,
my load of the universal human fate,
lonely, but looking up, hoping, for a
better world than the one we've got,
if I might be blessed to find the words,

for words can create a world, mold, shape it,
affirm what's human, set and clarify a goal,
words, change and shape a world, ideal,
in a humble human way, not utopia,
if men will but choose to change, after
thought and prayer, change their actions,
mirroring endless ripples of eternity.
Through tears I saw the moon shine brightly,
become truly a mirror of my dreams, and then
a light shone out, flashing across eons of
space, moonbeams pulling me in, taking me up,
carrying me toward its brilliance, raised, drawn.
I rose on photons of reflected light, toward
the mirror of the moon, blind Borges far behind,
the Simorgh become Light, transporting me,
carrying me to another time and place.

BOOK XI

THE ARGUMENT

Out of moonbeams into Africa. A cave beyond ancient,
Blombos Cave, on the Southern Cape, 72,000 years ago, bifacial
stone points, seashell necklaces, tools of bone, cross-hatched
chunks of ochre. From a midden in the dunes, *Homo sapiens*
outside the cave. Moon over what would one day be the Indian
Ocean. Ezeulu, a priest, a compound in Igboland, a dirt floor
and a kola nut. Wearied by a long journey, the Persona must
choose sacrifice. Ezeulu to the Poet of the Moon. Drums, song,
dance, feet pound the earth, the village moves, masks. A Griot
woman, Sogolon, Sundiata's mother, robes and a calabash
flowing in the air, takes the Poet into the heart of darkness, a
dense jungle, a village in a clearing. Mbeku, the Flying Tortoise,
lifts the Poet of the Moon to Skyland, back to the Moon, out of
America, out of Africa, back to the Moon.

A wise man, a shaman, he seemed, alone,
in the light of the full moon, gazing at the sea,
from the height of a cliff, looking back up at
the moonbeams, intent on both, unaware of
my presence in the sand dunes to the south,
as intent on him as he on the waves
and endless surf, the sea churning through the
millennia that separated me
from him, ancient father, before ancient,
older than Adam, seventy thousand years
and more, dawn before dawn, Blombos Man
on the African Cape, refugee from the
searing droughts to the north, desiccating
the African continent, little bands of
early man, sheltered in the savannas,
in the caves along the beaches of the Horn,
a bountiful Horn of Plenty, shellfish

brain food for millennia, nourishing
the mind, the Dreamtime of humanity.
I was as alone as he in the moonlight,
set down by translucent beams, transcending time
and an ocean, mind the only reality,
consciousness, drawn to itself, mind observing mind,
meditating on its own mystery,
from a vortex in the predawn darkness,
illuminated with a brilliant moon
and a trillion stars, metaphors of our nature,
rising up, surging, above and below
the daily level of life, quotidian.
Out of the vertigo, hiding below,
I watched him from behind milkweed plants,
on a shellfish midden, shells of every type
of mollusk that the sea has to offer,
strewn about in piles, heaping mounds,
fish bones and guts, a stench of rotting carcasses
that draws the flies of day. I knew he was
our father, naked with painted ochre reds
and a necklace of small seashells on his chest,
some bits of bone, rattling as he moved,
slightly about, watching and viewing the moon,
and then back again to gazing at the sea.
I wondered if he had seen me coming down,
on moonlight beams, and then dismissed the thought,
with a wry smile. The wind was blowing off
the southern ocean, what one day would be called
the Indian Ocean, Australia far away
and to the east. Voyagers, one day, too,
around this Horn, would sail, Camões writing
The Lusiads, Magellan, Vasco de Gama,
the Portuguese, Dutch, Spanish, and English to
China and Japan, every land of the East,
yet unknown, unnamed, labeled in modern time.

We stood so far before all of them it seemed
absurd to think of negligible "history."
I felt the gods had brought me there on wingéd feet,
reverence and humility washing over me,
like the surf over the rocks below, wearing
away on our planet, all that's ephemeral,
the surf of time leaving nothing behind.
I thought who is this primordial man?
And then I knew he was each one of us.
All the shades and hues were in his dusky,
ochre-covered body, his genome, at root,
its base and stem, from which we've grown,
untraceable, perhaps, but all his actions
and artefacts tell us now he was like us,
not a mere ape in a tree, or climbing down
from one, but upright and thinking, trying,
at least, more than many of us today.
The tip of his spear was upright, too, base in
the ground next to him, its finely wrought
stone point a work of high technology,
the cutting edge, in every sense, mastery
of thought and design, symbolic in itself,
in unknown ways, so it appears, some think.
His matted hair and mostly hairless chest,
contrasted with his bushman face which looked
human in the moonlight. As he continued
to work away on something, my thoughts too
flowed on, amazed by where and what I saw.
Behind him up the cliff was the opening
of a cave, in front of which a fire flamed,
and I could see another figure, clearly
woman, dressed like him, moving about, picking up
a child, nursing, an old man and woman
sitting on rocks to the side, weak and frail,
given by the woman something from the fire.

A little group, they seemed, a family flitted
through my mind, acts of kindness, togetherness,
like a story around an ancient campfire.
I thought I saw something different from
animals eating their young. Nature red in
tooth and claw, outside the glow of that fire.
I felt it was a privilege just to watch,
sheltered in the dunes below, so close,
while Blombos Man worked on, pondering.
Some internal, personal struggle was
going on inside his head, a need to know,
his consciousness grappling about, for
such he clearly had, as in his artefacts,
dressed in, and equipped, with their regalia,
their full equipage already his attire,
imagining and planning and creating,
what a memory he stood there accessing,
all of which I, myself, could barely guess at.
    The sky was beginning to show traces
of light in the east, definitely dawn
was approaching. I could tell he noticed,
perhaps had even before me, a suburbanite
on a wildly romping journey around
the world, through time. A spring breeze blew from
the east, and he seemed excited, reaching
into a pouch he wore on a waist string,
pulling out something, grasped in his hand, held up
in front of him, looking at it, turning it
to see it better in the dim morning light,
the moon still visible in the lightening sky.
And I too could see the chunk of ochre,
a reddish rock of pigment, held in his
outstretched left hand, as he moved it,
crosshatched markings appeared, a pattern, abstract,
a meaning obscure, but with an eye on

the moon, and the receding tide, he reached
back into his pouch and withdrew a stone,
flaked to a point, and began to etch another
mark onto the chunk, like some early road
surveyor, one I saw once along a
freeway, his eye at his scope, clipboard in
his hand, jotting down the latest measurement,
a new roadway forward in his mind,
cars and trucks barreling into the future.
I stood astonished by that hominid,
at what we were already, in that land
before time, a named continent, so much else.
And then Blombos Man began to chant in
a guttural tongue, if not a language,
I could not decipher, but emotion
filled the sounds, as he looked back up to
Mother Moon, from Mother Earth, in
Mother Africa. Shivers went through me,
and I, too, prayed, yearned for this man, and species,
to make it, over all, on this planet,
through the long corridors of time and space,
to find the necessary sustenance
and care, shelter, all that's needed, to sustain
the race, frail as we are, our existence
dependent on so much beyond our control,
life hanging in the balance, as on those rocks.
I worshiped with him the Moon, and felt it deep,
deep as the endless ocean we stood before.
Emotions I had never felt swept over me,
carrying me along in human sympathy,
with that small band of *Homo sapiens*,
worthy it seemed of the name. And then a voice
was raised from the cave, startling me,
while Blombos Man thrust his tools back into
his pouch, grabbed his spear, clambered up the cliffside,

away from the rocks overlooking the beach.
I saw him join the circle, taking something
from the woman, a piece of food, sitting down.
I was all alone in the milkweed bushes,
elated, marveling at what I had seen,
scarcely knowing what to do, turning away,
walking across the midden to the east,
skirting around piles of empty shells.
I made my way among the rocks and cliffs.
Nearer the ocean I stopped to gaze out at
its vastness, endlessness, far beyond my ken.
I stood transfixed, all alone, for what seemed
an eternity, before and after,
extending in every direction.
What could it all really mean? Who am I?
How did I get here and where am I going?
   Sounds and rustling in the bushes to my left.
A man stepped out, bushman, darker, African.
His markings in a whitish chalk, dressed about
the same. He stopped a distance from me,
then held out his arm. I found the gesture
so familiar and reassuring I smiled,
and he, pleased by my reaction, smiled back.
I moved forward, reached and grasped his wrist.
Together we rose above the Western Cape.
Far below us lay Africa and the sea,
into the heart of Africa we flew,
dry savanna, deserts, mountains, jungles,
another ocean on our left, already
traversed by other means, I thought. We flew on,
this man and I. My guide gazed firmly ahead,
intent on some distant destination
of which I had not the slightest clue.
Soon we were flying up a coast, land below
and swinging far ahead out to the west,

West Africa with the curvature of
the Earth, a great river, the Niger,
I recalled, flowing far into the sea.
Northward we swung, into the continent,
both green and sere, Nigeria, or so
they call it today, then Igboland, I learned.
I clung to the African man like a
baby chimp to its mother, descending,
as from the height of a great jungle tree,
deeper into the heart of Africa,
some unknown time and place, sailing lower,
down where villages appeared, scattered about.
He chose one, gently setting us near it,
in a clearing, by a cluster of mud huts,
with grass roofs, and there we stood together.
Not too far, I could see people in a field.
He turned and said, "I am Ezeulu,
priest of the village of Umuachala
and of Ani, the Earth Goddess.
The poets of the moon called me to bring
you here to Igboland, as you can see."
Without waiting for a reply, Ezeulu
went toward and into a compound,
past a type of shrine of some sort, outside,
my following his lead, into a simple hut,
bending low as I entered, onto its
earthen floor. He motioned me to a seat,
taking another. A wave of anticipation
swept over me, though mingled with weariness,
my journey so long around the world.
I could not but feel exhausted and tried
politely to hide it from my host.
Out of a bag, he took a kola nut,
cracked it for me, his guest, in welcome.
I eagerly chewed the nut, finding it

reviving, wondering when I had eaten last.
His proud face and dark eyes looked intently
at me, sizing me up, as I chewed. Though
wondering about my host, given all I had
been through, I trusted his gracious humanity.
I wasn't all that different from this priest.
He carried a burden, and so did I,
both seekers, so it seemed, entered my head,
driven by the thought of duty for the good
of others, trying to serve the community,
in, at times, human and misbegotten ways.
I worried I might unburden myself
too much to him and lose face.
   Finishing the kola nut, Ezeulu said,
"You have come a long way, from the moon, they say.
How was it there? And you return?" Answering
his own questions, continuing, "We all
will return. It is only a matter of time.
It is what we do here and how that matters.
In the place before time a man receives
his gifts and talents, his character, indeed,
his portion in life, even before he comes
into this world, though he chooses, too, somehow.
Chukwu, the great source of life and being,
overseeing man's *chi*, one's guiding spirit,
resides in a man's compound to the end.
O Poet of the Moon, you chose your chi.
Now you must keep choosing to serve him.
'If a man agrees, his chi agrees.'
You made a primordial bargain.
'Fear that the first word gets to Chukwu's house.'
Poets are the bearers of chi, memory,
servants of recall. Remind the people of chi,
a ray from the high regions of the sun.
You spoke and bargained with your chi at the

moment of your creation, enlisted
with Chukwu to improve creation.
You chose and agreed. You must keep choosing,
or you'll end up a priest of a dead god,
disgraced by his own actions, in the eyes of
his people, pushed aside by them, not heeded.
Sacrifice yourself for their good, serve them.
Only you can choose, as once you chose in
the realm before time. Always embrace your chi.
Chukwu allows you the freedom to choose.
Yes, it is futile, as I knew, but I had
to set the example, try to show the way.
Often that is all that Chukwu asks.
That alone can be enough for a man."
  Ezeulu stopped and held back his head
and shoulders, looking quietly at me.
And I thought of Chukwu, as the Ibo say,
the Great Chi, the Great Source of Life and Being.
The Yoruba know him as Oludumare,
Supreme Being, many ministers below;
and the Yoruba also call him Olorun,
the Owner of Heaven, Eleda, the Creator.
The Edo speak of Osanobuwa,
In a Class by Himself, alone and beyond,
God Who Is Source and Sustainer of the World.
The Nupe people call upon Soko,
the Great One, He Who Dwelleth in Heaven,
and the Tso revere Ci, Owner of Us,
the One to Whom We Belong,
the Bambara of Mali speak of Faro,
All-Powerful, Too Distant for Humans,
the Ewe-speaking have Nana Buluku,
Ancient of Days, while the Ashanti say
Nyame, the Supreme God, and the
Bacongo, He is Made by No Other,

No One Beyond Him Is, no images,
no idols, the Supreme Spirit, high above all,
not the animism and fetishes
of the missionaries, but One Supreme Being.
They're all Chukwu; they are but One.
Not even the desire to propagate
the religion, no founder or reformer,
like Buddha or Christ or Confucius,
yet loyal worshipers, unorganized,
in essence, the pattern is the same,
the Sanatana Dharma of Africa,
continent of diffused monotheism.
One could stand on the moon for eternity
reciting the names of the Transcendent One.
I rubbed my forehead and ran my fingers
through my hair, pondering his many names.
I had listened carefully to Ezeulu, every word.
After these moments of reflection, replied,
"I know I'm supposed to play the role of
the white man, but I only think of myself
as human, one of many, from planet Earth."
He interjected, smiling, "Don't we all."
I smiled too, kindly laughing together,
"We have the genes of every human being
who ever procreated on the planet.
I know my DNA is out of Africa,
and have the test results to prove it.
It's not some kind of cheap romanticism.
You welcomed me as brother, not stranger.
Why must I play the role of one now?
I thought we had moved beyond all that.
We're all a mixed bag of good and evil.
Africa is not the heart of darkness,
no more than any other place on Earth,
no more particularly savage than the rest.

All destroy and shun, ostracize the other,
expelling the Osu, Burakumin,
outsiders and heretics, Jews and Dalits,
Blacks and Indians, foreigners, strangers,
slander and libel, infidel, apostate,
Takfir and *Damnatio memoriae*.
We cracked the kola nut together.
Why should I play the white man now? For you
or me? I've already had my heart ripped out.
To me, the moral is Chukwu made us all.
Why should I suffer for others' bigotry?"
    Mulling over my words, Ezeulu finally said,
"They think you're white. It doesn't matter
that you know you're not. All they can see
when they look at you is a white man."
I retorted, "That's their problem. Not mine!"
"Oh, yes it is! Life has made it your problem.
You must accept it. You must play this role,
for their own good, the only way beyond it.
But only if you are willing to accept it.
You must choose it. It is your chi."
Uneasy, I squirmed on the seat, wanted
to escape, anywhere else on Earth would do.
I thought of the people I saw working,
coming in together, down the lane.
I felt a deep pang at my fate, yet knew
Ezeulu was right, while I struggled
to think of another way. Eventually,
I nodded to him, chose to submit.
A measure of relief swept over his face.
He then poured me a cup of palm wine,
saying, "You will sleep and have a vision,"
leading me to a cot when I had finished
the cup, thinking of my ancestors, back into
Europe, forty-five thousand years ago,

arriving after a long trek from Africa.
I summoned them now as my witnesses,
like Ezeulu's own ancestors in his
shrine outside, the heads of the priests hanging
from the rafters, skulls unearthed and retrieved.
I soon fell into a deep sleep, a trance.
There were drums, speaking with one voice, from under
a timeless ogbu tree, near the marketplace,
with elders sitting about, talking, honored
sacred masks and figures danced.
The masks of my ancestors, innumerable,
back for thousands of generations,
swirled and flew about in my mind,
and Ezeulu was in my dream speaking
before the elders, arguing, it seemed,
"He needs his head. Yes, it is our custom,
but how will he speak back on the moon?
The poets will not understand our ways.
He must speak to humanity for us too.
He is a foreigner, though our brother.
I will hang his head in the shrine, a vision,
and this will fulfill the way of the ancestors,
his ancestors and ours. They will be at one,
honor his struggle with his own people."
And then in the dream, Ezeulu painted
me with white chalk, half white, half black,
with a circle around the opposite eye,
half man, half spirit, antinomies complete;
and Robert Hayden was looking on, wearing
a bow tie, indignantly saying,
"I'm not about to play African dress-up.
Things are just going way too far for me,"
but Hayden too was painted as I was.
I forgave him and reached out to grasp his arm,
but he faded back beyond the Quantum world,

with the blowing of Roland's horn, leaving me
alone in one of love's lonely offices,
rising above my pain for the good of others,
looking back at Ezeulu, trusting him,
standing over me now, where I lay.
He intoned in a sonorous voice,
"We would hang your head in the shrine but have
given up that custom, yet recall it in
honor of you, in vision, Poet of the Moon.
And so I say here that you are a man.
I enter the shrine, even in this vision,
with your head, holding it as I hold it now,
and there pray, to Ani, Earth Goddess,
for you are a man full of memory.
We shall carve your mask. Thus we honor you,
and your journey through the regions of the gods.
Tell the people what it means to be human.
'A man must dance the dance of his time.'
'He is a fool who treats his brother as a
stranger. Are you not our brother?'
Now you are ready to speak to mankind.
Tell them what you have learned from the Igbo."
Then my head was restored to me somehow,
and I stood on the two good legs of my genes,
forty-five thousand years worth and more,
even Blombos Cave. I was not a white man,
but a man, among other men, my brothers
and sisters, all around the Earth, and Africa.
I belonged with Africans and they with me.
And I awoke and was again myself,
through sacrifice, made whole, one with creation.
Better than losing one's head for good,
like so many people on planet Earth.
Time passed as I lingered over the vision
I had been allowed, that my chi had brought me.

Ezeulu soon walked back into the room,
saying, "Poet of the Moon, we all are healed.
Now I understand. We can all be angels
or savages, choose the heart of darkness,
if we lose the human heart of the people,
become cold to human suffering not our own.
The people live in the village. Leaders
who forget the village are unworthy
of the people." A shiver ran through me.
Ezeulu led me out of the mud hut,
into the compound, where we could now hear and
see, down the lane, a drumming and dancing throng
of people, coming our way, some in brightly
colored dress, traditional and modern,
festive, a flute joining in, song rising.
The pounding sound of feet on the ground moved
jubilantly toward us, male and female,
voices taking spirits with them, antiphonies
of harmony, swaying and rocking masks,
young and old, children dancing with the rest.
In the tropical morning, a woman
presented me with a string of cowries,
slipping it over my head as I bowed,
and an old man with a walking staff
handed it insistently to me, though I feared
he needed it more than I, Ezeulu watching.
Words were beyond me. Silence seemed best.
Respect for the people of Umuachala.
    A woman stepped forward from the people,
a two-stringed instrument on her shoulder,
a West African griot's calabash,
colorful beads and a satchel around her neck.
A striking woman of presence and mind.
In front of the entire village, she held
out her arm to me. With a glance to

Ezeulu, who urged me forward, I moved
to where I could reach her wrist and grasped it.
She lifted us toward another realm.
Above flowing rivers and dense jungles
and mountains, the griot woman flew,
her robes and calabash streaming behind,
her proud face left me wondering who she was,
and to what she led, towards the east.
The farther we flew the more I noticed her
expression change to one of anxiety
and pain, tension, foreboding I knew not what,
but hoped there was some purpose in her design,
that somehow had brought her to be my guide.
Though I wanted to ask her who she was,
I kept silent before her struggling mind,
biding my thoughts until she set us down
on a small mountainside, rising above
surrounding jungle of deep vegetation,
trees and plants unknown to me. As I took
my bearings, I could hear sounds, too, of birds,
and other creatures I had never known.
Deep into Africa she had brought me.
Then she said to me, "I am Sogolon,
King Sundiata's mother, the good sorceress,
of ancient Mali, from the griot tradition.
The poets of the moon ordered you here,
into Africa's heart of modern darkness,
stirring painful memories for me, though I was
among the fortunate women, stalked by
hunters I fended them off with porcupine quills,
none here, worse than Homer's Penelope
pursued by avaricious, lustful suitors.
The Congo has lost the ways of the past.
No sorcery can remove this misery,
only renewal of the heart of man."

With her queenly bearing, she walked, leading me
through the jungle, down a high hill, to a
small clearing, from which we could see a village
farther down, of clustered compounds and huts,
surrounded by fields of crops of some kind.
In the humid morning, her calabash
still upon her shoulder, she stopped, took it,
and began to play, high notes of lute-like
music, joining the jungle birds in the glade,
while an ethereal song began to pour
from her heart. "Griots are the memory
of Africa, historians of their people,
of their kings and tribes, the wisdom of elders,
passed on to younger generations,
through ornaments of song, calabash and drums,
the kora and flutes, and balafon.
The music of the soul, griots the vessel
of secrets that are many centuries old,
far back into the dim past, royalty
forgotten but for griots, memory
of all mankind, the teaching that tames the beast,
keeping alive the example of human
nobility, the future springs of immortality,"
ending with her arms thrown wide and head full back,
as though appealing to the gods of the sky.
She paused, allowing the birds to carry on
the reverberations of her song in theirs.
   Breaking her silence, she said to me, "Woe to
a time that forgets the measure of man,
for then people fall to the darkest depths,
and not even I could defend myself
against attackers with all my herbs and potions,
even porcupine quills could not drive away
such men reduced to rapacious beasts."
Her voice broke, pure tears falling from her eyes,

as she turned toward the village, pausing
briefly in anguish, seeking the path forward.
Quietly, I stood, uncomprehending still,
but deeply moved by the poignancy of
her plaintive song and heartfelt grief, sensing some
tragedy lay before us. Wiping her eyes,
she set out through the bush. I followed
without a word, not knowing what to say,
until we again broke through jungle into
a wide clearing that at the far end held
the village compounds of round thatched huts
of mud brick, set on a rise of the land.
And there she started to talk about the woe,
about the coming of soldiers, warring tribes,
Hutus and Tutsis, Rwandans, Ugandans,
Congolese, and many factions, the loss of
human love, all caring cast to the winds,
and as she spoke she began to change before
my eyes, from an older woman of
traditional dress to a modern woman
of equally striking composure and beauty,
an elegant African beauty, dressed
in the finest international fashion,
from Paris, Italy, Tokyo, or New York.
Her lipstick and make up and stylish hair
revealing a beautiful young woman,
excoriating the men of her time,
who forgot the human spirit, without king
or chief, or guiding elders, hate and greed
ruling in their place, sought power and control,
minerals and oil, diamonds, copper and metals,
things of the world, not the soul. Millions slaughtered,
black Africans again enslaving Africans,
raped into submission, before their fathers,
husbands, and children, as in a nightmare,

the nightmare of life in this world run amok.
Shaking her head, she gave me the calabash,
saying, "Africa is more than the calabash."
Then stepping apart, she leaned back her head,
a black jewel, as black as the blackest black
of space, a universal jewel of great price,
a living universe of womanhood,
in her deepest mystery, feminine jewel,
a cipher all men seek to solve of every hue,
a daughter of Sogolon, as she were, namesake,
saying, "I, Sogolon, see a vast refugee camp,
spanning this valley, through the country,
the continent, the world, out of the dark heart
of humanity, standing by, watching, moved
and unmoved, all complicitous, all lacking
the will to stop the brutalization
of village women, vulnerable, weak, frail.
Why do you all stand by and watch on TV?
Everywhere everywhere everywhere on Earth,
the loss has first taken place in the human heart,
for the heart of darkness exists everywhere,
not only Africa, by any means,
everywhere women are brutalized and raped.
Man become an animal, an old and
terrible sight, every manner of violence
and bloodshed unleashed, ever perpetrated
by the human race, concealed behind the
tribal dress, the military uniform,
the three-piece suit, sucking the bones and marrow.
Here is what is in man that destroys women.
Here is what destroys man, making him a beast,
worse than a beast, a sick and evil thing.
O Africa, O humanity, I sing
the deepest grief for the young, the innocent,
the gentle children done unto death,

hacked with machetes and pango blades,
shot and bombed, burned in their homes and villages,
for the insane ideas of their parents
and the world." And then a young African man
appeared by her side, quietly listening,
her equal, dressed in a suit, a cell phone
in his hand, slipping it inside his coat.
Glancing at him, she began to sing again,
"Heal, O Africa, I, Sogolon, a daughter
of Sundiata's mother, a modern woman,
a mother who has suckled at her breast,
cry out, heal, with all the power of my spirit,
heal, embrace the healing medicine,
potions and herbs, amulets, before the
judging presence of the past, bend down in
shame and repentance, hear the voices
of guiding elders, grandmothers and mothers,
daughters and sisters, wives and babies,
hear the fathers of village traditions,
hear their one voice: 'Rise up, struggle, strive
to remain human, to be worthy of
more than a rapacious beast, worse even
than jungle animals. Cease murdering,
torturing, raping, pillaging, and the
plundering of all decency from
Mother Earth, for even she you have not
restrained yourselves from brutally raping,
with the help of foreign corporations.
Even now your victims lie prostrate, gasping
for what may be their last breath. Awake from the
destructive nightmare of your madness. Awake!
Before it is too late!" Sogolon ended
her song. I stood mute, dumbfounded, overwhelmed
by her appeal, no man exempt from her
scathing condemnation of human evil.

Sogolon stepped toward me in her high heels
and fashionable elegance, a confident
young woman, self-possessed and strong, fiery
with righteous indignation for her gender,
for the justice of her cause in Africa.
"Poet of the Moon, do not forget what you
have heard and seen. Take it back to the moon.
Let it suffuse your deliberations.
Out of Africa, all mankind once flowed,
the fountainhead of the global tribe.
All that was and is human stemmed from here.
Westerners can think we Africans are the
most savage of all human beings on Earth,
but who slaughtered millions all over Europe?
Japanese can think we're uncivilized,
but who slaughtered people all over Asia?
Others have their gulags and debacles.
None of us are innocent, pure, 'civilized,'
a heart of darkness reigns in the human heart,
cold to the suffering of others.
May Chukwu guide you on your journey,
inspire you with words to help retrieve the
human vision from those who have betrayed it,
from the mass grave into which it has been thrown,
before it is too late for humanity."
And with those sustaining words of blessing,
she and her companion turned and disappeared,
determined, pledged to fight together for
a better future for women, for all Africa.
And I, I was alone, so close to horror,
on the edge of human suffering and misery.
    Before fear could overtake me, I saw,
to my surprise, a large tortoise, an Igbo
tortoise, coming out of the jungle where
the couple had just recently entered.

They might have even passed one another.
He had feathers on his legs and was flying,
with a sly grin on his face, landing right in
front of me, sizing me up, from head to foot.
That flying African tortoise, Mbeku, greeted me,
"You must be the Poet of the Moon.
White as the moon, you stand out around here.
I, Mbeku, shall take you beyond Skyland,
where I was wont to fly, even up to
the moon. I have been commanded to fetch you.
They better have a mouth-watering feast
for me up there, or I might throw you back down."

O Reader, I could tell, after all I'd seen,
this was not an ordinary tortoise,
not the kind Earth dwellers usually meet.
But somehow I had to get back to the moon,
and Mbeku, alone, grinning, held out his
scaley leg. I stepped forward and seized it.
Far towards Skyland we soared, beyond Africa.

BOOK XII

THE ARGUMENT

Mbeku, the flying African tortoise, like the last stage of a Saturn V rocket, hurtling out of Earth orbit into a quarter of a million miles to the moon, 25,000 mph, clutching the Persona in his feathered arms, his cracked shell pointing backwards at the moon, pirouetting, twirling, in the weightlessness of space, in brilliant white sunlight, in the blackest black of eternity, through timelessness, into the future. Back to the Sea of Tranquility, back to the descent stage of the Lunar Module of Apollo 11. Fourth time on the moon, our hero, the Poet of the Moon, twice as many times as any astronaut, after a long journey, arduous quest, an ordeal. The far side of the moon, as dark as the dark night of the soul. The starry cosmos, a universe of galaxies, sextillions of stars. Lunar sunrise. Earthrise. The end of Nihilism and Scientism, the unity of science and religion, reason and intuition, the two cultures reconciled, entangled by the unity of the Imagination. The unity of Unity, oneness, our fragile, delicate Earth, four dimensional in its fullness, floating through eternal timelessness, a new panorama rising before humanity, rising above the moon.

M beku twirled like the last stage of a
Saturn V rocket, end over end, a
graceful ballet in space, pirouetting,
pas de deux, dual being becoming Being,
journey toward Essence, shedding time and space
for absolute time and space, beyond the
physics of time and space, contracting
the Earth horizon, ever smaller, in
itself, breaking free of its atmosphere,
through the thin layers, beyond stratosphere,
ever finer, rarified, ethereal,
Mbeku's shell our protecting module,

commandeering the way forward, into the
blackest black of space, Earth, home, blue-white globe,
floating four dimensionally across eternity,
out of time, into relativity,
how now to count time where time has no meaning,
immortal, eternal, on course, 25,000 mph,
headed for lunar rendezvous,
his cracked and crazed shell aimed at the moon,
holding me in his feathered arms, like all
of Africa hurtling into the future,
de-accelerating with a mid-flight burn,
gravity pulling us down relentlessly,
Mbeku landing at the Sea of Tranquility.
   All the poets were gone. Only we were there.
I asked Mbeku where were all the poets.
He, smiling deviously, said, "First you must
go on one last voyage, alone, by yourself.
No one can accompany you on this journey.
No guide can lead you. The test is yours alone,
to pass or fail, understand or despair.
Are you ready for it? Only you can choose,
and you may reject it. I will take you back
to Earth, if you prefer." He stood quietly,
mischievously, challengingly looking at me,
a daring, taunting expression on his face,
that African tortoise toying with me!
Not playing, I stayed calm and kept a straight face,
while I wondered what it was he was up to,
what was up his feathered leg, what dread trial.
I had already lost my heart and head,
and didn't want to hazard life itself.
I was already so worn down by trials.
And then resignation welled up in me,
ah, my fate, inescapable, so it seemed.
I broke off my defiant mood, gave in,

somewhere deep in my soul, there on that plain,
the Sea of Tranquility, near the module,
where I had sat in zazen when last there,
now strangely alone, but for a taunting tortoise,
mocking me as though he were from wonderland,
even *Alice in Wonderland*, Mock Turtle,
the poets dispersed to another realm.
I shook off my daze and looked at Mbeku,
saying, "I accept. I choose whatever trial,
ordeal, path of suffering, yet is my fate,
deemed necessary. Whatever you or the
Power of the Universe, the Great One,
sets before me. I am ready. Tell me!
I long to prove myself before Him.
Let it begin." With a sly glance, Mbeku
on his hind legs in the lunar dust,
released a sort of triumphant laugh,
addressed me saying, "O Poet of the Moon,
you have obeyed the Parliament of Poets
and traveled around the Earth, from Earth to
the moon, four times voyaging, and now
it is decreed, your final test, supreme,
surpassing all others that you have endured,
purgation and preparation, sacrifice
of self, to serve mankind, if possible,
with mighty words of epic song and vision,
worthy of your day, hard won, brought back home.
You must choose to travel to the dark side of
the moon, far from the sun's shining light,
life-giving radiance of the solar system,
without which no life can survive, flourish,
heroically shoulder this trial now for
the sake of your truest self, the true Self
of all humanity, and there you will
receive a blessèd sight beyond all imagining,

more glorious than the visions of poets
and seers of every land and time,
every people and race, throughout the eons
of human existence, beyond them all."
   I looked above and behind Mbeku
and there, again, high in the lunar sky,
floated Earth, a mere golf ball in the blackness
of space, a brilliantly lit blackness, far away,
home, so far away, the mandala of our time.
Resolve rose up in me; no longer despair, but
determination, consecration to my task and duty.
Mbeku mockingly waved a feathered leg,
on that vast desert of the moon. I mocked back
defiantly, and I found that I was
lifting off like the ascent stage of the
Lunar Module, headed back to space,
far above the moon in seconds, propelled
into lunar orbit, towards the dark side,
alone, even Mbeku gone, left behind,
alone in the brilliant blackness of space,
the inscrutable whiteness turned to blackness.
   As into some ancient cave, primordial,
Franco-Cantabrian, even Blombos Cave,
so many millennia ago, recent,
compared to the moon, I sped around the
surface of the planet, slipped around its edge,
entered its eerie shadow, the sun eclipsed
by the moon, spectacular, leaving behind
all that I knew and understood, familiar
landmarks long gone, into a vortex of
darkness, vertigo of the mind, hurtling,
falling down around into the gravity
of the moon, drawn, pulled into the shadow
of a region dark, inaccessible
to the eyes of man, so few have ever

seen, as in a dream, and so the moonscape
changed, became even more rugged, tortured,
pummeled with craters everywhere, gigantic,
crowded together, overlapped, interlaced,
a monstrous moonscape of the mind,
as though the soul had lost its way in the dark,
thrashing about, hammering the surface,
struggling to break free of false conceptions,
contemplation leading to futility,
frantically in despair, beating the surface,
the dark night of the soul overwhelming all,
like a sneering Mephistopheles,
inflicting its inner turmoil upon the moon.
I laid my hand on my painful chest wound.
I know the feeling well, cursing everything,
God Himself, worse than Job in dust and ashes,
his conventional friends, niggling pedants,
sack cloth and moon dust, shaking my fists
against it all. I too have clung to self,
my petty vanities, fantasies, blaming
them all on Him, Her, Beyond beyond,
darkest shadowed dread and despair,
Nihilism's ghoul come back, oh, once more,
before me in the tangible image of the moon,
no longer a mysterious, shining orb,
silent, eternal, bright and serene,
but a fearsome battle of the mind, the soul,
the universe struggling with itself,
psychomachia, as though I were looking
at my darkest moments, I gazed below,
flying forward in my orbit around
the backside of the moon, until I realized
that, just so, such a false sense was the splitting
of the soul into the false worship of science,
Scientism, the idol of modernity,

the chopped up parts of the human psyche,
body and soul, science and religion,
reason and spirit, the rational and
irrational, material and spiritual,
all those false dichotomies, when we are one,
one human essence, full, complete, unified,
undivided, not two cultures, but one,
decreed by the Great One who made us all
and everything, even our tools and
instruments, inner and outer, with which
we study all creation, up to and
beyond the moon, the starry cosmos, for
man is not an object or a wage slave, but Soul.
And then that enlightening thought made me
think to lift my gaze up from the battered moon,
and turn around, there in the dark, from the
eerie shadow, away from the seemingly
tortured moonscape, out to what lay behind me,
the great universe that I felt must be there,
sensed, and, lo, when I did, my eyes met with
the most glorious sight of creation,
the cosmos stretched out in every direction,
for now in the moon's shadow I could see
billions, trillions, nay, sextillions of stars,
beyond brilliant, more distinct and shining
than anything visible from Earth.
All the stars of Abraham, all the heavens
of the universe that he had seen from Earth,
the Lord God blessing him and all his seed,
the seed of the people of the Earth,
for all are His children and His offspring,
all the men and women of the good Earth,
for all eternity, the seed of Abraham.
With Hagar and Ishmael, make the pilgrimage,
surrender, run with her in search of Water.

Oh, no atmosphere there dimming my view,
as though I had the eyes of Abraham,
an Ultra Deep Image of eternity,
unfolding blossoms of galaxies of
every type and form, spiral, cluster, blazar,
globular, elliptical, dwarf, radio,
every shape and size, oriented on
every plane, though relative to what
I knew not how to judge, but to me, the Earth
out of sight, as well as the moon, my gaze,
my consciousness, a floating awareness
in the eternity of space, but a drop
out of the eternal Ocean, gazed and gazed
at the Image of the Glory of God,
made manifest, Invisible Essence,
Lord of All Names, Maker of the Heavens,
Handiwork of God, transported into Light,
the Light of the Universe, beyond words,
I gazed and gazed and gazed, in awe,
like Job or Arjuna, before the Mystery
of the Divine Being, Beyond, Beyond, Beyond,
beyond my power of words to describe,
but felt deep in the soul where words are
no longer needed, as in prayer we rest
in God, His Presence, Shekhinah, beyond
the murmur of syllables and sounds,
exalted above description, uttered in
this immensity, the All-Glorious Horizon,
Lord of Being, now mine eye seeth thee,
Thou Art That, I Am Whom I Am,
as Above so below, below Above,
the flight of the alone to the Alone,
Truth is One, sages call it by many names,
Intimation of the Lord of Creation,
the Most Exalted, the All-Glorious,

Indra's net strung with jewels throughout the cosmos,
O Universe become conscious of itself,
melted and merged into Unity,
O Creator of the Heavens, all created things,
I testify that Thou art God and that
there is no God but Thee, Lord of all Being,
Creator of all things visible and
invisible, the kingdoms of Earth and
Heaven are thine, O Lord of the Worlds!
   And in the peace beyond understanding,
beyond time, in the still moment, eternity,
I was carried, sustained, guided around
the back of the moon towards its edge,
to the sudden burst of lunar sunrise,
dawning and sweeping away the star-studded
universe with all its endless galaxies,
vast worlds beyond human numbering,
beings unknown but logically existing,
for how could we be the only creatures
in such a bounteous expanse of space?
What is woman? What is man? Together,
hurtling on a rock through the universe?
Before the Galactic Year is out,
come round again the spinning Milky Way,
humankind must explore and colonize
elsewhere in the universe to survive,
for the curve of evolution has been bent,
for man must explore every new frontier,
voyage out like Sindbad, Old Man of the Sea.
Let us work on our soul to prepare
for the long journey into the unknown,
the ultimate frontier of humanity,
returning through the blackest black of space,
the cosmological constant of existence,
learn how to live together in peace.

Awed by the brilliance of the white sunlight,
its purity unknown in our atmosphere,
above the Earth, unscattered, undimmed,
its solar wind seeming to carry me
around the edge of the moon, I saw next
a sight of such awesome beauty that I wept
with joy, elation, reverence, our planet,
Earth, rising above the inert lunar crust,
Earthrise, home, the blue-white globe of beauty,
floating in space, far off, beckoning again,
terrestrial sign, symbol of life, of all
we know and love, oceans and mountains,
trees and streams, forests, Great Lakes, what the
Indians called "large water," *Michigami,*
the steadying Hand of God upon the Earth,
billions of people, rising, rising, above
the moon's stark, cold, desolate expanse of rock,
a vision worthy of humanity, for
this is the way things should be, really be, are.
I thought what a joy to be alive!
Enrapt and fortified by the sight, I flew on,
deeply aware of what I had seen and felt
on my lone voyage around the dark side
of the moon, journey of life, into
one glorious sight after another, yet
impenetrable, beyond my powers fully
to absorb and understand, sights I felt
infinitely privileged to view, struggling
to understand, make sense of my journey
to and around the moon, my orbit bringing
me back where I became aware of
the Sea of Tranquility, far below,
my descending, as on ethereal wings,
space wings, traversing the vast regions of
our shining satellite. I gently landed

near the Lunar Module, like a Greek demigod,
Perseus, wingéd sandals on my feet,
firmly alighting on the lunar soil,
without a trace of moon dust kicking up,
as I took a few steps to a complete stop,
amongst a throng of poets, returned, assembled
once more, it seemed, to greet and parley,
drawing back, clearing a circle, for my landing.
I realized I held something in my left hand,
standing, as in the public square of the moon,
as even in the piazza of Florence.
I raised my left arm outward to find
suspended from my grip, the gorgon head
of Medusa, its horrid head of gore
dripping repulsive black blood into the moon dust.
I dropped it with my sword in revulsion,
thudding, shriveling into the substratum.
All watched in silence, still, a pageant played out.
Shakespeare's noble Prospero coming to mind,
"The rarer action is in virtue than
in vengeance, my reason against my fury."
I slaked my bloodlust that day upon the moon.
  Deep anticipation filled me for their words,
after all that I had been through, during
my long journeys to and from Earth, since I last
met with them on the moon, or elsewhere on Earth.
How I longed to hear their words, gain advice,
win my release from the arduous ordeal
that they and the blesséd Muses had set
before my soul, supreme trial of everything
I had ever read, thought, or believed,
of everything I had ever been down there,
on that blue-green planet, Mother Earth.
I glanced around wondering who would speak first,
finding familiar faces, poets I'd long

read and known, assembled once again.
Cervantes, far back, stood holding his lance,
quietly eyeing me, Rocinante gone,
clustered about by a crowd of Spanish poets,
as in a dream with Pedro Calderón,
Francisco de Quevedo, San Juan de la Cruz,
Lope de Vega, an imaginative crew.
A stolid Emerson stood nearby, Whitman
and Thoreau, Jones Very and Dickinson,
an unlikely match; T. S. Eliot;
Hawthorne, viewing from afar "Earth's Holocaust";
E. A. Robinson, "The Man Against the Sky,"
Countee Cullen, Hayden, and Langston Hughes.
All around, from India's far-off land,
Vyasa appeared with Kalidasa,
Tulsidas and Tagore, Jayadeva,
Vidyapati, with other Vaishnava poets,
griots and shamans, seers from the Americas,
Black Elk and Chief Seattle, hoop dancers,
hooping the cosmos in a hoop of peace,
the poets of all the planet, it seemed.
Du Fu too had brought all the Chinese poets.
From Europe, all were present, Baudelaire,
Leopardi, Goethe, Pushkin, Malinkowski,
with Rilke, Hermann Hesse, and Thomas Mann.
Dante, Boccaccio, and Petrarch, throngs from
every nation looked at me, as I at them, quietly.
No one answered my gaze with a word of
welcome or acknowledgment, but only
gaze met gaze. I looked again at Cervantes,
who, after all, had started all of this,
thinking he might sally forth once more,
but, no, he chose not to pick up the gage,
so silence deepened all around us,
while I struggled wondering if I should speak

with gratitude for their many lessons.
I shook myself a bit, making it clear
I was about to speak, pulling myself
up to my full stature, encircled on the moon,
the Lunar Module behind me to the right,
and there I saw Tolstoy standing with a
group of Russian and French writers, Milosz nearby,
and Bellow with a group of Jewish writers,
Isaac Bashevis Singer, Yiddish masters.
Jane Austen and Akmatova, Murasaki,
Scheherazade, Elizabeth Barrett Browning;
I noticed and nodded to Jules Michelet,
Rousseau, whose *Confessions* mean much to me,
Voltaire and Victor Hugo, and Stendhal.
Feeling encouraged that they were all there,
seeming to be waiting to hear from me,
I felt emboldened, swept my eyes over
their heads and began, "Masters, you know
I have sat at your feet and done your bidding,
trying to the best of my ability.
I call on you to acknowledge as much.
Alone, usually unaided, truth be told,
I have followed your example and your words.
I accepted the quest you placed before me,
though it cost every drop of my life-blood.
Agonies I endured, humiliation
for service to the Muse, sacrifice of self
in the bitterest situations. I boldly dare
any one of you to deny it. You know
you can't. You've turned me into someone other
than a petitioner. So blame yourselves
if you don't like it. I'm not here now to beg
and crawl. You've taught me that. Broke me and placed
in my hands the Golden Bough, the Flaming Torch,
the Garland, the Rose, the Sacred Bow of old,

standing with Oedipus in the Sacred Grove.
Like Crusoe, my message in a bottle.
I stand here among you rightly won.
Not the foible of an hour, but a lifetime
cast before the gods, the Muses, a burden
that only they can place upon a soul.
I honor your names that mankind not forget
the power and vision of epic song.
I've done this, as you know, not for myself,
but for service to the great Traditions
you yourselves served, what is human,
what is worthy of the human being,
the glories of the soul. The Unknown One
calls us to embrace and serve, now more so
than ever, the entire globe. I've learnt
your lessons and stand ready to hear the words
of any one here who thinks otherwise.
Let him or her speak. I reserve but the
right of conscience to respond, the right of all."
    Then the lunar silence deepened, a silence
greater than any known on Earth, a stillness
from the deep eons of time before time,
timelessness marking time, as my words lingered
above the lunar scene, poets of every
land and age stood by, the best and brightest
of every culture, challenged by me,
to acknowledge that I had won my worth
amongst them, the fairest poet's laurel,
if I could but return to Earth, write it down.
So it seemed to me, tears of emotion
welling up and overflowing at the thought,
as I stood there firm upon the moon,
in the Sea of Tranquility, no more
tranquil scene in all the universe,
except in the inmost moment of prayer.

Had I not had my heart ripped out, casting
an accusatory glare toward Octavio Paz,
with his Spanish and Mexican compañeros?
Had I not been beheaded in Africa,
glowering at the griots and shamans,
next to Okigbo, Chinua Achebe,
and all so many more times of pain and woe?
If there had been air upon the moon,
my words would have resonated,
as all the poets of the Earth assembled,
there in Parliament, clearly took in and
thought about what I had said, I, even I,
the poet they themselves had set upon
a journey through time and space, decades ago,
seeking answers to all the numbing riddles
of modernity, East and West, around the globe.
I challenged any one of them to deny it.
Like Cervantes in *Journey to Parnassus*,
some poets will scowl at me for putting
them in my poem, others for leaving them out.
Yet had I not cast all my lot on one book?
Seething inside, I thought, I've done as you taught!
    At last, someone stirred to my right and stepped
forward to speak, Tolstoy, my truest master,
accompanied by Emerson and Tagore.
Standing near me, where all could see him, Tolstoy,
his long beard and peasant smock apparent
against the Lunar Module and desolation
of the moon, began, "I speak for all
convened here in this Parliament of Poets.
We are here for consultation. Our goals
are one. We called you to the task, acknowledge
you have been given the favor of the Muse.
You bore every burden she and we have placed
upon you, and no poet here denies that,

though poetasters down there on Earth shall
certainly snipe and complain, niggling here
and there, in effete coteries and so-called
MFA programs, the dole for would-be poets.
But beware, O Poet of the Moon, of
the poet's sin," casting an eye askance at
Dante and Milton. "For the Muses are
unforgiving of those who gainsay their grace.
You have done what all the great amongst us
have done. The laurel is yours. Here upon
the moon. But we must remain here and cannot,
and do not, speak for the Earth. You must earn
it there by returning, remembering,
writing it down there, for the people, reaching
and touching their hearts through words of poetry,
a vision that they know as, and call, their own,
if it be the wise Apollo's wish.
In token of that day we see before you,
a challenge in itself, we trust, you shall
accomplish, we recognize one of our own.
The laurel is yours. We bestow it freely,
the epic laurel so rarely ever won,
cautioning again you must write it down.
You were allowed to breach the Gate of Horn,
but soon you must choose which way to return.
We will not force you through one or the other."
I asked, "How can I choose but the way I came?
Back through the Gate of Ivory, way of maya?"
Ignoring my questions, Tolstoy continued,
"Every one of us called you here to train you
for the task. Unbeknownst, you carry its
fertile seeds and flowers near your breast.
Take them now and before us all, here before
the Earthrise of our home, we love and revere,
plant them and see if they will grow and flourish,

for the soil of mankind is ever fertile,
no matter how lost and hopeless it may seem.
Always the world awaits the poet who can
find the right words, more so now than ever.
Plant them here in the Sea of Tranquility
and watch them grow." There Tolstoy ended.
I gasped, wondering at his words, but followed
his command, for all my braggadocio,
trusting my master to know better than I,
having brought my arrogant self all this way.
Job was right. I have to earn it down there.
The true Odysseus arrives on shore.
Stepping away from the Lunar Module,
through the crowd, opening a path beyond
the American flag, furling in the wind,
like the U of M flag on Hadley Rille,
I walked out with my African staff,
thinking on the way of Bob's Black Spear,
not for me a thyrsos topped with a pine cone,
the calabash bouncing on my shoulder,
and stuck the staff in the ground, freeing my hands,
so I could kneel down, digging in the dust,
carefully planting, as I did when I was
a boy in my family's garden, tending work
of generations coming back to me,
gardeners from Surrey, caring for the soil,
for Englands green and sceptered isle.
Just so caringly, I planted The Green Stick,
a golden leaf now grafted upon it, placed too
Faizi's flower, Rumi's reed, the red oleander
firmly in the lunar ground, patting down
the seemingly inert material around
them at the base. A greater contrast could not
be found in all the universe, four shoots
from the fragrant Earth, planted in

that unlikely terrain. Forgetting my staff,
I walked back to Tolstoy, a griot slipping
off my shoulder, as I passed, Sogolon's
calabash, I letting her have it, smiling.
Returning to Tolstoy, Emerson, and Tagore,
Whitman, too, drew close, out from the others.
We all looked back toward the little garden,
as it were, and there, already, amazingly,
The Green Stick inexplicably had taken root
and began to grow, drawing the frozen
water out of the charcoal-colored dirt,
as though the goddess Gaia had waved her wand,
rising not merely into a stick of scrub
but soon a majestic tree, a lunar tree,
a laurel or larch, hazel or sycamore,
cypress or willow, hawthorn or genome tree,
bearing the Golden Fleece of Jason,
the Golden Apples of the Hesperides,
a world tree towering above us, like the
tree of knowledge, or Yggdrasil grown back,
upon the moon. And below, the flowers had
sprouted, blue flowers and red oleanders,
blooming, spreading into a lush ground cover,
accompanied by a bed of green reeds,
as on a river bank or bubbling brook,
swaying in the breeze, fresh air redolent
of another clime, the fragrance of Earth,
where all that is beautiful and human resides,
bringing to the lunar desolation
an earthy aura, green leaves and lush flowers,
signs of hope in a place that had never
known what it means. And then to my astonishment,
my African staff began to grow, into
an ogbu tree, sacred tree of life, branches
reaching to the sky. The African griots

began to play the calabash, joined by all
the minstrels, rhapsodes, gandharvas, apsaras,
lyres and pipas sounded and melded
into a global blend of world music,
the music of the spheres, the solar system,
the harmony of man and creator,
raised around the trees of humanity.
And then I saw it high above the trees,
high above the curved lunar horizon,
the Earth, near the topmost branches, like an
adornment, almost a star upon the trees,
lofty trees of ancient spirit on the moon,
four-dimensional, in the blackest black
of space, floating, a tiny soap bubble.
All our hopes and dreams, everyone we knew
or had ever known, residing there,
looking like a delicate, luscious fruit,
high above us all, the poets of every
land and time, standing in awe, naturally
drawn together into a circle, like an
Indian medicine hoop, around mystic trees,
beyond words, experiencing it together,
our hearts in union with the glory of
the beauty, the beauty of Mother Earth,
far away, but with us, too, it seemed.
Some now held hands, or arms around shoulders.
We felt as one, tranquil and serene,
full of love, an indescribable love
for our planet, Mother Earth, and all her
people, her many cultures and nationalities,
languages and beliefs, religions,
all its many flowers and trees, animals,
all the variety of life on Earth.
They all seemed symboled there before us,
the Rose Image of who and what we are,

how we grow and blossom in even the
harshest conditions, if we will but choose
to cherish and cultivate our garden,
in this universe, fragile as a flower.
Many now were weeping, tears streaming down
in unabashed emotion, joy, gratitude.
I felt it too, a lump in my throat and
pressure at the eyes. And then Tolstoy,
tears wet on his white beard, stepped forward,
walking into the circle near the trees.
Momentarily, Tolstoy closed his eyes,
and then opened them, raising his arms,
gazing above the trees, lowering them,
as the two trees became one gigantic
redwood tree, like those that have grown on Earth
for a hundred and fifty million years,
all around the world, not just California,
before us all, the tree of life and the tree of
knowledge growing together, in the end,
into one tree, the hidden Root of all roots,
become the mystical tree of Sefiroth,
the Celestial Tree of all creation.
All eyes then saw the hoopoe and fellow birds
come flocking in, flying around and settling
on the redwood tree, like Birds of Paradise,
signs of the Lord of All the Worlds.
Soon they rose from the tree and became
One Bird, the Simorgh, a bird of astounding beauty.
She arose from the lunar east like the sun,
brilliant, resplendent, joined by three other birds,
each aligning itself on a point of the
lunar compass, around the tree, high above,
the phoenix bird, as out of the ashes,
in the west; Fenghuang, the Chinese phoenix,
in the east; and the Russian Firebird,

in the north. Their long streaming feathers
gracefully furled and swayed in the solar wind,
as they beat their wings, flapping them,
churning up a breeze that began to ruffle
the branches of the redwood, swaying and shaking
the boughs until the cones and seeds loosened
and flowed from the tree, swept by their fanning
multi-colored wings toward Mother Earth,
a great chain of being returning to Earth,
on the currents of space, the eddies of wings,
man the main actor in the drama of life.
All the poets stood silent, awe-struck, in tears,
as before a miracle, the miracle of life,
the gift from the Lord of All the Worlds.
Homer and Virgil, Dante and Milton,
Vyasa and Valmiki, Basho and Saigyo,
Bai Juyi and Du Fu, Rumi and Attar,
Borges and Paz, griots and shamans,
Milarepa, out of his Tibetan cave,
Kabir, too, all the way from Kashi,
all the poets and singers of all the ages,
the masters of the traditions of humanity,
from the antler-man and Blombos Cave,
we all stood there, and I, I was not alone.
All humanity stood there with us.
We were not alone. We all felt it.
The Love of the Unseen Essence, encircling us.
We were wrapped in the arms of the universe.
We gazed above the foliage at our home,
the Earth, a round hoop of beauty, dancing
across an endless field of space and stars.

GLOSSARY

This glossary is a necessarily modest effort to aid the reader unfamiliar with some of the riches of world religion and culture. There are many comprehensive sources for those interested in going beyond these sketchy definitions. One might also use Google.

Atman. Soul. "Atman is Brahman," the time-honored expression.
Avalokitesvara. The most highly regarded Bodhisattva of Buddhist tradition. Became known in China as Guan-yin and Kannon in Japan.
Ayodhya. Ancient capital and site of the temple of Rama.
Balafon. A West African xylophone.
Bodhisattva. One who foregoes enlightenment in order to lead others to it, the ultimate act of compassion.
Brahma. Creator of the universe.
Brahman. The universal, cosmic unity or energy.
Calabash. African stringed instrument made from a gourd.
Dharma. Ethical and religious law, duty, and custom.
Darshan. A view or sighting of a god, often through a statue.
Devata. Deity and sometimes temple dancer.
Gandharva. Heavenly musician.
Griot. Poet and recorder of history in Mali and West Africa.
Hanuman. The monkey god in the Indian epic the *Ramayana*, part monkey, part man, devoted to Rama.
Indra. King or leader of the Hindu gods.
Kalpa. A cycle of eons, an enormous period of time.
Kami. Japanese pre-Buddhist traditional gods.
Karma. Actions and deeds converging in the present, shaping future events.
Koinobori. Kites flown in Japan patterned after carp fish, swimming into the wind, against the hard currents of life.
Krishna. An incarnation of Vishnu, especially his concern for human beings.
Mandala. In Hinduism and Buddhism, a cosmic map or diagram, in the form of a circle, divided into quarters.

Maya. The world as illusion.

Moksha. Release from samsara, the wheel of existence, by uniting one's inner self with Brahman. The goal of life.

Mudra. Hand gestures carrying symbolic meaning.

Naga. Mythical water being.

OM. The sacred syllable in Indian religious traditions.

Pir. A Sufi master.

Rama. An incarnation of Vishnu and model of virtue.

Samsara. The cycle of birth and rebirth.

Sangha. The order of the Buddhist community.

Satori. Sudden enlightenment.

Sefiroth. Tree of, from the Jewish Kabbalah.

Shekhinah. The presence of God, as upon the altar of Solomon's Temple, and discussed in the Kabbalah.

Shiva. Destroyer and Preserver of the universe, Lord of Dancers, "Shiva Nataraja." Contrary to popular belief, "Shiva also is viewed as a manifestation of Vishnu in the *Bhagavata Purana* and the *Vishnu Purana* (4th c. CE)." Wikipedia.

Sun Wukong. The Monkey King in Chinese Buddhist folklore and legend.

Thyrsos. The rod or cane of the Greek god Dionysus, also known as Bacchus.

Ti'en. Heaven, underlying everything Confucius taught.

Vajra. Thunderbolt and lightning. A metaphor for enlightenment.

Vishnu. Preserver of the universe.

Xuanzang. The scripture-seeking monk of the Tang Dynasty, the crucial link in Buddhism between India and China, who traveled to India and back from 629 to 645 CE.

Yoga. A discipline having many traditional practices and forms.

Zazen. Japanese name for the traditional cross-legged position during Buddhist meditation.

CPSIA information can be obtained at www.ICGtesting.com
Printed in the USA
BVOW08*1347260516

449566BV00001B/3/P